# LITURGICAL THEOLOGY

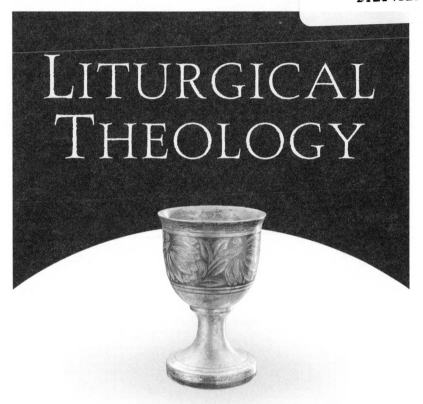

The Church as
Worshiping Community

## SIMON CHAN

IVP Academic

An imprint of InterVarsity Press
Downers Grove, Illinois

*InterVarsity Press*
*P.O. Box 1400, Downers Grove, IL 60515-1426*
*World Wide Web: www.ivpress.com*
*E-mail: mail@ivpress.com*

*InterVarsity Press® is the book-publishing division of InterVarsity Christian Fellowship/USA®, a movement of students and faculty active on campus at hundreds of universities, colleges and schools of nursing in the United States of America, and a member movement of the International Fellowship of Evangelical Students. For information about local and regional activities, write Public Relations Dept., InterVarsity Christian Fellowship/USA, 6400 Schroeder Rd., P.O. Box 7895, Madison, WI 53707-7895, or visit the IVCF website at <www.intervarsity.org>.*

*All Scripture quotations, unless otherwise indicated, are taken from the* Holy Bible, New International Version®. NIV®. *Copyright ©1973, 1978, 1984 by International Bible Society. Used by permission of Zondervan Publishing House. All rights reserved.*

*Design: Cindy Kiple*
*Images: ©Kirill Smirnov/iStockphoto*

*IISBN 978-0-8308-2763-3*

*Printed in the United States of America ∞*

**Library of Congress Cataloging-in-Publication Data**

*Chan, Simon.*

 *Liturgical theology: the church as worshiping community/Simon*
*chan.*

  *p. cm.*
 *Includes bibliographical references and indexes.*
 *ISBN-13: 978-0-8308-2763-3 (pbk.: alk. paper)*
 *ISBN-10: 0-8308-2763-3 (pbk.: alk. paper)*
  *1. Liturgics.  2. Church—History of doctrines.  3. Public worship.*
 *1. Title.*
 *BV176.3.C43 2006*
 *230'.04624—dc22*

                                                                           *2006013019*

| **P** | 23 | 22 | 21 | 20 | 19 | 18 | 17 | 16 | 15 | 14 | 13 | 12 | 11 | 10 | 9 | 8 | 7 | 6 |
| **Y** | 28 | 27 | 26 | 25 | 24 | 23 | 22 | 21 | 20 | 19 | 18 | 17 | 16 | 15 | 14 | 13 | 12 |

*For*

*the Rev. Dr. Joseph Frary,*

*teacher and friend*

# CONTENTS

# ACKNOWLEDGMENTS

This book would not have been possible without the help of many people. First, the project would have remained stalled had not the principal of Trinity Theological College, Dr. Ngoei Foong Nghian, agreed to release me from all major administrative duties of the college.

Thanks to my colleague, Dr. Jeffrey Truscott, for reading chapters one through three and making helpful suggestions. Dr. Joseph Mangina of Wycliffe College, Toronto, read a slightly different version of chapter four and offered many insights. Dr. Joseph Frary, who introduced me to the liturgy more than a quarter century ago, read chapters five through seven. It is therefore "very meet, right, and [my] bounden duty" that I dedicate this book to him. Needless to say, I bear full responsibility for any of its shortcomings.

Our librarian, Michael Mukunthan, has been most helpful, acquiring all the materials I needed, including some out-of-print books.

Finally, as usual, my wife's attention to other details of life has freed me to write. This is a rare gift. I could not ask for more.

# INTRODUCTION

In recent years a number of evangelical theologians have subjected the modern evangelical movement to close scrutiny and found it wanting.[1] Thinking evangelicals would hardly dispute David Wells's indictment:

> In entering the mainstream of American cultural life, [evangelicals] were brought face to face with the great shaping forces of modern life, and one of the immediate casualties was their sense of truth in both private and public life. Almost immediately their capacity to think theologically about themselves and their world also disappeared.[2]

Wells enumerates a number of signs of evangelical capitulation to the ways of the world. Christ as personal Savior has less to do with the objective truth of what he did than with how a person feels subjectively. Many church services have become one huge entertainment, in which there is no mention of sin and what is offered as gospel is "the therapeutic model of life."[3] There is the "professionalization" of the clergy, evidenced by its impermanence and marketability. Ministry is no longer a lifelong calling but another career that follows a certain "career path" like any other profession. If it does not work out, one moves on to another job.[4] The professional minister must have some marketable skills. This means that the focus of theological training is no longer on the knowledge of God as an end in itself (what Edward Farley calls "theologia")[5] but on "know-how." Thus it is not uncommon to find the modern theological curriculum dominated by practical subjects like counseling, church administration and leadership. When ministry is defined professionally, there is really nothing left in the ministerial profession that distinguishes it from other professions.

Preaching finds its echoes in secular teaching and counseling. Evangelism finds its echoes in sales. Pastoral counseling finds its echoes in the efforts of the case worker. Church ritual finds its echoes in the formal procedures of the court and legislature. And the administration of the church programs finds its echoes in the management of countless secular organizations.[6]

Similarly, Mark Noll has noted the failure of evangelicalism to critically engage modern culture.[7] Noll attributes the intellectual demise of modern American evangelicalism to three factors. The first is a revivalism that both promoted a new style of leadership focusing on the revivalist and undercut the traditional authority of the churches and thus helped to foster "individualism and immediatism."[8] The second is the separation of church and state. The disestablishment of the church meant that each church had to compete for members, which in turn necessitated the practice of revivalism, the "free-market economy" in church life. This gave great dynamism to church life, but it also promoted individualism and a focus on "spiritual matters" apart from the intellect. Truth must become "practical." These two effects resulted in the third: a synthesis of Christianity with popular culture in order to survive in the marketplace.[9]

The tendency to accommodate to popular culture is in fact not new, nor is it unique to modern evangelicalism. David Bebbington's study of evangelicalism in the last two and a half centuries has revealed a similar tendency. The "optimism of grace" of the Wesleys and the "reasonable faith" of Philip Doddridge reflected the optimistic temper of the Enlightenment.[10] Similarly, the Keswick Movement's emphasis on the surrender of the will in the cultivation of the "overcoming life" and its appreciation of nature as an avenue of divine revelation owed as much to nineteenth-century romanticism as to Scripture.[11] One might expect that the holiness movement of this period, with its emphasis on not being "of this world," would have provided the distance for a more nuanced critique of the world, but this was not the case.

That the evangelical movement is recognized to be in crisis cannot be denied. What we might want to question is how the crisis is being addressed. Here, we find that evangelicals have been generally long on analysis and critique but short on answers. Noll, for instance, thinks that for evangelicalism to be renewed, it has to change its attitude. "For evangelicalism as a whole, not new graduate schools, but an alteration of attitudes is the key to promoting a Christian life of the mind."[12] Furthermore, according to Noll, many of the distinctives of evangelicalism are not even the essentials of

Christianity. In other words, evangelicals are majoring on the peripherals rather than on what is central to the Christian faith.[13] Noll, however, is hopeful that evangelicalism, while stifling the mind, carries within itself the seeds of renewing the mind. Its central practice of preaching the "born-again" gospel entails a doctrine of total transformation of creation. "The scandal of the evangelical mind may be addressed by the scandal of the cross."[14] In a similar vein, Wells thinks that the answer to the theological vacuity of the evangelical church is to be found in the recovery of truth, not so much truth as abstract ideas and propositions as the truth of God's action in history, carried in the gospel concerning the life, death and resurrection of Jesus Christ.[15]

While these are significant recommendations, they do not go far enough. How are evangelicals to change their attitudes? How are the essentials to be recovered? How do we go beyond truths as abstract ideas and propositions? I would like to suggest that what evangelicals need is an adequate ecclesiology if they are to discover resources to deal with the longstanding problems that the critics have identified and quite ably analyzed. Attitudes can be reshaped only by a strong traditioning community; essentials are discovered in the Great Tradition of the church—the "one, holy, catholic and apostolic" church—that all Christians profess to believe in; and only within a church that is catholic and alive are truths traditioned and received as a living faith and not as abstract ideas and propositions.

Now, many evangelicals are aware of their ecclesiological deficit. In fact, one of the recurring criticisms of evangelicalism is that it has no adequate ecclesiology. This point was already highlighted in the "Chicago Call" made by a group of evangelical theologians as long ago as 1977. Of the eight articles in the call, six deal more or less directly with the church. The first article is "A Call to Historic Roots and Continuity." It confesses the failure of the modern evangelical churches to recognize the "evangelical impulse" present throughout church history in the Eastern Orthodox and Roman Catholic churches. This is closely related to the third article, "A Call to Creedal Identity," which among other things reaffirms "the abiding value of the great ecumenical creeds and the Reformation confessions." Articles 5 and 6 call evangelicals to "sacramental integrity" and "spirituality," noting the importance of the sacraments of baptism and the Lord's Supper and the need for a more broad-based spirituality. The "Call to Church Authority" (article 7) highlights the perennial problem of divisiveness and the need for accountability to the larger church, while the final article, "A Call to Church

Unity," deplores "the scandalous isolation and separation of Christians from one another" and urges evangelicals "to return to the ecumenical concern of the Reformers." The Chicago Call urges evangelicals to focus on a wider vision of the church. The resources needed for a vibrant evangelical faith are to be found not just in a return to Protestant orthodoxy, as Wells proposed,[16] but in the Great Tradition of the church, which includes patristic and medieval resources.

More recently, in his sequel to *No Place for Truth,* Wells recognizes the need for evangelicals to develop an ecclesiology. Wells speaks of the need for "the evangelical church to be the church" and for the church "to be an alternative to post-modern culture,"[17] yet his book provides no theological explanation of what the church is. Wells seems to assume that changing the church involves simply changing the people and especially the leaders who together make up the community called church. Again, Wells recognizes that theology can be nurtured only within the church, "the place where biblical knowledge must be learned, developed and applied."[18] The church must be bold to speak the truth and not surrender to all the subjective "truths" characteristic of postmodern culture. But how does the church learn "to speak its own language, the language of truth and understanding"?[19] How does it become a "counterculture"? We cannot answer these questions without a clear understanding of what the church is. When Wells speaks of the church, he seems to mean no more than a group of believers banding together for certain God-given tasks and concerns. Ultimately, the church is created by the action of those who profess the name of Christ. The church is essentially a collectivity. About the closest Wells comes to speaking of the church theologically is a passage at the end of his *God in the Wasteland.* The individual Christian must be

> embodied in a structure that gives corporate expression to private spirituality, in which the lone thread is woven into a fabric. In this sense, the local church creates its own Christian culture, its own set of values and ways of looking at the world, its own hopes and dreams, which, because they are corporately held and practiced, become normative.[20]

This is similar to what MacIntyre says about "communal practices."[21] But such a framework for the church remains essentially sociological. We need a theology of the church that gives a sound basis for the individual to be embodied in the ecclesial structure. Otherwise the church would just remain another social organization, an entity of our own making, or, as in the case of many a modern evangelical church, a community created by the skill of the preacher.

One who has taken evangelical ecclesiology a step further is Donald Bloesch.[22] The sixth volume of his magnum opus, a seven-volume series called Christian Foundations, is devoted to the church.[23] Bloesch quite obviously is seeking to develop an ecclesiology that takes cognizance of the larger Christian tradition, and one of the consequences of this is a greater evangelical awareness of the place of the sacrament in the life of the church. He upholds its objective character as a means of grace, arguing that the sacrament not only reveals but "confers" grace through the action of the Holy Spirit.[24] He is sympathetic to the Mercersburg theologians such as Philip Schaff, to whose memory *The Church* was dedicated.[25] He is also generally sympathetic to the landmark document of the Faith and Order Commission of the World Council of Churches, *Baptism, Eucharist and Ministry,*[26] but would like to add his own caveats. Bloesch is wary of a "sacramentalism" that would detract the church from what he perceives to be its central focus: the proclamation of the Word.[27] But when Bloesch speaks of the centrality of the Word, what he seems to refer to is the *preached* word in contrast to the sacrament.[28] Consequently, Bloesch cannot escape the rationalism that has dominated Reformed theology since the seventeenth century and that culminated in the nineteenth-century Princeton school of theology.[29]

This comes through most clearly in Bloesch's understanding of worship. Worship is a "creative response" to God's self-revelation.[30] The qualifier *creative* is telling; it seems to suggest that worship is largely a human construct, something worshipers could do creatively rather than "pathically" by letting revelation shape their response.[31] This is confirmed when we examine Bloesch's recommendation for an evangelical order of worship. One will not fail to notice some arbitrariness in the way the order is constructed. For example, Bloesch suggests that the reading of Scripture "may on occasion" include the Old Testament, Gospel and Epistle. Is the public reading of Scripture simply a matter for us to decide? Is there no theological basis for liturgical reading? While preaching is expected to go on every week, Communion is celebrated once a month, "thereby giving time for the necessary inward preparation."[32] This seems to be letting a pragmatic rationale dictate the frequency of eucharistic celebration. Is this consistent with a theology of church as Word *and* sacrament?

Underlying Bloesch's ecclesiology is his singular emphasis on the church's *distinction from* Christ rather than both the church's distinction from and its identification with Christ.[33] Bloesch is concerned that anything that suggests identification will "compromise the biblical doctrine of *solus Christus*."[34] A more adequate conception of the church could have been derived if Bloesch had recognized that the centrality of Christ is not compromised when the church upholds Word and sacrament equally in its worship, because such a worship is centered in Christ as the incarnate Word. In my view, Bloesch's noble effort falls short of the ecclesiology needed for a thorough evangelical renewal.

Another evangelical theologian who has subjected evangelical ecclesiology to sustained critique is Stanley Grenz. In my judgment he has come much closer than most to the crux of the problem. Grenz notes that the evangelical movement is largely a parachurch rather than a church movement.[35] The visible form of evangelicalism's "(non)ecclesiology" is the "voluntary society," in which the congregation is the ultimate source of authority.[36] The "born-again" experience that unites evangelicals has tended to highlight the value of transecclesial fellowship rather than ecclesial structures. This means that what is really important to evangelicals is the "fellowship of all genuine believers" regardless of which visible churches they come from. The visible church thus becomes "soteriologically irrelevant."[37] In other words, what evangelicals could offer is a docetic ecclesiology where the "real" church is perceived as spiritual, inward and invisible and has no direct correlation with the visible church. But what evangelicals need, according to Grenz, is a "theological ecclesiology" that sees ecclesial life as existing in perichoretic union with the triune God through the Spirit. This is what gives the church its true mark as the church of Jesus Christ.[38] It is by living within the trinitarian life that the church discovers its "primary identity."[39]

My book is, in a sense, a follow-up to Grenz's proposal, seeking to present a vision of the church as an ontological reality and to show that it is on the basis of such an ecclesiology that sound ecclesial practices can be developed. But why has ecclesiology remained largely undeveloped among evangelicals? I think there are at least two historical reasons. One is evangelicals' aversion to abuses of power in a hierarchical church, especially through the abuse of sacramental grace. Martin Luther's experience of a corrupt system looms large in every evangelical's mind whenever the question of church structure is raised. The typical evangelical response is to develop a "free church" type that is free from external control. Free church ecclesiology has become so much a part of the evangelical culture that it has even been set forth as the ecclesiology that is most compatible with evangelical spirituality.[40] Another reason is evangelicals' historical experience within mainline Protestantism. Historically most modern evangelical churches, especially in North America, are products of controversies within mainline denominations that have gone liberal. The deadness of the denominations is often associated with "dead liturgy." The churches that broke free from denominational restraints also broke free from their liturgical traditions.[41] We have here a case of throwing away the baby with the bathwater. This is largely a carryover of the Dissenting tradition, going back to the Puritans.[42] If evangelicalism is to develop a theologically coherent church, it has to move beyond its traditional boundaries. It has to recognize, in the words of Thomas Howard, that being "evangelical is not enough."[43] It needs to take seriously the proposals in the Chicago Call and even go beyond them.

I suggest that if evangelicals are to overcome the ecclesiological deficit that lies at the heart of the movement, they need to go beyond discussions of forms and structures, types of church government and so forth, and probe the ontology of the church. This is the focus of chapter one. From this ontology we discover that the nature of the church cannot be understood apart from its calling as a worshiping community. It is through worship that the church is decisively shaped *as* the ecclesial community. That is to say, the church that is the creation of the triune God is also formed by its action of corporate worship (chapter two). But if the church is to be definitively formed by its corporate worship, it must discover what are the normative components or structure through which worship is concretely expressed. This necessitates a consideration of the shape of the liturgy (chapter three). In chapter four, the relationship between the liturgy and ecclesial formation is further nuanced in light of the postmodern question regarding the way church practices form the church. I will argue that the practice of the liturgy provides the basis for all other ecclesial practices. This chapter provides a transition to the next three chapters, for with them it sets out a basic theological framework for understanding the liturgy. While they present what I hope is an accurate summary of the meaning of the church and its liturgy as found in the larger Christian tradition, my concern is to highlight those features that have significant bearing on the evangelical ecclesiological deficit. Thus I have emphasized the ontological nature of the church in light of the reductive tendency in evangelicalism.

Ecclesial renewal, however, cannot be achieved simply through theological arguments and reflection. There must also be an adequate knowledge of appropriate liturgical practices. This is the concern of the next three chapters. Chapter five discusses the practice of *initiation* as essentially a process of training and preparing new converts to become full members of the body of Christ. One key feature of this process, also called the catechumenate, is to help new converts enter meaningfully into the church's liturgy. The process culminates in postbaptismal instruction, known as *mystagogy*. Chapter six seeks to deepen worshipers' understanding and appreciation of the Sunday liturgy. It may be regarded as a further elaboration of mystagogical instruction. Understanding, however, is only one part of liturgical formation. If the church is to develop a vibrant liturgical spirituality, it must also consider the part that worshipers have to play and how the liturgy is to be carried out. These are the concerns of the final chapter.

My aim, however, is not to offer practical tips for conducting worship but to help evangelicals have a better understanding of these practices so as to make meaningful participation possible. One of the reasons many churches have abandoned good liturgical practices is a failure to understand *why* these practices developed.[44] Sound liturgical practices may not have an immediate effect on worshipers, but if we know that they are right practices, then the absence of any obvious immediate effects should not prompt a quest for alternatives with greater crowd appeal. Instead, we should be looking for ways to improve the practices. We persevere in them because they are true; and the truth not only sets us free from the pressure of false demands that the world imposes on the church but also makes us into the people we know God wants us to be.

Finally, a word is in order regarding the approach I have taken. What I present here is by no means a fully developed liturgical theology but an outline of what a liturgical theology that evangelicals could meaningfully appropriate might look like. What emerges may not be to everyone's liking. This is to be expected, considering that even among evangelicals who could be described as liturgical in their orientation, a wide range of views is held. The Anglican evangelical Christopher Cocksworth identifies a spectrum among evangelicals within the Church of England, from those on the right "with Reformed theological ideals still high on their agenda" to those on the left "with more avant-garde experiments in liturgical or activist directions."

Within this broad spectrum different views regarding the efficacy of the Eucharist are entertained, from those who argue for a more affective role to those who advance a more objective or effective role.[45] Given this range of possibilities, I have sought to highlight mostly the points of convergence within the Christian liturgical traditions rather than their differences. Similarly, my critique of evangelical ecclesiology says nothing about the high regard I have for evangelical Christianity as a whole. Christianity would not be the vibrant faith that it is in many parts of the Third World today without the evangelical contribution.[46] If my critique is severe, it is because the tradition is worth correcting.

# Part One

—

# FOUNDATIONS

# — 1 —

# THE ONTOLOGY
# OF THE CHURCH

C rucial to any ecclesiology is the question of how the church is to be understood in relation to creation. Is the church to be seen as an instrument to accomplish God's purpose in creation, or is the church the expression of God's ultimate purpose itself? The way we answer this question has far-reaching implications. If the church is essentially instrumental, then its basic identity can be expressed in terms of its functions: what it must do to fulfill God's larger purpose. But if the church is God's end in creation, then its basic identity can be expressed only in ontological rather than functional terms.

These two conceptions of the church entail their own ways of reading the biblical narrative. According to the instrumentalist view of the church, biblical history should be understood in terms of a linear creation-fall-redemption-consummation narrative. This has been the way the unity of the canon has been understood throughout much of Christian history and could well be called the "standard canonical narrative."[1] According to this "standard" narrative, God's ultimate purpose for humanity is shown in his creating humankind in his own image and likeness. The content of this image and likeness is usually identified with certain distinctive human qualities like rationality, eternity and capacity for communion, which give to human beings their inherent dignity. The Fall disrupted God's original purpose, while the work of Christ is to redeem the fallen creation and bring to final consummation God's original purpose for creation.

Within this structure the church broadly conceived as the covenant people of God is seen as a means to fulfilling God's original purpose in creation.

Creation becomes the basis for understanding the nature and role of the church. The church is only a subspecies of creation and must discover the clue to its identity within the created order. The classic example is H. Richard Niebuhr, whose "Christ and culture" typology understands culture as the neutral, all-embracing reality (reality *sui generis*) within which Christians must configure their identity in terms of Christ *against*, Christ *of* or Christ *for* culture.[2] Many modern ecclesiologies continue to operate on this Niebuhrian typology. We see this, for instance, in Daniel Hardy's concept of community. While Hardy, as a Christian, recognizes the givenness or divine origin of "social transcendentals," he rejects the gifts of God as primarily ecclesial and opts for a "'general sociality' or created sociality present in the human condition."[3] This implies that the church derives its basic identity from the larger world. Christian experience becomes only a specification of a larger human religious consciousness.

But in recent times this construal has been subject to sustained critique.[4] The problem with this narrative is that it tends to treat the bulk of the Old Testament as parenthetical material. If God's original purpose is found in the creation account, why is not more said about it? Why did God's dealings with creation as a whole come to a sudden halt after the first eleven chapters of Genesis? Why does the Old Testament devote what seems like an inordinate amount of space to the calling of one man (Abraham), one family (Jacob's) and one nation (Israel) out of a host of individuals, families and nations? Such an elaborate narrative seems incongruent with the main storyline if the election of Israel is meant only to provide a *background* for understanding God's work of restoring creation.

A better way to conceptualize the Bible's narrative coherence is to see creation as forming the backdrop for God's elective grace and covenant relationship rather than vice versa. God created the world in order that he might enter into a covenant relationship with humankind. And he accomplishes this with the call of Abraham and culminates his elective purpose in Jesus Christ and the church. This covenantal relationship always involves the election of a people from among humankind. The purpose is not to consign the rest to reprobation (as taught in scholastic Calvinism) but that through the elect the rest of humankind might be blessed (Gen 12:3). Creation, then, does not express God's highest intention for the world but should be seen as the *means* by which God's grace of election could be realized. God has always intended his relationship with the world to be a graced relationship, not just a "natural" relationship. Human creatures are meant to be more than creatures: they are to be God's people, living in full knowledge of and relationship with God as Father, Son and Holy Spirit.

Sin, however, disrupted this relationship and must be overcome. The revelation of God in Christ addresses this problem. But Christ's coming is not primarily focused on the sin problem. Even if humans had not sinned, Jesus Christ would still have needed to come in the fullness of time, because only through that revelation is covenantal relationship realized in the fullest measure—as communion with the triune God. This newer "storyline" has found support in what is called nonsupersessionism, which sees the church of the New Testament as standing in continuity with Israel as the one people of God rather than displacing Israel.[5]

Implied in this newer canonical narrative is another way of looking at the relationship between the church broadly conceived and creation, and that is to see it not as another entity within the larger creation but as prior to creation. The church precedes creation in that it is what God has in view from all eternity and creation is the means by which God fulfills his eternal purpose in time. The church does not exist in order to fix a broken creation; rather, creation exists to realize the church. To be sure, the church's coming into being does require the overcoming of sin, but that is quite different from saying that the problem of sin is the reason for the church's being. God made the world in order to make the church, not vice versa. Scripture itself testifies to the logical priority of the church over creation by referring to the church as chosen in Christ before the creation of the world (Eph 1:4), or to Christ who was slain before the foundation of the world (Rev 13:8).[6] The world, as Robert Jenson puts it, is the "raw material" from which God will bring the church to perfection in Christ.[7] The church is not an entity within the larger culture but *is* a culture.[8]

The church's priority over creation carries two implications. First, it does not have a purely creaturely existence, and second, its basic identity is to be found not in what it *does* but in what it *is*. This means that only as we probe its ontology can we properly understand its true nature and role. The church, unlike creation, is not "external" to God but is, as it were, "internal" to the life of the triune God *(opus ad intra)*. It is, according to Sergius Bulgakov, a "divine-humanity." It is a divine-humanity because of its organic link with its Head, Christ. This organic unity between Christ the Head with his body the church is usually designated by the term *totus Christus* (the total Christ). It is prior to creation precisely because it is the body of *Christ*, the Second Person of the Trinity, and its *historical* existence is brought about by the action of the Holy Spirit. The Spirit's presence in the church is by virtue of its being a divine-humanity.[9] Such a presence is different from his presence in a world that is purely creaturely (unless creation is conceived pantheistically). The theological basis of this understanding of the church could not be more succinctly summed up than in the words of Jenson: "Christ is personally the second identity of God, and the *totus Christus* is Christ with the church; therefore the church is not in the same way an *opus ad extra* as is the creation, even when it is perfect in God."[10]

If the church's existence is not purely creaturely but a "divine-humanity," then we need to spell out its link with the triune God more precisely if we are to understand its true nature and function.[11] For the role or function of the church grows out of its ontological status as a divine-humanity. This ontological status is sometimes expressed in the concept of Mother Church, made famous by Cyprian: "He who has not the Church for his mother, has not God for his Father." That is to say, the church is our nourishing Mother, and we are entirely dependent on her for our existence as Christians. We are not saved as individuals first and then incorporated into the church; rather, to be a Christian is to be incorporated into the church by baptism and nourished with the spiritual food of the body and blood of Christ in the Eucharist. Failure to understand this fact has led to a reduction of the church's role to a largely sociological one of a service provider catering to individual believers' spiritual needs.

We will explore the church's ontological relationship with the triune God in terms of three biblical images or metaphors: the people of God, body of Christ and temple of the Spirit.[12]

## THE PEOPLE OF GOD

To call the church the people of God is to recognize that it exists in continuity with the ancient covenant people of God, the people of Israel. That covenant is summed up in the oft-repeated promise of God throughout the Old and New Testaments: "I will be your God and you shall be my people." It is the most comprehensive term that includes even the Israel "after the flesh"; that is, even those who are not Abraham's descendants according to faith in Christ continue to be addressed in the New Testament as the people of God (Rom 9:1-5; cf. Rom 11:1-2).[13] According to Paul in Romans 9—11, what makes the church different from Israel is that it is a people brought about by God's grafting of Gentiles (the wild olive branches) into the natural olive tree. In other words, the church did not replace Israel. The existence of the church must be understood in terms of its relation to the irrevocable election of Israel. This nonsupersessionist view goes against the more commonly held *supersessionism*, which says that the church supersedes Israel as the covenant people of God in order to fulfill the instrumental purpose that Israel failed to carry out—to bring redemption to the world.[14]

There are important implications of the two different ways of reading the biblical narrative, some of them political and social. (One immediately recalls how a supersessionist view was used by the church to persecute Jews.) We will, however, limit ourselves to their theological implications. Douglas Harink, in his critique of N. T. Wright's supersessionism, has noted that the latter operates on the assumption that Israel's election was purely instrumental, namely, as a means to bring redemption to a fallen creation. Harink questions the instrumental understanding of election from such key passages as Isaiah 40—55 and Romans 9—11 and presents a convincing case that "God's election of Israel [was] for God's sake and for Israel's own sake." "God did not call Abraham in order to deal with the problem of Adam"; on the contrary, the biblical narrative is better understood if creation is seen as "primarily to provide a world-historical *background* to the main story, which is about Abraham and his descendants."[15]

The nature of the election of Israel is important because it provides a theologically coherent account of my earlier assertion that the church is prior to creation. It is from the church's continuity with Israel as the chosen people of God that we understand the church's own election as people of God, that is, as God's "polity" or "public" as opposed to the polities of "this world."[16] Lesslie Newbigin describes this as the "logic of election," that is, God's using a particular "tradition of rational discourse" as an instrument of his universal intent.[17] Wright's approach, in contrast, presupposes a linear creation-fall-redemption narrative and views Israel, the covenant people, as the instrument by which the fallen creation is restored. The covenant people exist to serve a higher purpose revealed in creation, and this is thought to be Paul's own comprehensive worldview![18] But as Harink points out, this is a "worldview of late modernity."[19] If Israel serves only a functional purpose, then the church, like ancient Israel, is just as dispensable. The church too could be superseded! If the election of the whole people of God is not seen as an end in itself and for God's sake ("to the praise of God's glory," Eph 1:6, 12, 14), the tendency is to see the church as simply one of a number of entities whose legitimacy is to be established solely based on their ability to serve a higher, all-transcending goal—a goal largely defined by modern secular reason (Niebuhr's "culture"). Relevance to the world becomes the main criterion by which the church defines its raison d'être. But if the church is a divine-humanity, chosen in Christ before the creation of the world,[20] then its raison d'être is not derived from the world; instead, the world must derive its raison d'être from the church, by dying to itself and being reborn into the polity of the church. This is the significance of Christian baptism, of which I shall have more to say later.

There is another aspect of the biblical narrative of Israel's election that is significant for our understanding of the church as the people of God. To recognize the church as the people of God is to recognize a people with a history—a history of ups and downs, of successes and failures. It is to recognize that the church is a pilgrim church, a church on the way, a church that has not quite arrived. Against this backdrop of a church with a checkered history runs a parallel idea that within such a church there exists a smaller group of true and faithful people: the remnant. In Romans 9—10 Paul argues that the "hardening" of Israel was part of God's elective purpose, so that Gentiles may be grafted into the one natural olive tree. This hardening does not mean the rejection of Israel, which is still "God's people" (Rom 11:1-2). The proof of its acceptance is the existence of the remnant themselves, who are not to be understood as the few "true and faithful" as opposed to the masses who are lost but are, rather, "the representative part of the whole, the very means by which the whole of Israel (including the hardened portion) is already made holy."[21] Mutatis mutandis, the church as God's people is always a mixed body *(corpus mixtum)* made up of genuine believers and unbelievers until the final Eschaton.[22] This understanding has had a long tradition in the church since the Donatist controversy. Against this, the impulse toward a "pure" church consisting only of the remnant has always been strong in the free church tradition that many modern evangelicals share.[23] But it represents a failure to appreciate the sovereign work of God in election—that is, the objectivity of the church. Instead it presupposes that the success or failure of the church is ultimately dependent on human effort.

The people of God are a "peculiar people," chosen by God from eternity and distinguished by their "core practices," or what is traditionally called "the marks of the church."[24] These marks are variously conceived. For John Calvin, the marks of the church are Word and sacrament.[25] For Luther, they are the Word of God, baptism, Holy Communion, church discipline, church office, worship and discipleship.[26] In sum, the people of God are distinguished by their faith in Jesus Christ, and the unique quality of their community by faithfulness to that gospel.[27] In whatever ways the marks are conceived, the people's basic identity is shaped by certain practices that make them into a community that is "not of this world"; they become "resident aliens" and "a community of character."[28] David Yeago sums up the nature of this ecclesial community:

> [It] would have a distinctive and living communal culture, with its roots in Israelite narrative, gospel story, sacramental practice and the liturgical drama, a communal culture with at least sufficient density that converts and children would actually need a serious initiation into it. It would not achieve moral perfection, nor escape ethical confusion, but it would have its own distinctive ethos, shaped by its identity-defining stories, with its own definitions of the virtues and its own "take" on the structure of moral questions. In its evangelization, it would not plead with people to find room for faith in their lives; it would invite them to leave home socio-culturally speaking like Abraham of old, and be given new lives in a new country, in the assembly of the Messiah, the public order of the heavenly city. In so doing, moreover, it would necessarily rediscover what "conversion" is and what "catechesis" means.[29]

Yeago's description of the ecclesial community will show, as we shall see, how important the Christian liturgy is in shaping that community.

## THE BODY OF CHRIST

If the church is the divine-humanity, what is the ontological basis of such a reality? The church is the divine-humanity by virtue of its being the body of Christ. The expression *body of Christ* is more than a metaphor for some intimate social dynamic between Christ and his church. It is an ontological reality, as Christ is ontologically real. Thus Lutheran theologian Anders Nygren could write, "The Church is Christ as he is present among and meets us upon earth after his resurrection. . . . Christ is present in his Church through his Word and sacrament, and the Church is, in its essence, nothing other than this presence of Christ."[30] Or, as Gustaf Aulén puts it, "The church exists in and through Christ. Just as the church cannot be conceived of without Christ, so neither can we think of *Kyrios-Christus* without his dominion and the connection with that fellowship which belongs to him. . . . *Christ has become embodied in his church.*"[31] Geoffrey Preston sums it up most succinctly: "The relation of the Church to Christ is not 'like' that of a man's body to the man himself. It *is* that of Christ's body to the Lord Himself."[32] Between the ascension and the parousia the church is the embodied Christ for the world. It is in this sense that Christ could be said to be "bodily" present for the world. "That the church is the body of Christ, in Paul's and our sense, means that she is the object in the world as which the risen Christ is an object for the world, an available something as which Christ is there to be addressed and grasped."[33]

This ontological reality is designated by the term *the total Christ,* made up of head and members *(totus Christus caput et membra).* The church could therefore be said to be an extension of Christ, the way, the truth and the life, on earth.[34] Yet we must not so conceive of the church's identity with Christ as to deny that the church is also *not* Christ but distinct from Christ. Robert Jenson clarifies the distinction between identity and separation in terms of the church as "community" and "association," respectively. In the former the church is the "object-Christ" for the world; in the latter it is confronted by the same and subject to his correction.[35]

To conceive of the church is this manner usually makes evangelicals nervous.[36] There is the fear that to affirm the church's identification with Christ would give too much power to the church, and evangelicals for historical reasons are wary of such things as church hierarchy and, worse, a theologically sanctioned hierarchy. There is also a nagging suspicion that such a concept is a product of church traditions and has nothing to do with Scripture. But the question whether the church should be understood as a divine-humanity or as essentially a social organization has less to do with hermeneutics as with one's preunderstanding or worldview. The issue concerns boundary principles by which we seek to make sense of Scripture. If we accept the idea that the church is only a way of organizing ourselves, then all biblical descriptions about the church are likely to be understood as metaphorical descriptions of social realities—for example, sacraments are nothing but a "memorial" of what Jesus Christ has done for our redemption. But if we believe that the church is a transcendent reality, then we need to probe the biblical descriptions more thoroughly and discover their deeper implications. Given a historical tendency within evangelicalism to accommodate itself to the spirit of the times,[37] what appears to be the "obvious meaning of Scripture" may in fact be a result of implicit acceptance of the reigning "plausibility structure," namely, the secular assumptions of a post-Enlighten-ment age.[38] Acknowledging the church in its spiritual-ontological dimension without diminishing its sociological dimension, however, gives us access to spiritual resources to deal with the problems that plague the modern church.

One of the consequences of affirming the ontological relationship be-tween Christ and the church is the way communion is understood. The church is a communion because members are incorporated into the body of Christ; and the church becomes the one body of Christ by eating and drink-ing the body and blood of Christ. Long before Ludwig Feuerbach popular-ized the saying "You are what you eat," the church fathers understood this principle with respect to the Eucharist. In an Easter sermon addressed to the newly baptized who had just partaken of Holy Communion for the first time, Augustine tells them that in receiving the bread and wine, "you are your-selves what you receive." And what they are receiving is the reality that makes them into members of the one body of Christ. In an embellished ty-pology, Augustine shows how the baptized are made into the one body:

> In this loaf of bread you are given clearly to understand how much you should love unity. I mean, was that loaf made from one grain? Weren't there many grains of wheat? But before they came into the loaf they were all separate; they were joined together by means of water after a certain amount of pounding and crushing. Unless wheat is ground, after all, and moistened with water, it can't possibly get into this shape which is called bread. In the same way you too were being ground and pounded, as it were, by the humiliation of fasting and the sacrament of exorcism. Then came baptism and you were, in a man-ner of speaking, moistened with water in order to be shaped into bread. But it's not yet without fire to bake it. So what does fire represent? That's the chrism, the anointing. Oil, the fire-feeder, you see, is the sacrament of the Holy Spirit.[39]

In sum, ecclesial communion is first and foremost an essentially eucha-ristic communion.[40] When the church is understood as essentially commun-ion in and of the body of Christ, the primary focus of the ecclesial life is not church hierarchy but *koinonia* characterized by *agape*.[41] Far from opening the door to the reintroduction of "priestcraft" into the church, communion-eucharistic ecclesiology subverts that possibility by giving to church hierar-chy and orders a subservient role. As Sergius Bulgakov puts it, "First the church, then the hierarchy, not vice versa. As the body of Christ and the tem-

ple of the Holy Spirit, the Church is the fullness from which hierarchical ministry emanates."[42] Communion ecclesiology is less likely to result in a situation that we find in many an independent megachurch: the dependence of
the church on a single charismatic leader.

A second consequence of understanding the church as ontologically
linked to Christ its Head is the way we understand the Christian tradition.
For many evangelicals, tradition is only the human interpretations of Scripture at best or unbiblical accretions that distort Scripture at worst. The only
real value of tradition is pedagogical: the past might offer us lessons on how
we should or should not do things now; studying Christian history may yield
some positive lessons or, more likely, negative ones. In fact, relying too
much on our forebears might even have a harmful effect on present theological endeavors. The former president of Dallas Theological Seminary,
Lewis Sperry Chafer, speaks for many evangelicals at the popular level: "The
very fact that I did not study a prescribed course in theology made it possible for me to approach the subject with an unprejudiced mind and to be
concerned only with what the Bible actually teaches."[43] If Scripture is the
sole and sufficient rule of faith and practice, one needs to refer only and
directly to Scripture, without recourse to tradition. In short, evangelicalism
accepts an ahistorical view of the church supported by an ahistorical view
of Scripture, cut off from tradition.[44] As a result, the church is constantly being created by one's own action in the here and now on the basis of a Bible
viewed as a deposit of propositional truths and timeless principles that can
be transposed into any time and situation.[45]

Tradition, however, is a dynamic process. Alasdair MacIntyre has given a
helpful definition of the nature of tradition:

> A tradition is an argument extended through time in which certain fundamen-
> tal agreements are defined and redefined in terms of two kinds of conflict:
> those with critics and enemies external to the tradition who reject all or at least
> key parts of those fundamental agreements, and those internal, interpretative
> debates through which the meaning and rationale of the fundamental agree-
> ments come to be expressed and by whose progress a tradition is consti-
> tuted.[46]

Tradition is an ongoing *coherent* process ("an argument") in which certain core values of a community ("fundamental agreements") are advanced
through debates with critics from outside and interpretive refinements from
within. Like a person whose history and memory shape his or her identity,

the church as the body of Christ cannot be understood apart from its history and collective memory of Jesus Christ. Tradition is the means by which the church understands its true identity. We can make sense of what the church is now only because it exists in *historical* continuity with the church then. To repudiate that historical link is to put our own identification with the "one, holy, catholic and apostolic" church into serious doubt. Baptist theologian D. H. Williams puts this question to "suspicious Protestants":

> How can any church today claim a connection with the apostolic era when it has remained ignorant of and often rejected in practice the church age which followed the apostles and which was *the* critical period for the very formation of the New Testament, for the propounding of the doctrines of Christ and the Trinity, for the confessions of redemption and eternal hope—in short, for the development of what it is to think and live as an orthodox Christian?[47]

The New Testament was itself the result of more than three centuries of church life, reflections and discussion in councils. How can we accept the New Testament and reject that very process in the church that "canonizes" it? Without tradition, the present-day church cannot legitimately claim to be in line with the New Testament—*sola Scriptura* notwithstanding.[48] Without anchoring itself within the living and continuing tradition, the modern church will have no long-term collective memory, and therefore no self-identity, that will enable it to judge the novelties and fleeting fashions of the day in light of the enduring truth of Scripture which it purports to uphold. In fact, in the repudiation of its own past, the gospel of Jesus Christ that should give the church its coherent life story is reduced to disjointed snippets. The integrity and wholeness of the gospel—the gospel that gives evangelicals their name and basic identity in the first place—becomes fragmented into gospels of easy believism, health and wealth, and self-gratification.

In short, if the church is the living body of Christ ontologically linked to the Head, then tradition is the life of the "embodied Christ" through time. If Christ is the Truth, then tradition is the extension of the Truth, the progressive actualizing of the Truth through time until it reaches its eschatological fulfillment. But *how* is the church linked to Christ? The answer is found in the third image of the church.

## THE TEMPLE OF THE HOLY SPIRIT

The church as the temple of the Spirit in a most decisive way completes the other two images as people of God and body of Christ. If the church as the people of God are distinguished by certain "marks" or "core practices" as noted earlier, the church as the temple of the Spirit reminds us that these practices are not our own invention but are "the Spirit's concrete works through which he fulfills his own sanctifying mission in the triune economy of salvation."[49] The "marks," according to Luther, are "holy possessions whereby the Holy Spirit effects in us a daily sanctification and vivification in Christ."[50] It is the Spirit that makes these distinctive practices possible—practices that form the church. If the church is the body of Christ, a divine-humanity grounded in the narrative of the triune God, the Spirit's relation to the church explains how this body is constituted as a vibrant communion. It is the Spirit that links the church to Christ the Head, making it the body of Christ, the *totus Christus*.[51]

Again, if the church as the body of Christ is the extension of Christ the Truth and the embodiment of the true Tradition (which is Christ himself, the first Tradition sent from the Father), the church as the temple of the Spirit explains how this tradition is alive and moving inexorably toward its appointed End.[52] In other words, to speak of the church as temple *of the Spirit* is also to recognize its essentially eschatological character, since the Spirit is the Spirit of the "last days." This eschatological dimension of church is usually carried by another image: the pilgrim church. The church is constantly on the move, in need of being transformed by the Spirit until it is completely restored at the consummation of the age. As the Vatican II document on the church puts it:

> The promised restoration which we are awaiting has already begun in Christ, is carried forward in the mission of the Holy Spirit, and through Him continues in the Church. There we learn through faith the meaning, too, of our temporal life, as we perform, with hope of good things to come, the task committed to us in this world by the Father, and work out our salvation (cf. Phil. 2:12).[53]

The key to understanding the Spirit in the church is to see the Spirit in his own right as the Third Person of the Trinity. Jenson points out that the basic pneumatological problem today is the distinct identity of the Spirit as the Third Person. The Western tradition has suffered from a "pneumatological deficit" by defining the Spirit almost exclusively in terms of the *relation*, that is, the bond of love between the Father and the Son, so that the *personal* relation of the Spirit to the Father and Son does not come through. The I-Thou refers exclusively to the Father-Son relationship and does not include the Spirit's relation to the Son and Father.[54]

The reason the Spirit's identity as Third Person is not fully appreciated is that the trinitarian life is understood in terms of "relation of origin" rather than in terms of the End. The Father's identity is clearly distinguished as the One "without origin." The Son too stands over against the Father in the incarnation. But the Spirit as Person, while acknowledged, does not distinguish himself in relation to either the Father or to the Son.[55]

Where then do we see the Spirit as Third Person? According to Jenson, following Wolfhart Pannenberg, it is when he is seen in relation to the eschaton, from his being sent by the Father "in my (Jesus') name," which inaugurates the last days. "Scripture knows various active relations between the Spirit as whom God is future to himself, and the Father and the Son whose future he is."[56] It is in relation to the future that the Spirit as Third Person is clearly seen. The gospel story continues with the coming of the Spirit upon the church at Pentecost and the Spirit's continuing leading of the church into the future toward the consummation. The Spirit's coming constitutes the church by uniting the church to its Head, making it the body of Christ. "The Spirit finds his 'I' in the Son just insofar as the Son is the *totus Christus,* insofar as the Son includes and is included in his community."[57]

This construction of the Spirit's role in the church is extremely crucial, because it not only reveals the distinctiveness of the Spirit as Third Person but also reveals the intimate connection between the Spirit and the church. It is in relation to the church as *totus Christus* that the Spirit as Third Person comes to his own.

*The Pentecost event.* This brings us to a reconsideration of the nature of the Pentecost event. Pentecost has been usually understood as the event that empowers the church to continue the work that Christ left for it to do after his ascension. In other words, it is essentially the extension of Christ's mission on earth. What is often not recognized is that the coming of the Spirit into the church introduces something new that is not just an extension of Christ's mission on earth. Jenson notes the distinctive Eastern contribution to the discussion on this point: "Pentecost is an 'intervention of the Holy Trinity' that is 'new' over against the Resurrection and 'issues from the third Person of the Trinity' *in his own identity.*"[58] Pentecost is the birth of the church not as the people of God but as the body of Christ and temple of the Spirit.[59] The church, in Peter Brunner's words, becomes the "epiphany of the crucified body of Christ on earth." The church as the body of Christ could not have existed while Jesus was still bodily present on earth. It is as the believers are filled with the Spirit that they are constituted as the body of Christ and replace the earthly Christ, giving to "the body of Jesus, the pneumatic derestriction, the pneumatic presence, through which He reaches out to the individual and integrates him into Himself in a pneumatic and yet concretely historical event."[60]

The newness of the Pentecost event is seen in a church whose communion is marked by an unprecedented characteristic. Earlier I quoted the picturesque language of Augustine when he describes communion in the body of Christ as dough not just knit together with the water of baptism but baked by the fire of the Spirit before it could become "one loaf." The Spirit effects a communion that is concrete and universal in scope. The record of Acts 2 tells us that on the day of Pentecost the Spirit came and filled *all* who were present and they began to speak in other tongues (Acts 2:4). The Spirit was indeed poured out on "all flesh": sons and daughters, young and old, menservants and maidservants (Acts 2:17-18). Yet, the "all flesh" spoke many different languages that could be understood by those present in Jerusalem.[61] Unlike the Tower of Babel, where human beings trying to build their own "church" by a united effort brought confusion and division,[62] the Pentecost event unites people speaking many different tongues into one body. Members of this body thereafter "devoted themselves to the apostles' teaching and to the fellowship, to the breaking of bread and to prayer" (Acts 2:42). The Spirit has created a community that is truly catholic, transcending all ethnic, cultural and social barriers. It is a communion in which real diversity exists side by side with real unity, a communion that could truly be called a body with many different parts (1 Cor 12:12-31).

Paul's use of the analogy of the body with many different parts to explain how the *charismata* should be exercised in the church highlights another aspect of the Spirit as Third Person. The Spirit is distinguished as the Third Person not only as the *gift* from the Father that the risen Christ "poured out" on the church (Acts 2:33) but also as the *giver* of gifts (1 Cor 12:7-11), making the whole church a charismatic community. It is largely to the credit of Pentecostals that this dimension of the Spirit's work in the church is now receiving the attention it deserves. Unfortunately, sometimes charismatics are so fixated on the Spirit that the Third Person is in danger of becoming isolated from the Father and the Son.[63] The reason is their failure to locate the Spirit in ecclesiology, and the result is not *charismata* but charismania.

*The living Tradition.* If, as noted above, the church as the body of Christ is the extension of Christ the Truth,[64] then the truth as embodied in the church indwelled by the Spirit is not merely a bare repetition of the truth of Christ. It is the truth that is ongoing, dynamic and developing on account of the distinctive work of the Spirit. The Spirit who is the anticipation of the End keeps the church constantly on the move. The Spirit is the Spirit of *truth,* who embodies the Truth in the church as well as guides the church into all truth—to Christ himself (Jn 14:26).[65] The Spirit is also the Spirit of *life,* so that the truth is not a static deposit or some timeless proposition but the living Tradition, the life of the Spirit in the church. He is also the Spirit of the eschaton, the one who anticipates and opens the *way* to the End, who reveals something of the end to us now as a "foretaste" and who guarantees the church's fulfillment of its intended end. If Christ is the way, the truth and the life objectively considered, the Spirit is the subjective embodiment of the way, the truth and the life in the church which is the embodied Christ. To speak of the Spirit in such a manner is to recognize that the church as the living Tradition embodies a living and developing dogma[66] and, at the same time, that the development of dogma does not lead the church astray (as evangelicals fear) but follows the trajectory set by the gospel events: Christ's life → death → resurrection → ascension → Pentecost → parousia.

The progress of dogma has the character of a plot, the ongoing story of God's action in the world, and the story of the church is part of that development. But what is the church's story? It is the story centering in the Third Person of the Trinity: the sending of the Spirit. The coming of the Spirit, as noted earlier, constitutes the church by uniting the body to the Head. In this very act, as Jenson puts it, the "Spirit frees an actual human community from merely historical determinisms, to be apt to be united with the Son and thus to be the gateway of creation's translation into God."[67] The story of the church, therefore, could be said to be the story of the Spirit in the church. In this sense, the church could be called "the public of the Spirit."[68] The gospel that the church embodies and proclaims is public truth.[69] This is why Pentecost is so vital to the continuing growth of the Christian story. Without telling the story of the church, which is the story of the Spirit in the church, we have an incomplete gospel.

Herein lies the main weakness in Protestant and evangelical theology: it terminates the gospel story at the resurrection and ascension, so that the church is seen solely as the agent to retell or restate a story that ended with

Christ's resurrection. Protestantism has no sense of the continuation of the gospel into ecclesiology and pneumatology. When it comes to understanding the church, sociology takes over. As for the Spirit, he is seen as essentially One who helps the church to carry out some extrinsic task, even if it is conceived as a divine task, such as evangelism. If the Spirit is linked to the church in any way, it is to the invisible church, such as in the Spirit's bringing spiritual rebirth to individuals. The visible church is largely defined sociologically, while the "real" church cannot be identified with anything visible. Such an ecclesiology could only be described as docetic.

Against such a view, we need to see ecclesiology as an intrinsic part of the doctrine of the gospel of Jesus Christ, not an administrative arrangement for the sake of securing practical results. The story of the church is what it is because it is the story of the Spirit who constitutes it, the continuation of the triune economy of salvation. Ecclesiology and pneumatology therefore cannot be separated. Spirit and church constitute the third article of the Nicene-Constantinopolitan Creed.[70] In fact, it could be argued that the creed in its present form does not keep Spirit and church close enough together. In some earlier confessions and catechisms, the confession of the faithful is in the form of "I believe in the Holy Spirit *in* the Holy Catholic Church."[71] Their close relationship can also be seen when we examine the affirmation concerning the church: "We believe in the one holy, catholic and apostolic church." The one church is *one* precisely because it is united to Christ the Head by the one Spirit who indwells it, making it the one temple of the Spirit and the one body of Christ. The church is *holy* precisely because it is the temple indwelled by the Holy Spirit. The church is *apostolic* precisely because the Spirit guides it into all truth and preserves it from error by binding it diachronically to the apostles in an unbroken succession.

*The eschatological tension.* Through the Spirit, the church is taken up into the triune narrative, which will find its fulfillment at the parousia. Since the Spirit's coming inaugurates the "last days," the church exists in a kind of interim commonly described as the "already and not yet." This dialectic itself defines the distinctive nature of the Spirit's work in the church. "Pentecost is the Spirit's particular personal initiative to delay the Parousia: when the Spirit descends eschatologically yet without raising all the dead and ending this age, the time for the church is opened."[72] Douglas Farrow characterizes this period in which the "already-not yet" tension is held in perfect balance as the "ascension-parousia differential."[73] Between the ascension and the parousia Christ is not physically present, but he is present eucharistically through the presence of the Spirit. This is the unique ministry of the Spirit in the church age. The church at present is sustained by this eucharistic presence of Christ. This is why the Eucharist is so central to the liturgy of the church and the invocation of the Spirit is most particularly connected with the celebration of the Eucharist.

The real work of the Spirit is his work in the church. Only within the ecclesial context is the Spirit as the "firstfruits" of the new creation actualized. This actualization takes place in the Eucharist, where the "already" and the "not yet" are held together. In the eucharistic worship of the church, the Spirit actualizes the past through remembrance *(anamnēsis)* and anticipates the future *(prolepsis)* when created things are transfigured (or "transubstantiated," if you like). In this anticipation, something of the future—a foretaste—is realized as the Father is "called upon" (Greek *epiclesis*) to send the Holy Spirit in the Eucharist.[74] *Anamnēsis* and *prolepsis* are the two poles held together in the present as the church invokes the Spirit's presence in its eucharistic celebration. Or, putting it another way, the church *remembers* Christ and appropriates the benefits of his redemption through the Spirit. But the experience of "feeding on Christ to life eternal" anticipates the future and is also a *foretaste* of the future: the marriage supper of the Lamb, the healing of a broken creation, reconciliation and face-to-face communion. The Eucharist is where the past and the future are effectively brought together in the present through the *epiclesis*. We may say, then, that the *epiclesis* represents the most distinctive mark of ecclesial existence between the ascension and the parousia. That is to say, ecclesial existence is characterized chiefly by the church's calling for the coming of the Spirit as the *arrabon* (the foretaste or pledge) of the new creation. This is the only proper way to understand the relationship between the Spirit and the church: ecclesiology is essentially pneumatological and charismatic, and pneumatology is essentially ecclesial.

Without a proper conjunction of Spirit and church, however, the tendency is to resolve the already-not yet tension in favor of one or the other. This is exactly what we see in modern evangelicalism. Traditionally, evangelicals profess belief in the supernatural, but in their day-to-day existence the "scientific worldview" prevails. It is a two-tiered world in which the supernatural and natural realms are kept in separate compartments. The supernatural is effectively excluded from the ordinary world. Using a term from formal logic, missiologist Paul Hiebert calls it the "flaw of the excluded middle."[75] In more recent times, however, some evangelicals—the "Third Wavers" or the signs-and-wonders advocates—have swung to the opposite extreme. Before they saw nothing supernatural in the world, but now they see nothing else.[76]

Why do evangelicals have this tendency to swing from one extreme to another while acknowledging in theory the need to maintain the eschato-logical tension? Why do they end up with either "futurist dispensationalism" and cessationism on one extreme or a kingdom-now theology on the other?[77] The reason is that evangelicalism does not take into account the ec-clesial and, more specifically, the eucharistic context of its supernaturalism. Earlier I noted Mark Noll's belief that the "supernaturalism" inherent in evan-gelicalism—that God can transform the soul through the cross—is also the hope of the movement, in that it opens up the possibility of its own trans-formation, the creation of an "evangelical mind." But this supernaturalism itself is not adequate if it is understood to apply only to individuals and not interpreted within the ecclesial context, more specifically, within the context of the church's eucharistic celebration. For it is in the eucharistic celebration itself that the already-not yet tension is actually upheld by the whole church as it invokes the Spirit as *arrabon.*

Evangelicalism has a strong ontology of the person but not an ontology of the church. Without an ontology of the church, the relationship between Spirit and church cannot be understood ontologically either. The real work of the Spirit is assumed to occur only in the individual and not in the church. As a result, the transformation of individuals will have only marginal impact on the whole communal life. Individuals with their particular temperaments and lim-ited perspectives will not be able to maintain the eschatological tension. It is as members of the body of Christ, "members of one another," that each dis-covers his or her part in relation to the whole church. The church is more than the sum of its parts and transcends the parts. In the Eucharist it becomes that whole, and as church—the *totus Christus*—it is able to uphold the tension through both *anamnēsis* and *prolepsis* in the power of the Spirit.

Perhaps an example would be useful to clarify the above point. Scott Peck in *People of the Lie* has shown us how structural evil affects the way individuals behave.[78] As a person, one may actually be quite moral, but as part of a system, one's behavior could become quite unconscionable. One starts to absolve questionable actions with such excuses as "under orders," "company policy" and the like. Systems do shape our values either for good or for evil. If that is the case, the church as a structure of truth will have a deep impact on its members.

Recognizing that the church is more than the sum of its individual members, that its head is Christ the Truth, that it is energized by the Spirit of Truth and that it is given spiritual resources to advance the Truth, we see a "structure of Truth" that can decisively shape the individuals within it. It is not enough to work from the bottom up, that is, to change structures by changing individuals;[79] we should be working from the top down, that is, by being open to the Spirit's working "epicletically" in the body. This means being faithful to what the church is called to be: a worshiping community feeding on spiritual food and drink to become a spiritual body.

But instead of trusting in and being faithful to what the Spirit is doing in the church, some have devised marketing techniques to commend a pop version of the Christian faith to its *un*cultured despisers. They dumb down worship to make it "seeker friendly" and congratulate themselves for successfully bringing in a crowd. Or they devise spiritual techniques to control the Spirit, as some Third Wavers have done. These are strategies that Jesus himself would have nothing to do with. When one crowd of people had eaten free bread and fish, they decided to make him king. Perhaps they thought that making Jesus their king would ensure a continuous supply of bread and fish and oblige him to perform more miracles. But Jesus thought differently; he withdrew himself from them (Jn 6:15).

## THE SPIRIT'S MISSION IN THE CHURCH

This brings us to the nature of the church's mission. In light of the unbreakable link between the Spirit and the church, the mission of the church could be summed up as nothing but the mission of the Spirit in the church. The church's very existence could be described as the Spirit's constantly pushing the body of Christ forward toward the parousia, the final fulfillment. That is part of the character of the Spirit in the church beginning at Pentecost. His coming creates the "ascension-parousia differential," a period characterized as "the last days" in Peter's sermon at Pentecost (Acts 2:17).

The essential nature of mission is for the church to be the *body* of Christ. We can be available to other persons only as embodied beings, and the church as *totus Christus* is the embodied Christ made available to the world. To say "The church is the body of Christ" means that Christ as embodied is available to the world: "That the church is the body of Christ, in Paul's and our sense, means that she is the object in the world as which the risen Christ is an object for the world, an available something as which Christ is there to be addressed and grasped."[80]

The church's primary mission, then, is to be itself, which is to be "Christ" for the world. The church by its faith and life becomes, in Newbigin's words, "the hermeneutic of the gospel"; that is, by being true to its calling as church, the church explicates the gospel in the world.[81] But in another sense, the church is not a perfect embodiment of Christ. It is in need of reform. It is still "on the way" *(in via)* to perfection, "marked with a genuine though imperfect holiness."[82] This fact reminds us that the church is distinct from Christ. It needs to "feed on Christ" and be disciplined by Christ. And as Christ makes himself available to the church in the sacraments, the church in turn makes itself available to the world as the "embodied Christ." One can see why mission sustains the closest relationship to the Eucharist: the Eucharist *is* mission. It is mission in that it is making the church, the embodied Christ, available to the world. In its eucharistic worship the church is reformed to "go forth into the world to love and serve the Lord." The world does not know of any other Christ except the Christ that is embodied in the church. Thus to be the church is the greatest mission to the world.

Mission, then, must be defined in the largest sense, which is the fulfillment of God's ultimate reason for the church's existence: "to the praise of his glory." It is much larger than the narrowly defined idea of "winning souls." Neither is it trying to fulfill the goal of creation (as in Matthew Fox's creation spirituality).[83] The goal is to be the church as the full people of God (one of the three pictures of the church), uniting all in Christ. When the ascension-parousia differential is overcome, then Christ will deliver up the kingdom to God so that God will be "all in all" (1 Cor 15:24-28). Creation then will be consummated in the church as the comprehensive people of God enjoying "deification," *visio Dei* (vision of God) or communion with the Trinity. Thus the final eschatological vision is described in terms that hark back to God's original covenant with Abraham, Isaac and Jacob: "Now the dwelling of God is with men, and he will live with them. They will be his people, and God himself will be with them and be their God" (Rev 21:3).

But how is this vision to become reality? Practically, how is the church to become the people of God, the body of Christ and the temple of the Spirit? The answer is to be found in the church's worship.

# THE WORSHIP
# OF THE CHURCH

The problem of ecclesiology plaguing modern evangelicalism cannot be separated from the problem of worship. The two are integrally linked: error in one leads to error in the other. If, for example, the church is merely the result of a human decision to gather together in a certain way in order to advance some practical end, such as the salvation of souls, then worship is likely to be understood as a human construct to achieve that end. This pragmatic concept of worship underlies many of the so-called worship wars between traditionalists and innovators in today's church.[1] Often the structure of worship is changed without much thought given to its theological consequence. What is foremost in the minds of the innovators is whether the worship is "relevant" to modern people, whether it meets their needs, whether it will attract and retain a crowd.

What this shows is the need for a sound theology of worship that can guide the church's practice and ensure that its worship is truly the worship of the triune God and not hijacked to serve other ends. The first step toward establishing a sound theology of worship is to discover the connection between worship and the church. As noted in chapter one, the church was chosen in Christ before the creation of the world (Eph 1:4), but in its actualization, the church is the people called out by God's word to be the congregation of God's people. What we call the liturgy is the people's *common* response to that word, their acceptance of the Word, which constitutes them as the covenant people. This is the pattern we find throughout the Scripture. In the Old Testament, the *qahal* (assembly) was constituted by God's word to the people, who signaled their entrance into the covenant by a sacrificial offering. In the New Testament, it is the coming of the Word made flesh and the sealing of the covenant by Christ's sacrificial death. The coming of God's word to gather a people and the people's response to that word—that is the basic dynamic of worship and the constitution of the liturgical assembly.[2]

There is therefore no separation between the liturgy and the church. *To be church is to be the worshiping community making a normative response to the revelation of the triune God.* I shall expand on this statement by looking at (1) how worship is related to the church, (2) how worship constitutes a normative response, which raises the question of the relationship between worship and theology, and (3) how the response should be characterized.

## WORSHIP AND THE CHURCH

To be church is to be the worshiping community—this statement acknowledges that the church's most basic identity is to be found in its act of worship. But how does worship reveal the church's identity as church? The question may be answered in three ways. First, *worship is what distinguishes the church as the church.* This understanding carries two implications. First, if worship distinguishes the church from the world, to be church is ipso facto to be not-of-this-world. The church, as noted in the previous chapter, existing in the eschatological tension between the "already" and "not yet," shows itself to be basically oriented toward the new creation and therefore not-of-this-world. But in its worship, it especially shows itself to be opposed to what the world stands for and even to be, in Jean-Jacques von Allmen's words, "a threat to the world."

> Every time the Church assembles to celebrate the cult, to "proclaim the death of Christ" (1 Cor 11:26), it proclaims also the end of the world and the failure of the world. It contradicts the world's claim to provide men with a valid justification for their existence, it renounces the world: it affirms, since it is made up of the baptized, that it is only on the other side of death to this world that life can assume its meaning. . . . Christian worship is the strongest denial that can be hurled in face of the world's claim to provide men with an effective and sufficient justification of their life. There is no more emphatic protest against the pride and the despair of the world than that implied in Church worship.[3]

If we reflect on the church's doxologies, we discover them to have "an eminently polemic implication." When the church proclaims, "For yours is the kingdom and the power" (Mt 6:13 footnote) or "To the only wise God be glory" (Rom 16:27) or "You are worthy, our Lord and God, to receive glory" (Rev 4:11), these proclamations affirm the obverse side of its baptismal vow—its renunciation of the world, the flesh and the devil. In effect, the church is saying that the only true worship is the worship of the true God, and by so doing it exposes any earthly entity or ideology that claims the right of absolute allegiance as both pretentious and idolatrous.

The early church under persecution fully understood the radical claims it was making by the simple act of worshiping God on Sunday. During the Diocletian persecution, when a group of Christians were taken into custody for attending worship on Sunday and charged with acting "against the orders of the emperors and the caesars," their reply was, "We have been celebrating what is the Lord's *(dominicus)*" and "what is the Lord's cannot cease."[4] Sunday is the Lord's. It is the day of Lord's resurrection and of Christians' participation in the new creation; it is the day of the Lord's presence actualized in the eucharistic celebration. There is an inner assurance in their simple assertion. Against the mightiest political power of the day, these Christians discovered a greater reality, the power of an unquenchable life, concretized in their worship on the Lord's Day. Sunday then was not even a public holiday. But for the Christians it was the new point of departure to a new order of existence. So real was it that, like their predecessors in the first century, they felt the inner compulsion to "obey God rather than men" (Acts 5:29).

> The Christian cult is a basically political action: it reminds the state of the limited and provisional character of its power, and when the state claims for itself an absolute trust and obedience, the Christian cult protests against this pretension to claim a kingdom, a power and a glory which belong of right to God alone. That is why, in gathering together for Christian worship, men compromise themselves politically.[5]

The second implication is that worship could be said to be *the* defining characteristic of the church. In this world the church may be many other things: a voice of conscience in the community, a champion of the poor and oppressed, a preserver of traditional values and so on. But these functions are not what make it the church, for they could as well be taken up by other religious and secular bodies. The church's defining characteristic is its worshipful response to the call of God to be his people. This may explain why in the Scriptures Christians are sometimes simply called worshipers (Phil 3:3; 1 Tim 2:10; Heb 12:28; Rev 13:12-13; 14:11). Worshiping God is the hallmark of the people of God. The call brings forth the assembly of responders or worshipers, whose definitive and culminating act of worship is the eucharistic celebration (see next chapter). This explains why the Eucharist has always been reserved for only the baptized.

If worship is the defining characteristic of the church, it would explain why the Scriptures treat some of the basic activities of the church as essentially liturgical acts. Worship became a comprehensive concept qualifying many other actions. Not only must the spirit of worship pervade all the activities of Christians, including eating and drinking (cf. 1 Cor 10:31), but certain works—the preaching of the gospel (Rom 15:16) and service (Heb 13:15-16)—are seen as liturgical acts. The Hebrews passage reads, "Through Jesus, therefore, let us continually offer to God a sacrifice of praise—the fruit of lips that confess his name. And do not forget to do good and to share with others, for with such sacrifices God is pleased." Here the author brings together the "sacrifice of praise" and doing good to others as "sacrifices" acceptable to God. From the teaching of the gospel, we can readily see how this is so regarding the latter. According to Jesus, in visiting the prisoner, feeding the hungry and clothing the naked, we are doing these acts to the one whom we acknowledge as Lord. Sacrifices of time, food and clothing are actually offered to him (cf. Mt 25:40). But how is preaching a liturgical act? The implication of this is so far reaching that it merits a small digression here.

Quite clearly Paul in Romans 15:16 sees his missionary work among the Gentiles in terms of the worship of God: a priestly service of offering up the Gentiles as an acceptable sacrifice to God (cf. Rom 12:1-3, where he urges the Christians to offer up themselves as living sacrifices wholly acceptable to God). In his commentary Barrett notes that "Paul serves by acting as a priest for the Gospel of God . . . in order that the offering of the Gentiles might be acceptable."[6] Bringing people to God through the proclamation of the gospel is a priestly act of offering up an acceptable sacrifice.

To see the preaching of the gospel in the world as a liturgical act means that it is first and foremost a service rendered *to God*. Failure to understand the proclamation of the gospel from this perspective is one reason that evangelism is conceived of as largely a human-centered activity. Much of modern evangelization focuses on the *need* of sinners. We tell people to go and preach the gospel because souls are dying and going to hell, that the completion of mission will hasten the return of Christ and so on. The needs of sinners are, of course, a legitimate concern: Christ came into the world to save sinners, and Paul himself confessed, "I am not ashamed of the gospel, because it is the power of God for the salvation of everyone who believes" (Rom 1:16). These are texts with a strong evangelistic import. But do we see mission as also and *primarily* an act of worship? To see the preaching of the gospel as priestly implies that it is essentially a Godward act, an offering up of living sacrifices to God (cf. Rom 12:1). Mission is ultimately theocentric rather than anthropocentric.

There is another dimension in preaching that reveals its essentially liturgical character. We preach and offer up to God, yet it cannot ultimately be our work but the work of the Spirit. Note again Romans 15:16: the offering up of the Gentiles as an acceptable sacrifice is possible through the sanctification of the Holy Spirit. It is the Spirit's setting them apart, making them a "holy" people, that makes them an acceptable offering. In evangelical parlance, we cannot separate preaching from what the Holy Spirit does to turn sinners into God's handiwork. Lives are transformed so that they become, in Stanley Hauerwas's term, "a community of character." This does not just mean being "nice" people. What marks Christians as God's people is that they have become a community that worships God in spirit and in truth. This is what the church must aim at in mission. Mission does not seek to turn sinners into saved individuals; it seeks, rather, to turn disparate individuals into a worshiping community. The preoccupation of the modern church with numbers often misses the real goal of mission. Instead of turning out fine works of art, the modern church tends to model its mission on the mass-production factory. The church becomes an efficiently run factory. We then market the megachurch as the model of a successful church. Is it any wonder that grandiose strategies of winning the world for Christ have produced a bloated church whose ways and values are not very different from those of the world?[7] The ministry becomes departmentalized (again, like a mass-production factory), mission is left to church-growth specialists, counseling is done by professionally trained counselors, and the pastor serves as the CEO.

If the various "ministries" of the modern church are to achieve coherence, to become the one ministry rendered ultimately to God, we need to recover the neglected concept of priestly ministry. For it is as priest that the minister discovers the essence of ministry: to offer up to God an *unblemished* sacrifice, one that meets the demands of a holy God. This is one of the most conspicuous features of the Old Testament cultus. It is from that context that the

New Testament sacrificial language is derived. Thus the ministry of proclaiming Christ is to admonish and teach "everyone with all wisdom, so that we may present everyone perfect in Christ" (Col 1:28). We see here again the preaching of the gospel presented as a priestly act of offering up perfect sacrifices in Christ to God.

A mass of half-committed, fair-weather adherents or a group of psychologically well-adjusted individuals (which is what a mass-production church could hope to accomplish at its best) does not amount to a perfect sacrifice. Only God himself can define what is the perfect and acceptable sacrifice: it must be a sacrifice sanctified by the Holy Spirit. This is why the Old Testament cultus is carefully regulated: everything has to be done according to the revealed pattern "as the Lord commanded" (for example, Ex 25:9; 39:43; 40:16, 19).

The church's mission must ultimately be defined by its divine givenness and its Godward dimension, that is, as an act of worship. Only when mission is carried out as an act of worship will it truly build up the church. For only when the church presents people as unblemished sacrifices before God will it become the community of God's people. In the church's encounter with the triune God, it is formed into the community of God. In true worship we become the church.

This brings us to the second point: Worship not only distinguishes the church as church, *it also makes or realizes the church*. In one sense, this is the least disputed point about worship. Even those with a purely functionalist understanding of the church would agree that in the worship service people are being influenced in a certain way, even if the influence may be quite fleeting, in terms of, for example, mood creation or emotional and aesthetic satisfaction. In the liturgical tradition, what is realized in the worship is the church as an ontological rather than sociological reality. According to the Russian Orthodox theologian Alexander Schmemann, worship is the function of the church, and "its purpose is to express, form, or realize the Church—to be the source of that grace which always makes the Church the Church, the people of God, the Body of Christ, 'a chosen race and a royal priesthood' (1 Peter 2:9)." Worship is church "manifesting, creating and fulfilling herself as the Body of Christ."[8] The same idea is poignantly expressed by Jean-Jacques von Allmen: "It is in the sphere of worship, the sphere par excellence where the life of the Church comes into being, that the fact of the Church first emerges. It is there that it gives proof of itself, there where it is focused, and where we are led when we truly seek it, and it is from that point that it goes out into the world to exercise its mission."[9]

Unlike the pragmatic conception of the church, where practices are largely determined by what works in a given place and time, the liturgical tradition insists that the church is truly formed as church if it practices what truly constitutes the church. These practices have always returned to two things, Word and sacrament, and these will be taken up in the next chapter.

Third, *worship is God's action in the church.* While we speak of worship as our response (see below), it is strictly speaking not our action but the action of Christ in the church, or the action of the church as *totus Christus.* The church responds to the God who revealed himself in history and most supremely in the Word made flesh. The response itself is not based on our own decision. We don't decide: now that God has spoken, what should we do? The call brings into being the assembly that makes a true response because it is the Spirit of the Son in the assembly who rightly responds to the Father, causing us to cry out, "Abba, Father!" (Rom 8:15). In true worship there is an inherent fittingness of the response to the One who reveals himself as who he is, because it comes ultimately from the Spirit of God who indwells the body of Christ.

We can give a fitting response only because worship is the work of the triune God in the church. This is seen in the church's ancient liturgical prayers, which were invariably trinitarian: to the Father, through the Son, in the Holy Spirit. This early trinitarian pattern, before the onset of the Arian controversy, reveals the distinctive roles of the triune God in the liturgy.[10] The Father is the origin and goal of our worship; the Son is the One who reveals the Father and the mediator between God and humankind; the Holy Spirit is the power by whom Christ lifts up fallen humanity and leads them to the Father.[11] The revival of trinitarian studies since the late twentieth century has once again returned the church to this richer understanding of the work of the triune God in worship.

One of the finest examples of this approach to liturgical theology is Edward Kilmartin's *Christian Liturgy:* "Christ, in the power of the Spirit, is the source of the real communication between the liturgical assembly and the Father of all." He is the "chief speaker and actor of the liturgical assembly, who communicates with its members through the expression of faith of the Church of which he, in the Spirit, is the vital source. As a result the faithful are aroused and made capable of interacting with the Lord, addressing the

Father through the one mediator between God and humankind."[12]

The worship of the church is, properly speaking, the action of the triune God in the church. But it is divine action joined with human action: we need to assemble and engage in the act of worship. This is why assembling together is so vital to the life of the church: it is what constitutes the *qahal*. So important it is that in an early Christian document, the *Didascalia* (third century), we are warned that absence from the assembly "cause[s] the body of Christ to be short of a member."[13]

## WORSHIP AND THEOLOGY

To speak of worship as a fitting response implies that in the very act of worship we are participating in the God who is truth. Liturgiologists call this participation doing "primary theology." This idea is given cogent expression by Schmemann, for whom liturgical theology is "the elucidation of the meaning of worship"[14] and the "theology" in the phrase "liturgical theology" is not secondary reflection on the liturgy but "the faith" finding concrete expression in the liturgy.

> What it means is that the Church's *leitourgia* . . . is the full and adequate "epiphany"—expression, manifestation, fulfillment of that in which the church believes, or what constitutes her faith. It implies an organic and essential interdependence in which one element, the faith, although source and cause of the other, the liturgy, essentially needs the other as its own self-understanding and self-fulfillment. It is, to be sure, faith that gives birth to, and "shapes," liturgy, but it is liturgy, that by fulfilling and expressing faith, "bears testimony" to faith and becomes thus its true and adequate expression and norm: *lex orandi est lex credendi.*[15]

The formula *lex orandi est lex credendi* ("the rule of praying is the rule of belief") is derived from a fifth-century monk, Prosper of Aquitaine.[16] The formula can be taken in two ways. It could mean that the teaching or belief of the church arises from its practice of worship; it could also mean that the teaching of the church (usually in the form of the teaching office) gives shape to liturgical practice, in which case the rule of belief is the rule of praying *(lex credendi est lex orandi)*. There is a dialectical relationship between the rule of praying and the rule of belief, between worship and doctrine. Schmemann acknowledges this dialectic when he says that "faith gives birth to, and 'shapes' liturgy," but he gives greater weight to liturgy giving shape to doctrine. Geoffrey Wainwright has shown that in the history of the church sometimes doctrinal formulations follow liturgical practice and at other times doctrinal beliefs precede liturgy, or at least control the development of the liturgy.[17] On the other hand, Aidan Kavanagh insists on the irreversibility of Prosper's statement. The liturgy is "primary theology" from which "secondary theology" or doctrines are derived.

> [The] liturgical tradition [is] the dynamic condition within which theological reflection is done, within which the Word of God is appropriately understood. This is because it is in the Church, of which the liturgy is the sustained expression and the life, that the various sources of theology function precisely as sources.[18]

The issue, it seems, has to do with the way liturgy is understood from different perspectives. Historically, it could be shown that *lex orandi* and *lex credendi* sustain a dialectical relationship with each other: liturgy shapes doctrine and doctrine shapes liturgy. An example of the former can be seen in the early Christians' practice of according worship to Jesus, which played a key role in later christological doctrine.[19] The development of the doctrine of the Trinity is an example of this dialectical relationship. I have noted above that a trinitarian awareness emerged from the early church's experience of worship and the Persons' distinctive roles were expressed in its doxology: to the Father, through the Son and in the Holy Spirit. But the challenge from the Arians led the church to emphasize the equality of the three Persons, leading to a coordinated doxology: to the Father, Son and Holy Spirit. This coordinated doxology expresses an unambiguously trinitarian doctrine (a product, we might say, of secondary theology) that was to become the dogma of the church in the Nicene-Constantinopolitan Creed (381). Protestants are generally more favorably disposed toward the idea of doctrine's shaping worship. They might point to the promulgation of the doctrines of the immaculate conception of Mary (1854) and the assumption of Mary (1950) in the light of widespread liturgical practice as instances where scriptural norms have failed to have a decisive control over liturgical practices.[20]

But in giving to *lex orandi* a defining role Schmemann is not referring to specific liturgical practices, like the "orders of service" found in the prayer books of various liturgical traditions. He is referring to the basic *ordo*, that deep, abiding structure which expresses the living faith of the church. In this sense *lex orandi* is the liturgical equivalent of the apostolic witness to the paradigmatic encounter with Jesus Christ and is the basis of all subsequent belief. This *ordo*, severally called the "shape" or "deep structure" of the liturgy, has been shown to be more or less consistent throughout the history of the Christian church.[21] It is this basic *ordo* that must set the standard for belief. In this sense the rule of prayer *is* the rule of belief. The theology that is embodied in the *ordo* is called primary theology because it is immediate to the divine-human encounter, an integrated or personal knowledge—the knowledge of God. Kavanagh offers this example to illustrate the nature of primary liturgical theology:

> Mrs. Murphy and her pastor do not fail to be theologians at the point where the seminary professor who taught the pastor succeeds in being one. The professor is a secondary theologian. Mrs. Murphy and her pastor are primary theologians whose discourse in faith is carried on not by concepts and propositions nearly so much as in the vastly complex vocabulary of experiences had, prayers said, sights seen, smells smelled, words said and heard and responded to, emotions controlled and released, sins committed and repented, children born and loved ones buried, and in many other ways no one can count or always account for. Their critical and reflective discourse is not merely about faith. It is the very way faith works itself out in the intricacies of human life both individually and in common. Its vocabulary is not precise, concise, or scientific. It is symbolic, aesthetic, ascetical, and sapiential. It is not just something she and her pastor think or say, but something they taste, the air they breathe. It is a sinuous discourse by which they and those innumerable millions like them . . . work out the primary body of perceived data concerning what it really means when God pours himself out into humanity, into the world as a member of our race. Nowhere else can that primary body of perceived data be read so well as in the living tradition of Christian worship.[22]

Primary theology could be described as a form of "tacit knowledge," to use a phrase from Michael Polanyi. Polanyi often said that we know more than we can tell, and in trying to tell it we often tell it badly. The primary liturgical theology is a tacit form of knowledge that is fully expressed only in the act of worship. Yet some form of critical reflection cannot be avoided the moment worshipers seek to make sense of their worship encounter, as can be seen in Kavanagh's own "taxonomy of primary theology":

> The taxonomy is operationally rhythmic. It begins with the act of liturgical worship. This act precipitates change in the liturgical assembly, change which is not so much immediately apparent, perhaps, as it is long-term, even eschatological, and inexorable. To such change the assembly adjusts through critical reflection upon its own stance in faith before the God who gifts the assembly with its own existence and with a created world in which to stand and minister

before him. The faithful assembly brings all this with it to its next act of worship, an act which then precipitates further change and adjustment, recapitulating what went before.[23]

One could say that critical reflection arises ineluctably from the experience and, in a very decisive way, is determined by the experience. Yet it is only when the experience is reflected upon and made explicit that it can function effectively as a norm, that is, become liturgical *theology.*

Here is where the theologian comes in. There is no reason that the teacher of Mrs. Murphy's pastor in the story above could not also be doing primary liturgical theology if he happens to be a member of the same worshiping community, engaged in the same liturgical act. In fact, he may be able to reflect on their common experience more accurately and, along the way, correct others' primary expressions of their vital faith. Primary theology, in that sense, needs secondary theology if it is not to fall into error.[24] Making primary theology explicit is the task of liturgical theology. We should therefore not make too sharp a distinction between primary and secondary theology. What the church should guard against is a secondary theology that is done outside of the worshiping community, a theology that abstracts from and generalizes about the liturgy based on some supposedly "neutral" criteria.[25]

Secondary liturgical theology seeks to explain as fully as possible this primary experience of the church in its encounter with God which is expressed in its public act of worship. Its goal is "to clarify and explain the connection between this act and the Church, i.e., to explain how the Church expresses and fulfills herself in this act,"[26] to make explicit what worshipers know mostly in an implicit or tacit way. As such, it takes pride of place over other forms of theology, since its subject is the normative *ordo* from which all true doctrines must be derived. But for it to function well, liturgical theology must keep the explanation always focused on the church's act of worship, where primary theology is being done. When liturgical theology loses this central focus, the result is to substitute "right" doctrines for right worship *(orthodoxia).* Secondary explanations take the place of the central *ordo* and become confused with it. One example of secondary accretions is the way theories of the Eucharist (*how* the "real presence" is related to the bread and wine) came to dominate and crowd out what is central to the Eucharist, the "real presence" of Christ in the Eucharist itself—a point that was never in dispute between the Catholic Church, Luther and Calvin.[27] This intrusion of secondary explanations, together with the influence of the "scientific" method of doing theology, has led to liturgical theology's being reduced to explication of the meanings of specific rites, actions and rubrics, or commentaries on liturgical texts and forms of worship. The focus is on the "data of the faith," on doctrines per se, rather than the "total living experience of the Church."[28] The result is a divorce between worship and theology, leaving both impoverished.[29]

Study of the relationship between the *lex orandi* and the *lex credendi* has important ramifications for evangelicals today. In whatever way we understand the relationship, belief and worship are so inextricably linked that separation can only undermine the integrity of both doctrine and worship. Yet this divorce is exactly what we are seeing in many evangelical churches.

For the more doctrinaire evangelical, worship is only a *superadditum* to the service, a kind of embellishment of what should be essentially an exercise in systematic indoctrination. In these churches the entire service may consist of a song to get the congregation ready, a very long and well prepared expository sermon, and another song to round it off. In between these, some prayers are interspersed and the offering collected. In this worship format, truth is not part of living worship but is almost exclusively confined to the sermon. Truth then becomes only a matter of right belief, and the worship service is essentially a time for instruction. The operating assumption is that teaching people the right things will lead to right living. There is no understanding of the formative role of the ecclesial community through ecclesial practice.

Among the more charismatically inclined, considerable attention is given to getting the congregation into a "worshipful atmosphere." Here the emphasis is on practice. But no thought whatsoever is given to what impact such forms of worship might have on belief. The assumption is that they have none so long as no heresy is preached. What such Christians fail to realize is that when worship is not "right worship" (which is what *orthodoxy* means), it won't be long before belief itself is modified to fit a heterodox worship. The primary theology expressed in a heterodox *ordo* will quickly overwhelm an isolated orthodox belief, making it totally irrelevant to the life of the church. Right belief and right practice *(orthopraxis)* can only come from right worship *(orthodoxia),* and vice versa.

## WORSHIP AND THE DIVINE GLORY

True worship is always the church's response to God's initiative of revealing who he is, which in biblical language is called the divine "glory." And so in worship we "glorify" God, that is, acknowledge him for who he is. This response to the revelation of God's glory can be characterized in the following ways: First, it can never be something we do for God. Second, it is its own end. Third, it is a response to God's total character, more specifically to the triune God.

First, *worship can never be something we do for God.* All human attempts to initiate worship can only result in distorting the glory of God. The glory of God is the glory of his self-giving, and all true worship must begin with the truth that everything we are and have is a gift. Thus even when we present our gifts to God, we acknowledge that "everything in heaven and on earth is yours. All things come from you, and of your own do we give you."[30] By contrast, humanly contrived worship always proceeds from seeking after a deity who needs to be placated and from whom devotees could gain some favor with *their* gifts. This is the reason Luther was strongly opposed to the idea of the Eucharist as a "sacrifice." To suggest that the consecrated bread and wine are our offering to God is to return to the pagan concept that we can somehow gain our acceptance by God with our sacrifice. Luther put it in no uncertain terms: "The memorial might well be a thanksgiving, but the sacrament itself is not an offering, but is a gift of God."[31] Modern Protestants may still retain some concept of salvation by grace and not think of their works as some form of merit, yet a form of meritorious work is subtly introduced into many contemporary "prayer and praise" services. Worship itself has become the means by which one hopes to induce God to act on our behalf. It is not uncommon nowadays to hear "worship leaders" telling the congregation that praise will bring down the glory of God, or that if we wait upon the Lord long enough we will receive healing.[32]

Second, *worship is never meant to serve any other purpose except the glory of God.* The end of worship is worship. The church exists "to acknowledge God as God."[33] "Man's chief end," says the Westminster Shorter Catechism, "is to glorify God and enjoy him forever." The Calvinist tradition has such a strong sense of the glory of God as the ultimate end of all existence that in the old Calvinist ordination service the ordinand is asked, "Are you willing to be damned for the glory of God?"[34]

We live in a pragmatic world in which every meaningful activity has to have some useful purpose. But the very nature of worship lies in its "aim-

lessness." That does not mean that it has no meaning. The difference between purpose and meaning, according to Romano Guardini, is like the difference between a gymnasium and a forest:

> In the first everything is consciously directed towards discipline and develop-
> ment, in the second life is lived with Nature, and internal growth takes place
> in her. The liturgy creates a universe brimming with fruitful spiritual life, and
> allows the soul to wander about in it at will and to develop itself there. The
> abundance of prayers, ideas, and actions, and the whole arrangement of the
> calendar are incomprehensible when they are measured by the objective stan-
> dard of strict suitability for a purpose.
>
> When the liturgy is rightly regarded, it cannot be said to have a purpose,
> because it does not exist for the sake of humanity, but for the sake of God. In
> the liturgy man is no longer concerned with himself; his gaze is directed to-
> wards God. In it man is not so much intended to edify himself as to contem-
> plate God's majesty. The liturgy means that the soul exists in God's presence,
> originates in Him, lives in a world of divine realities, truths, mysteries and sym-
> bols, and really lives its true, characteristic and fruitful life.[35]

Guardini also compares the liturgy to the play of a child. Like play, the
liturgy has no purpose, yet it is full of meaning: "[Play] is life, pouring itself
forth without an aim, seizing upon riches from its own abundant store, significant through the fact of its existence."[36] The aimlessness of the liturgy
corresponds to a point made previously about the nature of the church: it
exists for no other reason than "to the praise of God's glory." In worship,
the church is actualizing its own nature as the "polity of the Spirit" whose
chief end is to glorify God. It is in the liturgy that we understand the true
meaning of being church.

Modern people find that concept difficult; it is much easier to believe that
the church must exist for some useful purpose, something more earthy,
more noble, such as restoring the fallen creation or serving humanity. Yet
difficult as it may be for modern, pragmatic people, it is when we actualize
the "aimlessness" of the liturgy that we know what it means for the church
to exist "to the praise of God's glory."

> If the idea of living "to the praise of God's glory" seems too vaporous to mod-
> ern ears, that is our fault, not the apostle's. Perhaps we need to heed his warn-
> ing to "Give up living like the pagans with their good-for-nothing notions"
> (Eph. 4:17). Perhaps the idea of living "to the praise of God's glory" is opaque
> to us also because we have reversed the relationship between the church and

the world that is spelled out in the Ephesian letter. We think that the church exists for the sake of the world, but that is not true. The world, indeed the whole universe, exists for the church. . . . The world exists as the arena in which the gospel of Jesus Christ, the crucified, risen, and ascended Lord of all, can be proclaimed, and as a source of fresh recruits for the royal priesthood of the redeemed world.[37]

While worship has no practical purpose, it does not mean that worship has no practical byproduct. This point is well made by William Willimon:

> Worship loses its integrity when it is regarded instrumentally as a means of something else—even as a means of achieving the most noble of human purposes, even the noble purpose of moral edification. *Leitourgia* must be celebrated for its own sake, not simply as a means of rallying the faithful for *diakonia.*
>
> However, it is true that while we worship God, we are also being formed into God's people. While we are attempting to see God, we are acquiring, as a kind of by-product, a vision of who we are and who we are meant to be.[38]

"We do not worship God in order to be better people,"[39] but as a matter of fact, certain good things do happen to people when they worship God in spirit and in truth. We may call these byproducts "intrinsic goods."[40] For example, in encountering the awesome God we learn the virtue of humility; in thanking God we form the virtue of gratitude; in worshiping together we develop cooperation. These byproducts are perhaps more apparent in certain forms of ritual that are meant to serve specific purposes—rites involving birth, marriage and death. When set within the context of worship, these "rites of crisis" are meant to show that these critical passages through life are carried out in God's presence and are meant to glorify God. As God seeks to make the church ("I will be their God, and they will be my people"), we in response do become the church, his people, by letting all of life be lived to his glory. We affirm our covenant faithfulness to God in these acts before him. In being his people, we show forth who he is: the God who acts to bring forth a people for himself (1 Pet 2:9). These rites set the norms for ethical behavior in the ecclesial community. Other members of the community attending a wedding learn what is to be expected in Christian marriage.[41] While worship is not *aimed at* making us into good people, it does, if done "in spirit and in truth," make us into a "community of character." I shall have more to say about spiritual formation through the liturgy later.

The effect of worship on life is another lesson we can learn from the nature of play. While worship, like play, is not aimed at anything practical, it has its unavoidable effects. Johann Huizinga in his classic study on play has shown that what we call culture has its beginnings in play. Play has a "civilizing function."[42] The play analogy may at first give the impression that in worship we are setting aside an hour of so out of the week to play a role that we quickly leave behind afterward to return to the ordinary, so-called real world. Worship then becomes an escape from reality. But in fact, when we are engaged in worship—when we are in "active participation" *(particepatio actuosa)*[43]—we encounter the God who sees us through and through. It is then that we are most truly ourselves, because we no longer need to present a "nice front." Most of the time in the "real world" we are less true to ourselves. At our workplace we need to appear nice and friendly when serving customers. Bosses have to appear caring toward their staff. It is in the "real world" that we are compelled to play the game of "let's pretend," whereas before God, from whom "nothing in all creation is hidden" and in whose sight "everything is uncovered and laid bare" (Heb 4:13), there is no need to pretend. We are truly liberated to be the persons we are meant to be. In the spirit of openness before God *(coram Deo),* we can truly open to one another and, hopefully, carry that true self back into our workaday world.

Third, *worship is response to God's total character.* In worship we recognize God for who he is; and who he is is what he reveals himself to be. Since Rudolf Otto's *The Idea of the Holy,* it is customary to speak of God's revelation in terms of the polarity of *fascinans et tremendum.* God's presence both attracts *(fascinans)* and fills us with fear *(tremendum).* He is both loving and holy. Paul in Romans 11:22 reminds the Gentile Christians, "Behold . . . the *kindness* and *severity* of God" (NASB). God is holy because he is "wholly other," that is, not in any way dependent on us. God is self-sufficient because he is the three-personed God. Holiness is who God *is.*

> "Holy" is the real name of God, of the God "not of scholars and philosophers," but of the living God of faith. The knowledge *about* God results in definitions and distinctions. The knowledge *of* God leads to this one, incomprehensible, yet obvious and inescapable word: holy. And in this word we express both that God is the Absolutely Other, the One *about* whom we know nothing, and that He is the end of all our hunger, all our desires, the inaccessible One who mobilizes our wills, the mysterious treasure that attracts us, and there is really nothing to know but Him. "Holy" is the word, the song, the "reaction" of the

Church as it enters into heaven, as it stands before the heavenly glory of God.[44]

At the same time this holy God is also love. For the triune life is also the life of mutual self-giving between Father and Son through the Spirit. Thus holiness and love, transcendence and immanence are the two poles that sum up what the triune God is in his essential being.

The wholly other God who is also the giving God also shares his love with his creatures. This manifestation of his holiness outside of himself, which is an act of love, is what Scripture calls his "glory." God's glory encompasses these two paradoxical characteristics, his holiness and love. To cite but one biblical example: the account of Moses' encounter with God. Needing assurance of Yahweh's continual covenant faithfulness after the golden calf incident, Moses asked God, "Show me your glory" (Ex 33:18). Exodus 34:5-7 is God's answer:

> Then the LORD came down in the cloud and stood there with him and proclaimed his name, the LORD. And he passed in front of Moses, proclaiming, "The LORD, the LORD, the compassionate and gracious God, slow to anger, abounding in love and faithfulness, maintaining love to thousands, and forgiving wickedness, rebellion and sin. Yet he does not leave the guilty unpunished; he punishes the children and their children for the sin of the fathers to the third and fourth generation."

God forgives wickedness, yet he punishes! The paradoxical nature of the divine glory is also reflected in various parts of the ancient Christian liturgy; I will give but two instances.[45] The Christian use of Psalm 95 (the Venite) to call the congregation to worship begins with a reassuring invitation, "Come, let us worship and bow down. . . . For he is our God and we are the people of his pasture and the sheep of his hand" (Ps 95:6-7). But this is immediately followed by a warning: "Today, if you hear his voice, do not harden your hearts" (Ps 95:7-8). Another is a phrase in the Eucharist, "The gifts of God for the people of God," or "Holy things for holy people." This is an invitation welcoming the people of God to the holy meal, yet it carries an implicit warning that the people who are welcomed must be set apart to become wholly for God.[46]

True worship must reflect the reality of who God is. That is, whatever the liturgical forms may be, they must conform to certain theological norms. But for many advocates of "contemporary worship" this fact is often obscured by attempts at ad hoc constructions of "orders" of worship that pay more attention to what the congregation demands than to what God requires. For example, in many charismatic services today worship is a continuous celebration. One gets the impression from start to finish that God is nice, accommodating and friendly, always expected to meet *my* needs and solve *my* problems. One gets to see only the divine *fascinans* without the *tremendum,* love without holiness, immanence without transcendence. This seems to be the predilection of our modern age. The "domestication of transcendence" is not only found among so-called progressive theologians;[47] evangelicals and charismatics are equally guilty of domesticating transcendence through their marketing strategies and seeker-friendly services. Perhaps we all need reminding that Aslan is "not a tame lion"![48]

But Christian worship is more than encountering God as *fascinans et tremendum.* To speak of the divine glory in this way is at best to speak in terms of a general religious category. Otto's description of "the holy," after all, belongs to the field of phenomenology of religion and might well fit any number of religions. Christianity as religion shares certain traits with others within the genus of religion. The uniqueness of the Christian religion is that the God who reveals himself is the triune God. It is this revelation of God as Father, Son and Holy Spirit that sets Christian worship apart from other religious worship, even from the Jewish faith in which Christianity has its roots. Christian worship is specifically the encounter with the triune God whose identity is revealed in the mystery of salvation, in the work of the Father sending the Son and the Spirit for the redemption of the world. This is why, as noted above, the traditional Christian doxology was *to* the Father, *through* the Son and *in* the Holy Spirit.

This brings us to the very heart of Christian worship and to what it means to do liturgical theology. The task of liturgical theology is to demonstrate

> how the liturgy serves in its particular way as transparency for the mystery of salvation. . . . The one mystery of Christian faith is the Triune God in his self-communication to humanity. . . . In different ways, the forms of liturgy express the conviction of faith that the Triune God, in their economic activity, is the mystery of Christian worship. Consequently, theologians are challenged to show how theology of liturgy can be formulated as theology of the economic Trinity.[49]

Edward Kilmartin sees the theology of the liturgy as essentially the theology of the Trinity in the life of the church. In other words, the criterion that establishes the truth of the liturgy is its correspondence to the work of the

triune God, which reveals who the triune God *is*. "Liturgical celebrations are
a medium of participation of the faithful in the economic Trinity, a medium
of Trinitarian self-communication. Liturgy, above all, is the work of the Trinity in its *execution* and *content*."[50] Salvation is the sharing of the divine life
of the Trinity by rational creatures. The grace of salvation is the grace of trinitarian self-communication.

The nature of this self-communication of the Trinity to creatures is as follows: The Father is the source of all self-communication, but he communicates always through the Son and the Spirit.[51] Kilmartin develops this self-
communication of the Father in great detail, in terms of what he calls the
"procession" and "bestowal" models. In what follows I shall summarize the
essential outlines of the two models and highlight their liturgical implications. The procession model is discovered from the *fact* of the incarnation,
the Word becoming flesh (Jn 1:14). This "Logos-Christology"—the sending
of the Son into the world in the economy of redemption—corresponds to
the generation of the Son by the Father in the immanent Trinity. It could be
described as a "descending" model. The bestowal model, on the other hand,
is discovered from the *event* of the incarnation, or the manner in which the
procession occurs. The bestowal model clarifies the personal mission of the
Spirit as seen in the Spirit's uniting the Word with human nature and sanctifying the human nature of Jesus (Lk 1:34-35), anointing Jesus at his baptism
and thus revealing Jesus' true identity to the world (Lk 3:21-22), and extend-
ing this anointing to the church in the Pentecost event. This bestowal of
the Spirit in the economy of redemption corresponds to the bestowal of the
Spirit between the Father and the Son in the immanent Trinity, where
the "Father bestows the Spirit on the Son and the Son bestows the Spirit on
the Father as answering love."[52] Within the bestowal model there is not
only the sending of the Spirit but also an ascending movement, the "return"
of the Spirit to the Father.

This return in "answering love" deepens our understanding of the prayer
of the church in three ways. First, the prayer of the church is the answering
love to the Father in the power of the Spirit. Just as the bestowal of the Spirit
upon Jesus is answered by Jesus' love for the Father by the Spirit, the
church's prayer is essentially the return of love by the power of the Spirit,
whom the Father bestows upon the church in Jesus' name.[53] The Spirit of
the Father is the Spirit of sonship, and by the same Spirit the church is able
to call God "Abba, Father" (cf. Rom 8:15).

Second, I noted in chapter one that the story of the church is the continuation of the triune economy of redemption. It is the story of the Spirit from the Father, poured out upon the church after the ascension. Pentecost is the Father's response to Jesus' intercession in heaven. The prayer of the church on earth, as in the *epiclesis* where the church calls on the Father to send his Spirit upon the eucharistic assembly, is the prayer of returning love that answers to and actualizes the high-priestly prayer of the ascended Jesus. Jesus prays to the Father to give the church the Spirit (Jn 14:16, 26); the returning prayer of the church is for the Spirit to be given in its eucharistic assembly. Thus, as is common in Eastern Orthodoxy, we could speak of the earthly liturgy as a counterpart to the heavenly liturgy. The earthly liturgy is based on and derived from the heavenly liturgy and is also the continuation of the heavenly. Christ's high-priestly work in heaven finds its continual fulfillment in the life and worship of his body on earth. But this does not mean that the heavenly and earthly liturgies could be simply equated, if the distinctive work of the Spirit between the ascension and the parousia is to be fully appreciated.[54] In the eucharistic assembly, the church is always made aware of an unfulfilled dimension as it looks up to the heavenly liturgy and also looks forward to Christ's eschatological return.[55] In looking up, the church finds its completeness ("already") in Christ, but in looking forward the church recognizes its incompleteness ("not yet") as it awaits the parousia, when Christ, by the power of the Spirit, will transform "lowly bodies" into the likeness of his glorious body (Phil 3:21).

Third, as Pentecost is the extension of the work of the triune God, all the actions of the church are, properly speaking, also the actions of Christ in relation to the Father in the power of the Spirit. This is the way God accomplishes his redemptive work on earth: it always involves a conjoint divine-human action or "synergy."[56] All liturgical actions are effectual because they involve the synergy of the Spirit and the church.[57] Creation by fiat or ex nihilo was the hallmark of the old creation, whereas creation by synergy is the hallmark of the new creation.[58] The foundation for understanding this coaction of the church and Christ is the mystery of the incarnation. The incarnation is the result of the action of the Spirit on a human agent, but the work of the Spirit requires a willing response from Mary ("May it be to me as you have said," Lk 1:38). This synergistic pattern continues in the incarnate Son, the God-man. In the perfect unity of the divine and the human in one person, we see that in "the least action of Christ God lives humanly and the human person lives divinely." "When Christ speaks, his listeners hear the man Jesus, and at the same time the Father utters himself in his incarnate Word."[59] So too, the work of the church as the divine-humanity is always a synergy. "Through this synergism, by which the Spirit of God impregnates the energies of creatures, they are drawn into personal communion with God and do the works of God."[60] The work of the liturgy is a synergy: it is the work of the church and at the same time the work of Christ in the church by the Spirit.[61]

All this is to say that worship is a work of critical importance for the life of the church and ultimately for the kingdom of God. It is no less than the continuation of the work of the triune God in the church until the eschaton. It is the progress of the gospel in the history of salvation. Worship is true to the degree that it corresponds to the work of the triune God and continues and extends the work of the triune God. In other words, there are theological norms in worship. If our worship does not reveal God in his holiness and love, transcendence and immanence, as *fascinans et tremendum*—in short, as the triune God—then it has fallen short of the glory of God. If it does not continue the action of the triune God, it is not worship in spirit and in truth.

Evangelical Christianity needs to address its severe liturgical deficits. It needs a liturgical theology that coherently explains the true meaning of worship and effectively realizes a true primary theology. When modern evangelical-charismatic churches arbitrarily construct their worship to cater to human needs and whims, they are doing primary theology. But it is a false theology, because it distorts our vision of the divine glory. This failure to understand what true worship is stems from a failure to understand what the church is. Conversely, a sound liturgical theology will also reveal the true nature of the church.

It is not sufficient, however, simply to affirm what worship is theologically. If churches today are to effect real reform, that theology needs to be given concrete expression in a liturgy, that is, in a clearly discernible structure. Without a liturgy, we will not be able to actualize our theology of worship in practice. This will be the subject of the next chapter.

# THE SHAPE
# OF THE LITURGY

The preceding chapter focuses on worship as the church's response to God's revelation in Christ, and yet this response is itself the work of the tri-une God in the church. The Spirit of God dwells in those who are made children of God and enables them to cry, "Abba, Father!" The response fits the revelation because it is a response in Spirit and in truth.[1]

This normative response, however, must be given concrete expression if it is to be actualized in practice; the way to actualize our theology of worship is through the liturgy. The liturgy may be described as embodied worship. It is worship expressed through a certain visible order or structure (thus the phrase "order of service"). There is general agreement among liturgiologists today that for all the variations in liturgical expressions, there is nonetheless a basic shape or *ordo* underlying these expressions. The convergence of various liturgical traditions in recent years, as seen in the use of the common lectionary and rites of Christian initiation, is in part due to the recognition of this normative shape of the liturgy discovered through the study of the liturgies of the undivided church.[2] The *ordo* is a consistent whole; what it reveals is a whole way of life of the ecclesial community. As Lutheran liturgiologist Frank Senn puts it, "Liturgy expresses nothing less than a world-view."[3]

To discover the shape of the liturgy, therefore, is to discover the true way of worship or the way of reorienting the church toward the Christian world-view. In short, a normative liturgy is the true way of becoming church. Among "pragmatic evangelicals," to use one of Robert Webber's categories, the question of truth concerning worship is not even raised, but this discovery is crucial if we are to have sound theological criteria for evaluating our worship. Unless our respective orders of service (and there could be many) conform to the basic *ordo,* we are not being shaped into the community we are meant to be.

The church throughout its history has recognized that this basic *ordo* consists of two parts, Word and sacrament. This two-part shape could be explored from a number of perspectives. First, we will examine the ways in which Word and sacrament are related; I conclude that both have their basis in the *incarnation,* the Word becoming flesh (Jn 1:14). Thus Christ could be called the "primordial Sacrament," and all true worship is fundamentally sacramental. Second, within the sacramental framework of worship, the Eucharist holds a special place as the "sacrament of sacraments." It is from the Eucharist that we come to a better understanding of the church as essentially communion. The liturgy, then, has a *eucharistic* orientation. Third, the Eucharist, which communicates the eternal reality, is always celebrated in time, in daily, weekly and yearly cycles. This means that within the liturgy, eternity and time, the "already and not yet," are set in an eschatological tension, giving to the liturgy its *eschatological* orientation. Fourth, the liturgy of Word and sacrament is set within two other essential acts: the gathering for worship and the sending forth into the world. This pattern reveals its *missiological* orientation.

## THE RELATIONSHIP BETWEEN WORD AND SACRAMENT

The church is constituted by Word and sacrament. This is the standard understanding of the church among the Reformers. "Whenever we see the Word of God purely preached and heard, and the sacraments administered according to Christ's institution," says Calvin, "there . . . a church of God exists."[4] Similarly, article 7 of the Ausburg Confession (1530) states, "But the church is the congregation of saints, in which the gospel is rightly taught and the sacrament rightly administered. And unto the true unity of the church, it is sufficient to agree concerning the doctrine of the Gospel and the administration of the sacraments." These two "marks" of the church reveal the true identity of the church *as* church. As Senn puts it, "The church is visible only where the people assemble to do those things that constitute them as the people of God—proclaim the word of God and celebrate the sacraments of Christ."[5]

The New Testament shows a church whose worship is structured around

Word and sacrament: "They devoted themselves to the apostles' teaching and to the fellowship, to the breaking of bread and to prayer" (Acts 2:42). The earliest account of Christian worship shows a similar pattern of worship. We have, for example, a description from Justin Martyr (c. A.D. 155) in the following words:

> And on the day called Sunday, all who live in cities or in the country gather together to one place, and the memoirs of the apostles or the writings of the prophets are read, as long as time permits; then, when the reader has ceased, the president verbally instructs, and exhorts to the imitation of these good things. Then we all rise together and pray, and, as we before said, when our prayer is ended, bread and wine and water are brought, and the president in like manner offers prayers and thanksgivings, according to his ability, and the people assent, saying Amen; and there is a distribution of each, and a participation of that over which thanks have been given, and to those who are absent a portion is sent by the deacons.[6]

Justin's description consists of two distinct parts. The reading, discourse and prayer segment is generally thought to be derived from the Jewish synagogue practice and hence is called the *synaxis* (Greek for "gathering"), while the Eucharist in the second part is believed to have its origin in the Jewish *chaburah* meal. Although originally *synaxis* and Eucharist were believed to be "separable," they occurred together "in the regular Sunday worship of all churches in the second century."[7]

*Word and sacrament inseparable.* Word and sacrament, although distinguished, are held together in a single rite from earliest times. It is crucial that we maintain their proper emphases within the liturgy as well as their indispensability to each another. Failure to do so will result in the dissolution of the eschatological tension so crucial for the church's existence. Reformed liturgiologist Jean-Jacques von Allmen clarifies the dual perils:

> If the sermon absorbs the whole of the service, the Church is forgetting that the Kingdom has already drawn near, and that it can live on the first fruits of the Kingdom, it becomes "de-eschatologized"; but if the Eucharist monopolizes the whole of worship, the Church is forgetting that the world still continues, it is trying to exalt the Church beyond this world and to uproot it from history.[8]

Historically, however, the church has shown a tendency to subordinate one to the other. Roman Catholicism, at least until relatively recent times, has tended toward subordinating the liturgy of the Word, so that little is understood of what goes on in the elaborate worship ritual.[9] On the other hand, Protestants have tended to give stronger emphasis to the Word and treat it as if it were separable from the Eucharist.[10] Others have so emphasized the Word that the Eucharist comes to play only a very marginal role. But as von Allmen warns, "We have no right to remain attached to a mode of worship which precludes the people of the baptized from assembling to obey the command: 'Do this in remembrance of Me.' We have no right to continue to celebrate our worship without re-integrating the Lord's Supper into it, or it into the Lord's Supper."[11] To regard the Eucharist as "optional," continues von Allmen, is to undermine our claim to catholicity.[12] Similarly, the evangelical Anglican Philip Seddon has noted that for many evangelicals the Eucharist is "a non-essential illustrative accessory, an adjunct, supplementary to the preached word" and is seldom observed on a weekly basis.[13] Yet John Stott reminded new Christians many years ago that "nearly every branch of the Christian Church agrees that the Lord's Supper or Holy Communion is the central service of the church."[14] If this is so, there is no sound basis for relegating it to a once-a-month ritual.

Two reasons are commonly given for infrequent observance of the Eucharist. One is that if the Lord's Supper were observed too frequently, it would lose its meaning. But according to a Reformed evangelical pastor, Leonard J. Vander Zee, this rationale betrays "the old gnostic tendency" to exalt the "spiritual" and denigrate the "material."[15] Further, the rationale assumes that the Lord's Supper is another commemorative event, like a birthday or wedding anniversary. But if the Lord's Supper is indeed a "feeding on Christ to eternal life," making us into what we eat, then there is no question about whether frequent Communion would cause a loss of significance. No one has yet complained that having three meals a day had eroded the significance of eating. (Some even insist on having more!) As Vander Zee puts it, "If God feeds and confirms our faith in the sacrament, then we deprive ourselves of the fullness of his grace when we sit around the table only once in a while. We need every nourishment that God provides, and to miss the meal not only snubs his gracious hospitality but creates spiritual anorexics."[16] Second, it is sometimes argued that Word and sacrament are merely two ways of communicating the same gospel. If what the sacrament conveys is already conveyed, in fact in a better way, in preaching, then the sacrament is quite extraneous in the regular church service. Sacrament, according to this view, merely "portrays" the gospel—and in a rather limited way at that—whereas preaching gives almost unlimited scope for the exposition of the gospel.

But this is to misunderstand the very nature of Word and sacrament and their distinctive functions in the liturgy. Not only is the sacrament more than the visible form of the Word, but each is indispensable to the other. Sacrament brings the proclaimed Word to its fulfillment. We come to know what the proclaimed Word is by actually entering into communion with the Real Presence effected by the Spirit in the Lord's Supper. Word without sacrament remains incomplete, and sacrament without Word becomes an empty sign. "If one cannot live by bread alone, neither can one live by word alone."[17] For just as the Word is completed in the sacrament, so the sacrament derives its meaning from the Word. As Louis Bouyer states, "Every sacrament is a *verbum visibile,* a word made visible, and every sacrament also essentially implies *verba sacramentalia,* the sacred words which give to the sacred action itself not only its meaning but also its own inner reality."[18] Word and sacrament cannot be separated. The whole liturgy of Word and sacrament is both God's Word and God's action for the sake of the church. Worship becomes less than what it is when one is emphasized at the expense of the other.

*As reflection and participation.* The relationship between Word and sacrament could be further elaborated in other ways. First, Word and sacrament correspond to the two essential ways by which a community is formed: participation (the sacramental dimension) and reflection (the verbal dimension). We are formed by being a part of a community and participating fully in its life. We learn the ways of the community the way we learned our native tongue: one grows up speaking the language of the community that speaks it. This participation is something people do habitually and unconsciously with others rather than reflectively or critically. The other way is to learn by critical reflection. If the church is a community whose basic identity is defined by certain theological criteria (the actions of the triune God) and where participation comes through a conscious decision, then critical reflection is especially important. "In such a society education into the moral life cannot come primarily from observing and practicing appropriate behavior of others. Instead, we will need an intellectual training in the rules or ideals themselves; training in how to apply and defend them."[19]

Both participation and reflection are essential for one to be properly initiated into the ecclesial community. If persons are formed only by participation in a community (as is sometimes the case with children growing up in the church), its moral values tend to be imbibed without much critical reflection. Participants' values could degenerate into unquestioned taboos; further, if challenged, they would not have the intellectual resources to respond adequately to the challenge. This is partly the reason some who grew up in the church end up rejecting the way of life in which they have been trained. An unthinking habit, no matter how deeply ingrained, can be undone in the face of a well-articulated worldview coming from a rival community. For many Christians today, that rival community is the "secular city" whose influence is felt far more strongly than that of the Christian community.

While the worshiping community forms spiritual habits and assimilates a "primary theology," it needs to engage in critical reflection on what it does to reinforce its implicit beliefs. The ancient church did this through the catechumenate, which explains the faith and practices of the church to those desiring to join the church before and after their baptism.[20] But here we seem to encounter another problem. The moment we start to think about what we are doing, we find ourselves unable to perform the action effectively.[21] Good drivers do not think about driving when driving. But they may need to think about driving when they want to acquire new skills. Then they need to practice the new moves consciously until they become habitual. The same can be said of good worshipers. They are truly worshiping when "lost in wonder, love and praise," not when thinking about the most profound definition of praise. But thinking about profound definitions is still needed if the community is to improve its worship. These two processes, participation and reflection, must be ongoing for a community to remain vibrant. The failure to understand these processes is one reason for the failure of evangelical spirituality.[22] It tries to build the spiritual life based largely on teaching and indoctrinating without understanding that it is not critical reflection as such but habits that constitute Christian living. Evangelicalism has created a largely hearing community rather than an aural-tactile community, a Word community rather than a Word-and-sacrament community. But the whole of worship must include hearing, singing and praying (Word) *and* seeing, touching, eating and drinking (sacrament).

*As revelation and response.* A second way of understanding the church as Word and sacrament is in terms of the basic dialectic of revelation-response. To say that the church is constituted by Word and sacrament is to say that the church is the result of revelation and response to that revelation. The primary nature of revelation is God's speaking his Word, which culminates in the Word becoming flesh. It is the Word that calls the assembly into being, to be the people of God existing in covenant relationship with him. That new covenant is sealed by the shedding of the blood of Christ, who, on the night before his death, instituted the eucharistic Communion of his body and blood. In the Eucharist we are realizing ourselves as the body of Christ made alive by his life-giving blood through the Spirit. In the Eucharist we become the people who are called out by the Word. The Eucharist is our response to the Word-becoming-flesh dwelling among us. The Word is always prior: Without God's speaking first, there would be no genuine response. This is why the basic structure of worship has to be Word and sacrament and not sacrament and Word.[23]

*As preparation and fulfillment.* Third, the church is constituted by Word and sacrament in that the Word prepares for and leads to the culmination of worship in the Eucharist. In a postconciliar document of Vatican II, we read, "The Liturgy of the Word prepares for and leads into the Liturgy of the Eucharist, forming with it one act of worship."[24] The Word proclaims, the sacrament accomplishes. It is in the Word proclaimed that faith is created, and it is in faith that the bread and wine are effectually received. The Word is completed in the Eucharist. The Word believed leads the people of God to the actual feasting on the body and blood of Christ. As Jean Tillard puts it:

> At the root of the church of God, word and sacrament are one whole. Without the word and the faith it arouses, the sacrament is only an empty ritual; without the Eucharist, the word does not lead believers into the depths of the "mystery." It is not by accident that the reaffirmation of the ecclesiology of communion at Vatican II coincided with the rediscovery of the role of the word and the renewal of the mission.[25]

There is a logical priority of Word over sacrament, just as there is a logical priority of revelation over response. But Word is not complete without sacrament. We hear the Word preached as a divine epiphany, and we respond by eating and drinking. Going back to Justin's description of worship, we notice six elements:

1. reading of Scriptures: Old Testament and New Testament

2. sermon

3. intercessory prayers for the people

4. bringing in of bread and wine

5. the great prayer of thanksgiving

6. Communion: bread and wine

Quite obviously, for Justin the Eucharist was the culminating experience of worship. The proclamation of the Word is completed only in the eucharistic celebration. Just as the prophets prepared the way for the incarnation of the Word, the liturgy of the Word is a preparation for the Eucharist. And just as the Word's becoming flesh constitutes the decisive moment of God's revelation, the sacrament of the body and blood of Christ is the decisive moment of the liturgy of the Eucharist. Thus von Allmen insists that "in a place of worship the pulpit must not overshadow the communion table."[26]

This process reveals the thoroughly eschatological character of worship. That is to say, the whole worship of the church is a movement toward fulfillment: of Word culminating in sacrament, of Word inspiring faith and thus preparing believers for the feast, which in turn points to the kingdom still to come. Again, in the words of von Allmen:

> Divine worship is an eschatological event. Its whole procedure is a sort of echo of the incarnation and a prefiguration of worship in heaven. It is an echo of the incarnation in that it includes, like the ministry of Jesus, what one could call a "Galilean" moment—centred on the sermon—and a "Jerusalemite" moment—centred on the eucharist. These two elements, indispensable in the ordinary worship of the Church, are conditioned by one another. The preaching of the Kingdom could not have been properly understood if Jesus had not sealed it with His blood; but neither could the crucifixion have been understood if Jesus had not prepared it by His prophetic ministry. The same is true of the relation between sermon and communion.[27]

To say that the Word culminates in the sacrament does not, however, imply that preaching itself has no spiritual effects. For it too is a sacramental act. It is God's Word coming in human words (just as the eternal Word is revealed in human flesh). But preaching must be shaped by and directed toward what is objectively revealed in the Eucharist: God's gift of his Son to be our spiritual food and the means of real participation in the communion of the triune God. If preaching does not have this eucharistic orientation and focus, it no longer qualifies as the proclamation of the gospel. This is what happens when worship is not shaped by the Eucharist. Preaching then takes a life of its own, and before long all sorts of "gospels" are proclaimed in the name of Christ.

Finally, to say that Word culminates in the sacrament suggests that they are not two discrete acts in the service but form "one single act of worship,"[28] part of the same continuum of worship. The reason for their singularity is that they are united around Christ. The liturgy of the church is patterned after the "liturgy" of the Son of God.[29] Both Word and Eucharist constitute a single rite because both have their basis in the incarnation and they share the same sacramental character. Preaching, too, is a sacramental act which in itself has spiritual effects. Reformed theologian von Allmen has most forcefully presented the case for the sacramental character of preaching. "Preaching is . . . speech *by* God rather than speech *about* God." It is "an echo of the humble and despised incarnation of the Word, an anticipation of the indisputable glory of that same Word."[30]

> Just as, in Jesus Christ, God remains fully Himself in a man, without that man being in consequence dehumanized; and just as this duality of nature does not infringe the unity of the person: so, in preaching, the Word of God resounds in, under and with the words of its messenger, without those words ceasing in consequence to be completely human.[31]

Because both Word and sacrament have their basis in the God-man, Jesus Christ, the "primordial Sacrament,"[32] Christian worship takes on what Geoffrey Wainwright calls "the Christ pattern" and is essentially sacramental.[33] All the sacraments point to this central reality of the incarnation, "the personal embodiment of the meeting between God and humanity."[34]

## THE EUCHARISTIC ORIENTATION OF THE LITURGY

All sacraments have this common feature: they are ordinary things and actions that communicate spiritual realities. They are "symbols" that "cast together" *(symballein)* the human and the divine, and this unity has its basis in the incarnation, the perfect union between the divine and human natures in the one person Jesus Christ. In the words of Geoffrey Preston, "Sacramentality is rooted in Jesus as the dialogue, conversation, meeting between God and man, and between man and God."[35]

But among all the sacraments the Eucharist holds a place of special importance. Not only is it the culmination of the liturgy, as noted above, but it is also the sacrament by which Christ gives wholly of himself to the whole church.[36] It concerns the *person* of Christ himself, whereas the other sacraments concern the *activity* of Christ in the church. This is why other sacraments are done with or in the presence of the Eucharist.[37] Further, whereas baptism and other "sacramentals"[38] deal with individual members of the church and their purpose is to integrate the individual into the church, the Eucharist deals with the church itself. The church "is fulfilled in the Eucharist and each sacrament . . . finds its natural end, its fulfillment in the Eucharist."[39] The Eucharist is tied to Christ himself in a way that no other action or event is. Just as Jesus tied himself to certain actions of his people, so that when we feed the hungry, for example, we are said to be doing it to him, similarly in the Eucharist Jesus has covenanted to tie himself to certain actions involving bread and wine.[40] In the Emmaus story of the postresurrection appearance, Jesus Christ was not readily recognized even by his own disciples but was recognized in the breaking of bread.[41] In the Eucharist we are entering into the life of Christ; through the Eucharist we are made his body—the communion between Christ and his people and among his people. This is why it is called the "sacrament of sacraments."

In the light of this fact, the worship of the church could be further characterized as essentially eucharistic. The worship of the church is essentially eucharistic because it is the Eucharist that makes the church uniquely what it is. The early church understood this principle by restricting the Communion meal to believers who were baptized and in good standing with the church. Not only catechumens but also those under church discipline were excluded from Communion, though they were not excluded from hearing the Word. Here we see the difference in function between Word and sacrament. The Word calls people to the church, whether unbelievers or erring believers, and seeks to form or reform them, whereas the Eucharist "defines the fellowship of the church."[42] It is indeed a communion meal and meant to be for those who are in full communion with the church— thus the invitation given at the meal: "Holy things for holy people." Even catechumens are deemed to be not yet in full fellowship with the church. As Peter Brunner puts it, they have worship "done on them" but are not "sponsors of worship."[43]

The sacraments as a whole and the Eucharist in particular demonstrate a certain givenness about the truth they signify. The people eating the Lord's Supper *are* in actual communion; anything less than the reality will not do. For this reason it is the means of church discipline. When Communion is withheld from one under discipline, the church is saying that there is a serious breach of truth in the person's life. Similarly, when it is withheld from those not yet baptized, the church is saying that the truth will not be fully actualized in them until they are fully incorporated into the body of Christ.[44]

*Eucharist as communion.* If the church is the extension of the work of the triune God (chapter one) and worship is the way to realize the church (chapter two), then the Eucharist is the supreme expression of the worship that realizes the church. Through the Eucharist the Spirit actualizes the communion between Christ and his body and between the members of his body. Communion is at the heart of the Eucharist. In much of church history, however, this was often marginalized and largely replaced by the focus on the mystery of the Real Presence. The result of the latter emphasis has been to encourage the development of an individualistic eucharistic devotion rather than an ecclesial communion.[45] For example, a prominent feature of late medieval piety and seventeenth-century Puritan devotion is the meditation on the Eucharist. The Eucharist came to mean largely a one-to-one communion between the believer and Christ. Instead of its being a public celebration, the Eucharist functioned as a means to arouse personal piety.[46] But the recovery of communioecclesiology in recent years[47] has restored communion to the center of the eucharistic celebration.[48]

Eucharistic communion begins with the fact of who we are and what we are meant to be "in Christ." First, salvation is not just "my own personal relationship with Jesus Christ"; it is "to be inserted into a body animated by the Spirit of God, the body of Christ, the Church."[49] To be saved is to become branches of the true vine (Jn 15:1-8) and stones in a building (Eph 2:20-22). This relationship with Christ as members of his body, branches in the vine and stones in a building also implies relationship with one another. Communion in the fullest sense is always one-and-many and many-and-many, and that relationship is effected by the Spirit, who joins the members as one body with the Head, engrafts the branches to the vine and cements the stones together to make one building.

> Whoever is "in Christ" and "in the Spirit" never is in a relation of one to one with God. Because life "in Christ" implies not only the other that Christ Jesus is, and under whose sway one lives, but also others, the members of the body of Christ to which one is not added but "associated" in the same way, Paul explains, as the eyes is associated with the hand, the weaker members with the stronger ones, so that "if one member suffers, all suffer together with it . . ." The life that is reconciled with God is led with others, and this by its very nature. It is not only a life *in the church* but—the nuance is of crucial importance—a life *from and by the church*.[50]

The communion that is triune in character is a unique communion that has no parallel in human communities. It is a communion that transcends all human distinctions, binding together Jews and Gentiles, bond and free, male and female (Gal 3:28). John Chrysostom, like many of the church fathers, used the analogy of the many grains that go into the making of one loaf of bread to emphasize not only the reality of communion in Christ but also the all-transcending nature of that communion.

> If some are endowed with worldly honors or the splendor of riches, if they take pride in their being highborn or having glory in this present life, here they are placed on the same footing as beggars and those in rags or, as it happens, the blind and crippled. And they are not indignant over this because they know that none of these distinctions apply in the spiritual realities where what counts is only the good disposition of the soul.[51]

Such communion is possible only because it is the work of the Spirit that animates the body of Christ. So according to Augustine's mystagogical teaching, if Christians are to live by the Spirit of Christ, they must be in the body of Christ. Just as "my body lives by my spirit and your body by your spirit," so "the body of Christ can live only by the Spirit of Christ."[52] As Christians feed on Christ, they are being energized by the Spirit or "baked" by the fire of the Spirit to become one loaf. The Spirit plays a critical role in the transformation. This is why the Spirit is invoked in the consecration of the bread and wine so that these gifts "may be to us the body and blood of Christ." The *epiclesis* does not necessitate any particular theory of how ordinary bread and wine become the body and blood of Christ. The prayer's assertion in its plea for the coming of the Spirit in the eucharistic meal is that *by means of* ordinary bread and wine God has given us real spiritual bread through the action of the Spirit.

> Hear us, O merciful Father, we most humbly beseech thee; and grant that by the power of thy Holy Spirit, we, receiving these thy creatures of bread and wine, according to thy Son our Saviour Jesus Christ's holy institution, in remembrance of his death and passion, may be partakers of his most blessed body and blood.[53]

The *epiclesis* is not so much a prayer for a miracle as an acknowledgment of a mystery—a mystery that has its basis in the Word becoming flesh, so that at the Eucharist we can truly say that that "which we have seen with our eyes, which we have looked at and our hands have touched," is indeed the Word of life (1 Jn 1:1). By feeding on Christ "by faith" at the eucharistic meal, we become the communion-ecclesia.

## EUCHARIST AS SACRIFICE

I noted earlier that the mission of the church, particularly the preaching of the gospel, is to be understood as a liturgical act: the offering up of the Gentiles as acceptable sacrifices to God. This is but one of many sacrificial acts that are summed up in the eucharistic sacrifice. The Protestant aversion to using sacrificial language in connection with the Eucharist has led to an impoverishment in their understanding of this sacrament of sacraments. One needs to be clear in what sense the Eucharist is *not* a sacrifice. It is not a sacrifice in the same sense as Christ's offering up of himself is a sacrifice for the sins of the world. That is the once-for-all, unrepeatable sacrifice. Our sacrifice can never be an offering meant to appease God and atone for sin. To insinuate that possibility in any way is, in Luther's words, to commit blasphemy. We cannot initiate anything in the Eucharist—nor even in non-eucharistic worship. We can only respond, as I have been saying all along, to God's initiative—and even that response is made possible by the indwelling Spirit. So any talk of sacrifice has to be understood in terms of response to God's great gift of salvation, the once-for-all sacrifice of Christ.

There are at least three sacrifices the church offers up to God during the Communion. If we follow what Gregory Dix calls the "four-action shape" of the Eucharist—offertory, prayer, fraction and communion[54]—it is obvious that the first sense in which the term *sacrifice* could be applied is the offering of our gifts to God with *thanksgiving*. The offertory is the first action involving the bringing of bread and wine to the Communion table. This is the fourth action in Justin's order. But in what sense it is an offering? It is interesting that one of the arguments Irenaeus used against the Gnostics was that the Eucharist (which Gnostic Christians also celebrated) itself shows the goodness of creation. Jesus' blessing of bread and wine was his way of teaching his disciples to offer up the firstfruits of creation to God so that they would be neither "unfruitful nor ungrateful."[55] In seeking to overturn the Gnostic argument by pointing out that in the eucharistic celebration we offer up the firstfruits of creation in thankfulness and receive through God's action the body and blood of Christ, Irenaeus teaches us an important lesson about the way God's creation gifts are to be received. They are to be accepted with gratitude and offered back to God with thanksgiving; God has returned them to us as spiritual food nourishing us to eternal life:

> For we offer to Him His own, announcing consistently the fellowship and union of the flesh and Spirit. For as bread, which is produced from the earth, when it receives the invocation of God, is no longer common bread, but the Eucharist, consisting of two realities, earthly and heavenly; so also our bodies, when they receive the Eucharist, are no longer corruptible, having the hope of the resurrection to eternity.
>
> Now we make offering to Him, not as though He stood in need of it, but rendering thanks for His gift, and thus sanctifying what has been created. . . . He stood in no need of them that they might learn to serve God: thus is it, therefore, also His will that we too should offer a gift at the altar, frequently without intermission.[56]

The Eucharist is so called because it is a thanksgiving for what God has done for us in Christ. God uses ordinary things to communicate spiritual food to his people. This thankful attitude formed at the eucharistic meal reverberates through all aspects of life. It is no coincidence that thanksgiving is associated with eating and drinking. Eating and drinking are basic to life, and we are to eat and drink in grateful acknowledgment that everything we have in life is a gift from God. Life in Eden began with and was ordered around eating (Gen 2:16-17), and in the new creation it will be consummated with another meal: the marriage supper of the Lamb.

There is something profoundly significant in this fact: what we regard as a very mundane activity is actually something that defines human beings' basic existence in relationship to God. Alexander Schmemann has aptly observed:

> In the Bible the food that man eats, the world of which he must partake in order to live, is given to him by God, and it is given as *communion with God.* The world as man's food is not something "material" and limited to material functions, thus being different from, and opposed to, the specifically "spiritual" function by which man is related to God. All that exists is God's gift to man, and it all exists to make God known to man, to make man's life communion with God. . . . God blesses everything he creates, and, in biblical language, this means that he makes all creation the sign and means of his presence and wisdom, love and revelation.[57]

Life, as God originally intended it, is meant to be wholly sacramental, wholly oriented toward thanksgiving *(eucharistia)*. Redemption restores this basic eucharistic nature of life, so that we may once again eat and drink to the glory of God (1 Cor 10:31). The thanksgiving is brought to its sharpest focus in the Great Thanksgiving prayer (the second of the "four actions"). Here is recalled the great work of redemption, what God has done for us in Christ and how the church must respond: with thankfulness. As an old gospel song puts it, redemption must be the "theme of our song." Thus we read in Revelation that the theme of the saints' celebration is the "Song of Moses" and the "Song of the Lamb" (Rev 15:3). But the attention focused on God in the eucharistic celebration should echo beyond the church walls into the world in our proclamation of the gospel and our daily living—in the *eucharistia* before every meal. Eucharistically oriented worship provides not only the model but also the means for the sanctification of all of life's mundane acts. We begin to recover what was God's original intention in creation. Life in the world was never meant to be bifurcated into a "secular" realm and a "sacred" realm, but all of life is to be lived "to the glory of God," and all of life's gifts are to be received with thanksgiving.

In many modern eucharistic liturgies, the offertory is also the time when the gifts of the people are received. This brings us to the second usage of *sacrifice:* thanksgiving is also expressed concretely in terms of *care for the poor.* Thanksgiving translates into the sacrifice of mercy and service. The writer to the Hebrews joins thanksgiving and service to others together as sacrifices pleasing to God: "Through Jesus, therefore, let us continually offer to God a sacrifice of praise—the fruit of lips that confess his name. And do not forget to do good and to share with others, for with such sacrifices God is pleased" (Heb 13:15-16). The New Testament seems to suggest that this was the standing practice of Jesus and his disciples. At the last supper with his disciples Jesus told Judas Iscariot, "What you are about to do, do quickly," and his disciples took this to mean that since Judas was in charge of the common purse, Jesus was instructing him "to buy what was needed for the Feast, or to give something to the poor" (Jn 13:27-29). This was not a novel practice but was derived from the Jewish practice of distributing a "basket for the poor" on the eve of the sabbath.[58]

Thus the earliest accounts of eucharistic celebrations also mention the care for the poor. In the account of Christian worship in Justin Martyr quoted above, Justin goes on to say:

> And they who are well to do, and willing, give what each thinks fit; and what is collected is deposited with the president, who succours the orphans and widows, and those who, through sickness or any other cause, are in want, and

those who are in bonds, and the strangers sojourning among us, and in a word takes care of all who are in need.[59]

Third, the church, in gratefulness for the gift of eternal life freely given and received, *offers up itself* as a holy and living sacrifice. As the *Book of Common Prayer* (1549) puts it,

And here we offer and present unto thee, O Lord, ourselves, our souls and bodies to be a reasonable, holy and lively sacrifice unto thee; humbly beseeching thee, that whosoever shall be partakers of this holy communion, may worthily receive the most precious body and blood of thy Son Jesus Christ; and be fulfilled with thy grace and heavenly benediction, and made one body with thy Son Jesus Christ, that he may dwell in them, and they in him.[60]

The offering up of the church as a living sacrifice is in response to the sacrifice of Christ offered once for all. In the Eucharist the church "is transformed into the sacrifice it celebrates."[61] This self-sacrifice is expressed concretely in service in the world: "Almighty God, we thank thee for feeding us with the body and blood of thy Son Jesus Christ our Lord. Through him we offer thee our souls and bodies to be a living sacrifice. Send us out in the power of thy Spirit to live and work to thy praise and glory. Amen."[62]

Service entails many things. I referred earlier to the proclamation of the gospel and the "offering up of the Gentiles" as sacrifices to God (Rom 15:16).[63] Service also involves the use of the gifts given by the Spirit to each member of Christ's body for the building up of the entire body (1 Cor 12—14). The problem in the church at Corinth, as commentators have noted, is a lack of real unity, that is, a lack of awareness of being the body of Christ.[64] In the chapter preceding the discussion of spiritual gifts in 12—14, Paul strongly rebukes them for failing to "discern the Lord's body" at the Lord's table (1 Cor 11:29).

The Eucharist provides the context for understanding ministry to one another, a ministry that should lead to the building up of the entire body of Christ. There is a fine balance that needs to be maintained if we are to avoid either of two extremes in this ministry. One is to so tie charisms to the priestly ministry that little remains for the laity to do. For instance, why should the gifts of healing be considered a priestly prerogative? This has been the weakness of traditional Catholicism and Orthodoxy, although currently attempts are being made to correct it. On the other hand, failure to exercise the gifts of the Spirit within a eucharistic context has resulted in the gifts' causing division within the body of Christ instead of edification. This has been the case with free church and Pentecostal traditions, although in recent years some from within these traditions have come to embrace the sacramental nature of worship and its effect on ministry.[65]

But the supreme sacrifice is the laying down of one's life for one's "friends" (Jn 15:13). It is suggested that John 13 is the Johannine Eucharist just as John 20:22 is the Johannine Pentecost.[66] The example of mutual service (foot washing) and the giving of the "new commandment" to love one another, by which all will know that "you are my disciples" (Jn 13:34-35)—these sacrificial acts are set in the context of a meal that was to be Jesus' last supper with his disciples (cf. Jn 13:1). Christ's own sacrifice will effect these sacrificial acts in his disciples: "the osmosis . . . between the 'sacrifice' of the Lord and Master and the 'sacrifice' of his disciples."[67] The theme of communion between Christ and his disciples continues in John 15 with the imagery of the vine and branches and culminates in the call to the disciples to lay down their lives just as he lays down his life for his "friends." Communion in the body of Christ is no less than loving to the point of death, just as Christ himself, in love, humbled himself and became obedient even to death (cf. Phil 2:8). This is how Paul understands his ministry in relation to the church: "But even if I am being poured out like a drink offering on the sacrifice and service coming from your faith, I am glad and rejoice with all of you" (Phil 2:17).

The Eucharist as communion and sacrifice has opened up a profound understanding of the nature of the ecclesial life. All sociological categories are transcended precisely when this life is understood as *eucharistic* communion and sacrifice. That is to say, the ecclesial life is strictly speaking not *our* life but the life that the triune God graciously shares with his people through the redemptive work of Christ, so that we become partakers of the divine nature (2 Pet 2:4) by eucharistically eating his flesh and drinking his blood (Jn 6:53-55). Further, we receive that life not by our effort but through the gift of the Spirit poured out on the church since Pentecost. It is the Spirit who unites the people of God to Christ, making them the body of Christ, branches in the vine, living stones of the temple; it is the Spirit who makes effectual by synergizing his work with the work of the people of God in the liturgy.

## THE ESCHATOLOGICAL ORIENTATION OF THE LITURGY

Word and sacrament point to and indeed sustain the utterly basic eschatological nature of Christian existence. As Wainwright has pointed out, the Word reminds the church of what is "still necessary": it still needs to proclaim the kingdom until it comes; the Eucharist meanwhile reminds it of what is "already possible" here: it has already received the firstfruits of the new creation.[68] Similarly, Schmemann argues for a "liturgical dualism" consisting of the *synaxis* (the service of the Word) and Eucharist as the basic configuration of the liturgy. Early Christian worship, Schmemann notes, was built on the Jewish pattern of synagogue service *(synaxis)* and the *chaburah* meal (Eucharist), because the first Christians understood themselves as fulfilling what was promised to Israel.[69] Precisely because of their understanding of inheriting the promise of God to Israel, their eschatological orientation did not dissolve their interest in time *(synaxis)*. The Eucharist highlights the eternal dimension of the liturgy. It is the actualization of "a past event in all its supra-temporal, eternal reality and effectiveness. . . . All theological theories of the Sacrament agree that its meaning lies in the fact that while it is performed as a repetition in time, it manifests an unrepeatable and supratemporal reality."[70] Schmemann sees this supratemporal reality expressed, for instance, in the *anaphora,* the lifting up of hearts to the Lord. The *anaphora* "is the ascension of the Church to heaven." It is not just about what happens to the bread and wine. It is first about what happens to us who are constituted the church and are "lifted up" and transfigured!"[71]

But the Eucharist is celebrated in time. The Eucharist is the "summit" or center of worship, but not its sole content.[72] The *ordo* of worship includes the temporal dimension as well, expressed in the cycles of daily prayers, weekly gatherings and yearly festivals. The liturgy of time connects worship to the natural cycles of this world. This "liturgical dualism" is based on the Christian understanding of the coming of the Messiah as the coming of the "last days," the revelation of the final age. But the special character of this age is that while the new is already here, the old has not been completely done away with. In other words, the church age, as we normally call it, is characterized by eternity-in-time, or, in more familiar language, the eschatological tension between the "already and not yet."[73] This juxtaposing of eternity and time is what Schmemann means by the calling the liturgy eschatological. "We can say that it is precisely the eschatology of the new cult which in turn postulates the old cult as the liturgy of time, since this eschatology is itself in relation to time, and only in relation to time can it be ultimately and truly eschatology, i.e., a manifestation and actualization *(eschaton)*."[74]

The vertical movement is set within the daily, weekly and yearly cycles of time, the natural rhythm that orders life in the world. The very structure of the liturgy expresses the eschatological tension: the church is in the world and yet not of the world. It is grasped by the eternal Truth that is Christ, yet it exists in a world of change, a world in which ordinary things (bread and wine) and acts (eating and drinking) carried out in ordinary time are somehow "transfigured" and made the occasions for the transformation of our mortal bodies into the likeness of Christ's glorious body (Phil 3:21). The liturgy, as Gordon Lathrop puts it repeatedly, "juxtaposes" the old and the new, the already and not yet, time and eternity.[75] This is because liturgy is the manifestation of eternity-in-time, of God's eschatological kingdom.

If we examine the liturgy connected with each of the time cycles, we encounter this eschatological tension throughout. Take the daily prayers or the "liturgy of the hours." Most modern liturgies of the hours have a fourfold structure consisting of an introduction, psalmody, intercession and conclusion.[76] Here we discover juxtapositions or sets of dialectic in the very structure of the liturgy. There is, first, the dialectic between the introduction and the conclusion: the introduction moves us from life lived in the world to liturgical time that is separated from the world, while the conclusion drives us back into the world. In psalmody and intercessions we encounter another dialectic, that of future fulfillment and present need. The psalms, "an idealized and comprehensive recitation of the relationship between God and God's people, . . . [capture] an eschatological moment in which we liturgically experience the fullness of God's love and fidelity." But the intercessions "bring us back to a soteriological 'need' in which we liturgically embrace the brokenness and interdependence of humankind."[77]

The daily rhythm of evening and morning prayers reminds us of the tension of the end and beginning.[78] The Christian life is lived in time—time that will end for us one day, an awareness that gives to our present life an absolute seriousness. We are reminded of the words of Paul:

> The time is short. From now on those who have wives should live as if they had none; those who mourn, as if they did not; those who are happy, as if they were not; those who buy something, as if it were not theirs to keep; those who use the things of the world, as if not engrossed in them. For this world in its present form is passing away. (1 Cor 7:29-31)

Yet the end is not quite the end, not "chaos and old night,"[79] but signals the beginning of something new, of hope and of "death . . . swallowed up in victory" (1 Cor 15:54).

In the Christian weekly cycle worship was moved from the Jewish sabbath to Sunday, the day of the Lord's resurrection. Sunday is the first day of the week, but the early Christians also called it the eighth day. By calling it the eighth day, the Christians understood the resurrection event as breaking through the earthly limitation of the weekly cycle. Sunday points to the transformation of time. It is one of the days of the week, the first day, yet it points beyond present time to the new creation, the kingdom "not of this world," the eighth day. "By remaining one of the ordinary days, and yet by revealing itself through the Eucharist as the eighth and first day, it gave all days their true meaning. It made the time of this world a time of the *end,* and it made it also the time of the *beginning.*"[80]

In the Christian year we discover the meaning of feasts: Advent, Easter, Pentecost and so on. And as in the daily and weekly cycles, in the Christian yearly cycle of feasts we discover the same dialectic of the now-and-not-yet, of eternity-in-time, of deep eschatological tension between the old and the new creation.

> For the man of the past a feast was not something accidental and "additional": it was his way of putting meaning into his life, of liberating it from the animal rhythm of work and rest. A feast was not a simple "break" in the otherwise meaningless and hard life of work, but a justification of that work, its fruit, its—so to speak—sacramental transformation into joy and, therefore, into freedom. A feast was thus always deeply and organically related to time, to the natural cycles of time, to the whole framework of man's life in the world. And, whether we want it nor not, whether we like it or not, Christianity *accepted* and made its own this fundamentally human phenomenon of feast, as it accepted and made its own the whole man and all his needs. But, as in everything else, Christians accepted the feast not only by giving it a new meaning, by transforming its "content," but by taking it, along with the whole of "natural" man, *through death and resurrection.*[81]

There is another way in which the eschatological orientation of the liturgy is conveyed through the liturgy of time. This is the practice of turning east. Ancient churches were built facing east; at baptism the candidate turns east; during the eucharistic celebration both celebrant and people face east. In turning east the church understands itself as the people of God who "set off for the *Oriens,* for the Christ who comes to meet us"; both are engaged in "the common movement forward" toward the eschaton, to await the time when the sun (Son) of righteousness will come with "healing in its wings" (Mal 4:2). Joseph Ratzinger insists that this is an essential "orientation" of the church in the Eucharist and should not be displaced by a face-to-face closed circle, even though nice theological reasons are given *ex eventu* to explain this new configuration.[82]

Everywhere we turn, as we celebrate the liturgy of life within the liturgy of time, the liturgy confronts us with the truth that Christian existence is basically eschatological. We face the same realities that everyone in *this world* faces, its joys and pains, its hopes and disappointments, its dizzying height of success and depth of failure, and finally death. But we are not like "those who have no hope" (1 Thess 4:13). We are on a journey from "this age" to "the age to come." We are already in the age to come while still in this age. This is the peculiar nature of our existence between Pentecost and the parousia. It is an existence that is perhaps impossible to realize by any other means except by doing the liturgy.[83]

This explains why evangelicalism, while readily acknowledging the eschatological nature of Christian existence, has failed to maintain the already-not yet dialectic in practice. It relies heavily on the spirituality or theological finesse of the individual and lacks a liturgical spirituality that would give normative expression to that dialectic. The shape of the liturgy not only provides the normative pattern for Christian faith (hence, *lex orandi est lex credendi),* it is also the means that gives normative shape to Christian living through the liturgy of time. The world may be deeply conscious of time marked by the clock and the movement of the earth *(chronos).* Within this *chronological* time frame many people aspire to fulfill their dreams—dreams that are largely fed by the consumerist culture. The people of God, however, live by a different kind of time. Through the liturgy of time, the church deepens its awareness of living in God's *kairos*. It is this awareness that gives to Christian living its distinctively eschatological orientation.

## THE MISSIOLOGICAL ORIENTATION OF THE LITURGY

When Schmemann argues that the liturgy itself expresses a concrete, primary theology, he also specifies what the nature of that theology is.[84] Speaking of the worship of the early church, he says, "It was born out of the Christian vision and experience of the World, the Church, and the Kingdom, of their fundamental relationship to one another."[85] That is to say, in the very act of assembling (church) on the Lord's Day (world) to break bread (kingdom), the church is concretely expressing its understanding of and realizing the intimate connection between church, kingdom and world.[86] But this fundamental relationship can be maintained only if the church does not lower the eschatological tension of living in this age and in the age to come. Eschatology sustains the mission of the church. The moment it resolves the tension either by becoming totally immersed in this world or by divorcing itself from the world, it ceases to be the true hope of the world, even when it is involved in all sorts of "mission" activities and programs.

In the liturgy, the church straddles the kingdom and the world and maintains its dual orientation toward both. Von Allmen compares this dual orientation to the heart's pumping blood to keep the body alive. At worship the church keeps a "diastole" beat toward the world and a "systole" beat toward God.[87] These two poles, von Allmen further argues, are preserved in the application of two key terms to the church's worship: *Eucharist* and *Mass*. Eucharist "connotes . . . a movement . . . of gathering together, of assembly, to become an offering of praise for that which God has done in Jesus Christ for the world's salvation." Mass, on the other hand, is the movement of going into the world when the celebration ends. "These two words describe the very movement of the Church in the world, the pulsation of her life in history."[88] The Supper is the "center" from which the church goes out to the world and to which it returns from the world with its "harvest" to offer to the Lord.[89]

If we use different imagery, the liturgy may be compared to a journey—a journey from this world to the heavenly kingdom and back to this world.[90] In the language of the liturgy, Word and sacrament are bounded by two other acts: the gathering and sending forth. As Christians leave the world to come together, they are "on their way to *constitute the Church*, . . . to be transformed into the Church of God."[91] The biblical paradigm for this journey is the Mount of Transfiguration. The disciples separated themselves from the world and ascended the mountain with Jesus Christ and then returned to serve. But the *basis* is the ascension of Christ. In the eucharistic prayer (the *anaphora*) the church is raised up to heaven to join in the heavenly liturgy: "We have entered the Eschaton, and are now standing beyond time and space."[92] It is from there that the mission of the church begins;[93] from there that Jesus sent the Holy Spirit to constitute the church as his Spirit-filled body; from there that, after being given spiritual food, the church returns to the world—back in "time"—to love and serve the Lord.

In the Eucharist, the church is involved in a deep paradox. It is most truly

and exclusively the church, since all but the baptized living in full communion are excluded from the meal. In that sense the Eucharist in itself is not
missionary.[94] Yet this separation and exclusiveness are not to exclude the
world but are, in Schmemann's famous phrase, "for the life of the world."
"The Church in its separation from 'this world' on its journey to heaven *remembers* the world, remembers all men, remembers the whole of creation,
takes it in love to God. The Eucharist is the sacrament of cosmic remembrance: it is indeed a restoration of love as the very life of the world."[95]

The church is most intimately related to the world precisely by being separated from the world, and by being separated it gives true hope to the
world. The church in the eucharistic celebration, as von Allmen has noted,

> is doubly sacramental, because she stands for the real Presence of the King-
> dom of God in and on behalf of this world, and for the real presence of this
> world before and on behalf of God, but of this world when it has rediscovered
> its "religious" link as being all-important, of this world when it is willing to
> admit its true nature as a creation of God, destined to glorify Him in Christ
> who has saved it.[96]

What this reveals is that the world "subsists" in the church.[97] The church
in offering up the firstfruits of creation *becomes* the firstfruits of the new creation (cf. Jas 1:18) and shows what God intends for the world to become.
The goal of creation is to become church: the church is prior to creation.[98]
The church does most for the world when it is least like the world, whereas
the church that tries very hard to be "relevant" to the world spells doom for
itself and for the world.

## CONCLUSION

We have looked at the normative shape of the liturgy in terms of the relationship of Word and sacrament. This basic structure is further shown to
have an eucharistic, eschatological and missiological orientation. These ori-
entations provide the theological criteria by which any liturgical order must
be evaluated. Only as the liturgy meets these criteria can it be said to be able
to truly form the church. There is, however, a further issue that we must address before we examine some of the constituent elements of the liturgy. If
the liturgy forms the church, how does it do it? This question has arisen because of certain hitherto unquestioned assumptions made regarding the relationship between ecclesial practices and spiritual formation by advocates
of the "new ecclesiology." To this question we must now turn.

# THE LITURGY
# AS ECCLESIAL PRACTICE

Much has been written in recent years on the importance of church practice in forming the ecclesial community.[1] This interest in church practice in part reflects the postmodern preference for the concrete and particular over generalizations and abstractions. The focus is less on what the church *is* than on what it *does*. This shift in focus is significant enough for the new emphasis to be called "the new ecclesiology."[2] According to Nicholas Healy, in traditional ecclesiologies the church is described in its idealized state rather than in its actual, concrete reality. Healy calls these "blueprint ecclesiologies," and they are inadequate precisely because they fail to take cognizance of the weaknesses and failures that are very much a part of the concrete church before the eschaton.[3] Too much concentration on an idealized concept of the church (represented, for example, by various "models")[4] may have actually prevented the church from fulfilling its basic tasks as a concrete existence on earth: the pastoral care of its members and its witness to the truth in the world.[5]

There are a number of positive features in the new ecclesiologies. First, the focus on the church in all its particularities is not meant to be reductionistic. Healy is emphatic that he is not looking at the church merely as a sociological or institutional reality; rather, its concreteness includes the active presence of the Holy Spirit as constitutive of the church. Concreteness is not just about the institution's being called to hand down a set of doctrines and practices to the next generation; it is about "a distinctive way of life made possible by the gracious action of the Holy Spirit, which orients its adherents to the Father through Jesus Christ."[6] In other words, ecclesial practices are as much the actions of members as the actions of the Spirit; they cannot be reduced to social phenomena.

Second, the focus on the concrete church necessitates a robust defense of Christianity's unique truth claims. After all, if the church is to be understood in its concrete existence, its specific truth claims must also be taken seriously. There is no attempt at fudging its differences with rival truth claims under some supposed "common religious experience" as is current in foundationalist apologetics. The Christian way of life in all its distinctiveness and concreteness can and must be shown to be consistent with its own orientation toward what it perceives to be the ultimately real. Yet this is done in a way that is not arrogant, since this ecclesiological apologetics must take into account the fact that the church, in its concrete existence, has weaknesses and sins.[7] The methodology and concerns of the new ecclesiology are well summarized by Stanley Grenz in his call to evangelicals to focus on the visible church as the way to evangelical renewal:

> The postmodern situation looks to the church to be the practical demonstration of the reality of its message, that is, to be the embodiment of the gospel invitation to enter into fellowship with God in the divine triune fullness. In such a situation, the ecclesiological question can no longer be answered merely by appeal to the true church as an invisible, spiritual reality, together with the denominationalist compromise. Rather, the postmodern, pluralist context calls for an apologetic evangelical theology that reaffirms the place of the church as a people and, in a certain sense, as a soteriologically relevant reality.[8]

The turn to the particular, however, has raised new concerns. As attention shifts to the concrete practices of the church, it is becoming apparent that the relationship between practice and ecclesial formation is not as straightforward as commonly assumed. Sometimes good practices in the church do not translate into good practices in the world.[9] Sometimes good practices may not have any apparent grounding in good beliefs.[10] Can we make sense of this lack of coherence between beliefs and practices even while acknowledging that they are closely linked? Furthermore, within the same community the same practice may not be understood in the same way, and this may result in members' being formed in unexpectedly different ways. What, after all, are good ecclesial practices, and what are not? How do we tell the difference? In other words, the postmodern understanding not only challenges us to acknowledge the existence of different communities but also raises the problem of the existence of diversity *within* each community, of which the church is one instantiation.

The problem of ecclesial practice briefly outlined in the foregoing paragraphs requires me to further nuance the previous two chapters' discussion of the relationship between worship and spiritual formation. I would like to suggest that the problem could be adequately addressed if it is understood in the light of the church's liturgy as the essential and primary practice. The deep structure underlying the church's liturgy conveys a primary theology that gives the practice of the liturgy its inner coherence and shapes the church into a coherent community. It is from this coherent liturgy that other secondary practices derive their significance as Christian practices. But in the final analysis, how the liturgy forms the community can be expressed only in terms of the mystery of grace—a mystery one inevitably discovers in the practice of prayer. It is from such a theology of the liturgy that we can develop a sound theology of practice.

Two main issues need to be addressed if an adequate theology of practice is to be developed. One has to do with the personal dimension of ecclesial practices and the other with the meaning of the practices. Healy has observed that even where constitutive practices of church life are concerned (the "clearly structured" sorts of practices, like the sacraments), there is a failure to establish criteria for determining if they are done well. "Repeated performance of behavior patterns does not, of itself, issue in the right formation of church members nor the acquisition of Christian virtues," unless "they are performed with appropriate intentions and construals."[11] He cites Reinhold Hütter's assertion that the core practices of the church are the concrete works of the Spirit as an example of this failure.[12] It is one thing to say that the Spirit "is the real agent who actually enables theological inquiry to be done fruitfully" but quite another to account for human agents' failure to carry out the practice properly. I think Healy's critique is fair insofar as we need an account of how the Spirit works vis-à-vis the human agent, so that we can say that a practice done in such-and-such a way (e.g., with right intention) and producing certain effects (e.g., a more prayerful life) is a sign of the Spirit's work. However, one must also ask: are all ecclesial practices dependent on their being subjectively appropriated for them to be rightly formative?

Perhaps greater clarity can be achieved at this point if a distinction is drawn between two kinds of ecclesial practices: those constitutive practices

that belong to the *esse* of the church and those that belong to its *bene esse*.
Practices of the first kind may be called *essential* practices, those that constitute the church as church. These essential practices or "marks" are Word
and sacrament.[13] The church is that community of people incorporated into
the body of Christ through baptism in the name of the Father, Son and Holy
Spirit. They live under the proclamation of the gospel and by the eucharistic
meal. To identify Word and sacraments as marks of the church is to say that
they are the *determinative* means by which the Spirit constitutes the church
as one holy, catholic and apostolic church.[14] In that sense they *are* the concrete works of the Spirit: Word and sacrament objectively form the church.
Where the Word is rightly preached (i.e., as it is consonant with the gospel)
and the sacraments rightly administered ("according to Christ's institution"),
there the church is objectively present.[15] They constitute the church by being
what they are in themselves and quite apart from the intention and other
subjective response of the one performing them.[16] There is, however, a subjective side to it as well, where Word and sacraments are personally appropriated. Here intention, "faith" and right understanding are required of the
people if they are to be formed. We may say, then, that practices that constitute the marks of the church have both an objective and a subjective
pole—a point I shall return to shortly.

Practices belonging to the *bene esse* operate somewhat differently. They
too are the works of the Spirit and constitutive of the church, but in a different way. Their Christian status depends on how well they are coherently
linked to the essential practices and the Christian belief system, and their
ability to form individual Christians depends on how they are personally appropriated through right understanding and intention. They are subordinate
to the essential practice, but that does not mean that they are less important,
for the failure to perform them well may affect the living witness or *bene
esse* of the church. Take the practice of hospitality. We could ask: what are
the criteria to establish a practice like hospitality as a *Christian* practice?
Here questions of intention and its link to the larger Christian framework of
belief are important (see below). We could say, for instance, that hospitality
is Christian insofar as it is done in the name of Jesus Christ, that is, as an
outgrowth of the total mission of Christ to the world, and that it forms us
when we perform it with right intention and understanding. Without such a
link it would not be appropriate to call it "Christian."[17]

A second issue has to do with the meaning of practices. It may be granted that ecclesial practices may not form one rightly unless their meaning is first understood. Healy is particularly critical of attempts at fixing the meaning of a practice by the practice itself.[18] According to Healy, most ecclesial practices, even the structured practices like the sacraments, do not convey an unequivocal or fixed meaning. Within the same ecclesial community different people may understand the same practice differently.[19] Again, this criticism is more apropos to the secondary practices than to the essential practices of the church. The marks of the church, particularly Word and sacraments, have a long tradition in most churches and carry more or less fixed meanings within those communities.[20] The Eucharist is a complex ritual involving the juxtaposition of signs *and* words. It contains within itself a whole web of meaning that, for anyone who participates in it regularly, is hard to miss. Its meaning is fixed "officially."[21] In this sense it is unlike an isolated practice like dipping one's finger into holy water or laying an anointed handkerchief on a sick person, unless these acts are properly set within a broader web of meaning.[22] This is not to deny that more could be said about the essential practices. This is why the ancient church had its catechumenate, in which the meanings of the essential practices were rigorously taught.[23] This is one practice we will need to look at in greater detail later.

Teaching the meaning of the practices is an important part of church practice itself. Hopefully, as one deepens one's understanding of a practice, one is more deeply formed by the practice. Further, the teaching includes inculcating right disposition and intention. How a practice is done is just as important as knowing what it means. In other words, besides understanding the meaning of the practices, we need to inculcate a spirituality of the practices if they are to become formative for the whole community. Ecclesial practices cannot be considered apart from the larger web of meaning (systematic theology) and the attitude and intention in which they are to be carried out (spirituality). But spiritual formation, as we shall see, is more than the application of the truth to oneself; it has an objective dimension as far as the essential practice is concerned.

In summary, the problem of ecclesial practices could be understood in terms of the distinction between the church's essential and secondary practices and the different ways in which these practices form the church. The essential practices of Word and sacrament are not discrete practices but are set within a complex liturgical structure. They constitute, as already noted in the previous chapter, the "shape" of the liturgy, so that we could say that the liturgy of Word and sacrament is the primary practice of the church. In worship the church is essentially the community making a normative response to the revelation of the triune God. It is from the primary practice of the liturgy that we can understand the real nature of other ecclesial practices. Further, it is from the liturgy that secondary practices are distinguished *as* ecclesial practices. How does the practice of hospitality, for instance, form us as the church of Jesus Christ? We need to go beyond seeing the ecclesial community as just an instantiation of dynamic, socially coherent traditioning bodies, like the ancient Greek *polis*. The key to understanding and appropriating ecclesial practices is to ground them in the liturgy.

## THE LITURGY AS THE PRACTICE PAR EXCELLENCE

Worship is the word of the people of God in response to the coming of the Word.[24] It is a response to God's initiative of revealing himself in Jesus Christ and the Spirit. In this act, as noted in chapter two, the church's identity as church is revealed. This implies that the practice of worship constitutes the primary practice of the church. The worship of the church, normalized in the liturgy, is what makes the church the church.

But how does the liturgy form the church? Earlier I referred to the church's essential practices as having an objective and a subjective pole, the former being determined by the objective marks of the church while the latter is their personal appropriation. I would like to elaborate on these two poles by employing a schema widely used in liturgical studies: the distinction between a "cathedral" and a "monastic" way of praying.[25] These two ways of praying could be said to correspond to the two poles of ecclesial practices and may help to clarify the nature of ecclesial practices. "Cathedral" prayer places objective emphasis on who God is through thanksgiving and praise. It is, in the strict sense, corporate prayer or the prayer of the church. "Monastic" prayer, on the other hand, aims at personal appropriation. It tends to be individualistic, meditative and devotional.[26] Cathedral prayer proclaims the truth objectively, while monastic prayer seeks to internalize the truth in one's own life. Perhaps the cathedral prayer in its objectivity has the tendency to become ritualistic, a tendency that monastic prayer seeks to overcome. But the two should not be treated as antithetical. There is no reason that the objective focus on God should be practiced in a detached manner, divorced from its inner reality and meaning. In any case, cathedral prayer conveys its own distinctive "experience" quite apart from conscious attempts at internalization. Cathedral prayer puts the individual into the corporate life of the church, while monastic prayer seeks to make the prayer of the church one's own.

The distinction between these two ways of praying is important if only to point out that the formation of Christian character should not be made to depend *entirely* on the Christian's personal appropriation through right disposition and intention, however important these may be. Often it is those objective "marks" that shape us subtly, even before we are aware of their formative effects. This is not an idealization from a "blueprint ecclesiology" but an experienced reality, as the Nobel laureate Isaac Bashevis Singer pointed out in one of his novels, *The Penitent:* "The deeds must come first. Long before the child knows that it has a stomach, it wants to eat. Long before you reach total faith, you must act in a Jewish way. Jewishness leads to faith. I know now that there is a God."[27]

This is especially the case if we consider Word and sacrament as the marks of the church. These practices are embodied in a liturgical structure that has remained more or less stable throughout the church's long history and that defines the basic content of liturgical prayer.[28] As prayer, the liturgy has the same determinative characteristic as ascetical prayer. That is to say, the liturgy itself, as the common prayer of the church, is determinative of ecclesial formation. But it forms us, not because we make the conscious effort to be formed by it through such ascetical acts as meditation, but by its own inherent power to form us and in its own distinct way. In Paul Bradshaw's words:

> Recalling to mind what God has done, we are interpreting our human experience in religious terms; we are making our credal confession of faith; we are proclaiming our gospel to the world; we are restoring ourselves and all creation to a relationship of holiness to God; and all this not for ourselves but so that God may be glorified.[29]

Theologically, this is what it means to call it the work of the Spirit. The actual gathering and celebration of the liturgy is where the church is made visible and realizes itself as church, the visible sign of the kingdom of God.[30] There is something decisive and determinative in the very act of gathering and celebrating Word and sacrament. As Schmemann reminds us, in worship the church is "manifesting, creating and fulfilling herself as the body of Christ."[31] There is a corporate spirituality that is realized in the act of worship, a spirituality that is more than the aggregate spiritualities of individual members. Over time this pervading "spirit" of the liturgy will have its unseen effect on individual members and form them into members of the body of Christ. Some understanding is needed, and we may safely assume that where Word and sacrament are properly carried out, true understanding is never entirely absent, even if it is mostly implicit and inchoate, since there is a "primary theology" present in the very performance of the liturgy.[32]

It is the liturgy of Word and sacrament culminating in the eucharistic celebration that lays the foundation for a theology of ecclesial practices.[33] It does so in a number of ways. First, it provides a *pattern* for understanding practice. The Eucharist exemplifies a way of doing things which involves action and meaning. It is not merely a set of coordinated actions but includes words. It is both word and sign. All practices must conform to this pattern if they are to be truly formative.

Second, it provides the *means* of establishing other secondary practices as ecclesial practices. It holds all the other practices in their proper place in the Christian community. It "distills the Christian meaning of the practices [such as hospitality] and holds them up for the whole community to see."[34] The Eucharist is essentially communion, and communion with God and others includes the practice of hospitality.[35] This is why the eucharistic celebration ends with the sending forth "to love and serve the Lord."[36] Christian hospitality grows out of the Christian understanding of life as essentially communion— which is grounded in the triune God in eternity and the triune God's sharing of his own life with his creatures in the economy of salvation. This sharing reverberates in our sharing with one another. This is why failure to share at the Lord's Table elicited a strong rebuke from the apostle Paul (1 Cor 11).

Third, the liturgical basis of practice can also be approached from the perspective of the Eucharist as mystery.[37] To better appreciate this point, we need to set it within the broader context of a theology of mystery. A theology of mystery begins with the most basic fact that God in himself is incomprehensible. Incomprehensibility belongs to the nature of God as God.[38] God is mystery in the sense that he is not an "object," or a "super object" existing alongside of other objects, but is the very ground of all existence. This truth constitutes the starting point of our theology[39] and is encapsulated in the traditional doctrine of divine transcendence.[40] Christian theology teaches that this transcendent God reveals himself and revelation is God's communication of himself *as* the incomprehensible God. Thus even in his revelation God remains hidden (Jn 1:18; 6:46; 1 Tim 6:16; 1 Jn 4:20). Christian theology seeks to express this idea in terms of the *theologia negativa*. In Protestantism it is most poignantly captured in Luther's *theologia crucis*. The *theologia crucis* underscores the fact that the God who reveals himself on the cross remains hidden in his revelation.[41] Karl Rahner sums up the concept of mystery and its importance for theology in this way:

> The essential and permanent incomprehensibility of God precisely as such must be the real reason why there is such a thing as mystery (or mysteries). And there can only be mysteries of faith in the strict sense where God as God, i.e., as incomprehensible, communicates himself. This real self-communication (as an event which simultaneously makes itself known) necessarily shares in the character of incomprehensibility which belongs to God.[42]

Even when we no longer see through a glass darkly, in the beatific vision, God's incomprehensibility cannot be superseded. Human existence, therefore, could be described as grounded in "the abyss of mystery," and human relationship with God could be characterized as openness to mystery.[43] To lose this sense of mystery is to lose what is characteristically the graced life.

It is in the context of a theology of mystery that we can understand why Christian beliefs are traditionally called the mysteries of the faith. God's self-communication is found supremely in the person of Jesus Christ. This revelation, however, does not mean that God can now be fully grasped, for what is communicated is no less than the mystery of the triune God. The economy of salvation, in fact, deepens the mystery rather than exhausts it. In the self-communication of the triune God in the economy of salvation we encounter the mystery of the incarnation: the God who is hidden in human flesh. We encounter the mystery of divine grace that transforms sinners to saints through the power of the Third Person, the Holy Spirit. These and other doctrines are rightly called the mysteries of the faith because they reveal to us something of the God who is incomprehensible.

At the heart of the church's practice is the mystery of the liturgy, culminating in the Eucharist, where we encounter the mystery of the triune God and his transforming grace. Worship is not just one of the many practices of the church; it is the church's definitive practice. To be the church is to be the worshiping community responding to the revelation of the divine mystery. This mystery underlies all other ecclesial practices; how practice forms us into graced beings cannot be explained by a mechanistic cause-effect relationship. To speak of practice changing us is inevitably to encounter the

mystery of grace. However grace is understood, whether as acquired or in-
fused, prevenient or concomitant, its transforming power is experienced as
a gift, never as something we deserve.[44] Sometimes a practice changes us
without any effort on our part (*sine nobis,* apart from us); at other times it
has no apparent effect despite our best intention. Grace can never be within
our control. This is why true Christianity must reject any form of spiritual
technology (as seen, for example, among some Third Wave charismatics),
which is but the modern version of the ancient Pelagian heresy. This is also
why traditional descriptions of grace are always in terms of bipolarities: prevenient and comcomitant, operating and cooperating, energy and synergy,
and so on. The doctrine of synergy has sometimes been mistaken for the
Pelagian heresy that the human will can contribute a part to human salvation. But properly understood, it simply affirms the truth that God's grace
extends to the transformation of the human will, so that it becomes truly free
for obedience. The doctrine was actually affirmed in the third ecumenical
Council of Ephesus (431):

> Assuredly free choice is not taken away by this aid and gift of God, but it is
> set at liberty. . . . For He acts in us that we may both will and do what He
> wishes, nor does He allow those gifts to be idle in us which He has given to
> be used and not to be neglected, that we also may be cooperators with the
> grace of God.[45]

In other words, we do the work, and yet it is ultimately the work of grace,
something freely given to us, something that we could only receive as a gift
(cf. Hütter's "*suffering* divine things"). We cannot predetermine the outcome
of our practices no matter how correctly they are carried out. For ultimately
it is grace that forms us and not practices per se, and yet it forms us not apart
from practice.

In view of this, real spiritual formation can be cultivated only in the
spirit of humble acceptance. Humility is the only appropriate posture for
the church to take toward the graced life. Humility is not one of the many
virtues to be cultivated alongside of others; it is the defining characteristic
of the worshiping community. This is the way the Christian spiritual tradition has understood it. In the Rule of St. Benedict humility is regarded as
the overriding and definitive quality of the Christian life.[46] It is the virtue
that makes all other virtues possible. Thus John Calvin, following Chrysostom, calls humility "the foundation of our philosophy."[47] St. Augustine,
writing to a young student, Dioscorus, has this to say about the way to at-

tain the highest good, that is, to know God:

> That way is, first, humility; second, humility; third, humility; and as often as
> you ask, I'll tell you, humility. It's not that I can't give you any other precepts,
> but that unless humility comes before, with, and after all our good actions, and
> is the goal we keep before our eyes, the pole we cling to, and the hole that
> contains us; pride wrenches everything out of our hands when we take pleas-
> ure in any good deed.[48]

Now, humility is simply the stance of the church at worship before the incomprehensible God. It is the foundational virtue as worship is the foundational practice.

*The subjective pole of prayer.* The posture of humility leads naturally to a consideration of the subjective pole of prayer, what liturgical scholars call "monastic" prayer. Prayer (and all ecclesial practices, for that matter) is true in so far as it is a *humble* response to the mystery of grace. To explore this, I will use a text from one of the most influential pioneers of monastic spirituality in the fourth century, Evagrius of Pontus.[49] What comes through clearly in Evagrius's teaching is a constant juxtaposing of human and divine action, of synergy and the mystery of grace.

Evagrius begins in his prologue with this statement: "The way of prayer is twofold: it comprises practice of virtues and contemplation." Contemplation is essentially an act of the intellect, which focuses attentively, without distraction (no. 71), on "the inner essences *[logoi]* of created things" and then passes on to "contemplation of the Logos who gives them their being; and He manifests Himself when we are in the state of prayer" (no. 52). Contemplation, then, is not an act of the discursive intellect but engages the whole person in the vision of God. Such a person could be called a theologian, one who knows God. This is how we must understand Evagrius's oft-quoted saying: "If you are a theologian, you will pray truly. And if you pray truly, you are a theologian" (no. 61). What Evagrius means is that the theologian is not a person who understands truth merely cognitively but one who embodies it in prayer, which is "the intellect's true and highest activity" (no. 84). True prayer calls for a certain disposition, a contemplative engagement with the Truth, the Logos.

This engagement requires rigorous effort. We need to be "pure and free from passion" so that the demons will not distract us from "sinister thoughts" (no. 73). "You cannot attain pure prayer while entangled in material things and agitated by constant cares. For prayer means the shedding of thoughts" (no. 70). True prayer comes with perseverance (no. 88). We grow in our prayer, that is, become more focused on "spiritual knowledge" of God (no. 86), by persevering in prayer and cultivating "attentiveness" (no. 149). Yet prayer is a gift. Sometimes God sends his angel, whose "presence alone . . . puts an end to all adverse energy within the intellect and makes its light energize without illusion" (no. 75). In support of this idea, Evagrius cites Revelation 8:3, which refers to the angel's bringing incense before God and offering it up with the prayers of the saints. Evagrius understands this to refer to the grace of prayer "energized through the angel" which "instills knowledge of true prayer, so that the intellect stands firm, free from all agitation, listlessness and negligence" (no. 76). In this way, prayer, "the energy which accords with the dignity of the intellect," is itself energized by the angel of God. There is a kind of synergy in prayer: in praying we are expending the energy of the "intellect," but at the same time it is energized by the angelic hosts. The mystery of grace is again seen in the way Evagrius juxtaposes prayer and the virtues. Prayer trains us in the love of God, such that even the very presence of an angel could not distract the saint who is pure in prayer from continuing his praying (no. 112). At the same time, the cultivation of certain virtues is necessary to make prayer effective, especially against the temptations of demons, such as the virtues of humility and courage (no. 96). In short, vices such as "gluttony, unchastity, avarice, anger, rancour" hinder prayer (no. 51), while virtues will advance prayer, especially the virtue of friendship with God (no. 77).

Evagrius's teaching on the practice of prayer is very much in line with the larger Christian spiritual tradition. It embodies a number of ascetical principles that are basic to any attempt at developing a theology of ecclesial practices. The mystery of divine and human action, so central to a theology of practice, comes through over and over again. Yet in much of the current discussion about ecclesial practices, surprisingly little is said about a theology of prayer.[50]

There is yet another feature of Evagrius's teaching on prayer which has an important bearing on ecclesial practices. This is his constant reference to the demonic (nos. 47, 68, 90, 91, 94-96, 134, 138, 139). As God's angel assists us in our prayer, demons are seeking constantly to hinder prayer through distraction and imagination, that is, by casting images into our mind, including even images of God (no. 74). This recognition of the demonic should warn us that ecclesial practices are often carried out imperfectly. While Evagrius tends to treat them as minor annoyances (no. 105) that can be kept at bay by continuing prayer (nos. 108-9), modern Christians cannot be so sure, especially when prayer (liturgical or otherwise) hardly features in their practices. However, if we are praying the prayer of the church (cathedral prayer) in a spirit of humility, we can be assured that we are engaging in a practice that is rightly formative.

*A spirituality of practice.* One of the rules of the spiritual life is that we need to engage in practice in a focused manner—with "active participation" *(actuosa participatio)* is how the Constitution on the Sacred Liturgy puts it.[51] Active participation requires, minimally, a certain level of attentiveness—what Martin Thornton calls "the technique of going to church."[52] And as one grows in ascetical proficiency, one's level of participation increases to include a deepening of understanding and, hopefully, purer motives: "right intention and construals." But we must not suppose that we are being formed spiritually *because of* our active participation. We must particularly watch against this tendency at the higher levels of participation, like understanding and intention. Intention itself is not the cause of grace, as if intention were some kind of merit that induced God to act. Rather, where spiritual formation occurs, God's grace and human actions are set in a dialectical relationship. This dialectic could perhaps be described as the practice of *imbibing* the spirit of the liturgy. Worship is what we *do;* yet imbibing is, strictly speaking, something we do "pathically," to use Hütter's term. That is to say, we do not grasp the mystery but are grasped by it. Another reason we must be wary of making intention too determinative is that one never quite knows when one is intending aright. Intention may be either conscious or unconscious. Below conscious intention lies a much larger reservoir of unconscious intention that is hidden from even ourselves. In view of its ambiguity, the Christian spiritual tradition discourages us from becoming too introspective over our hidden motives. In fact, nothing is more debilitating to one's spiritual formation than to be constantly wondering if one is intending aright.

Self-examination is, strictly speaking, not something we do by ourselves; we always stand "before God" *(coram deo)* in all our actions with our conscious or unconscious motives. God alone sees the heart, and sometimes he comes with friendly encouragement and at other times with "severe mercy," but always in friendship. The relationship is always a graced relationship.[53] It is in the context of friendship with God that we carry on our practices of eating and drinking and "by faith" feed on Christ to life eternal.[54] In cultivat-

ing relationship with God, and through God with others, we are formed
spiritually. Yet *how* that happens will remain as mysterious as how bread
and wine become the means of receiving the body and blood of Christ.

## CONCLUSION

Because worship is the defining practice of the church, it "provides the primary source for the nourishment of the Christian spiritual life."[55] Over time
worship will have a deep and abiding effect on the practitioners. In worship
we are doing something. We are reenacting the Christian Story, reliving its
reality, imbibing its truth. There is a certain newness or freshness in the
speaking and acting. We are not merely repeating some ideas from the past
but are engaged in a "rubric" or pattern of actions of re-presenting them in
the here and now.[56]

All these liturgical words and actions, however, are more than a socializ-
ing process; we are engaged in a practice that is strictly speaking not of our
own making. First, the practice is a *fitting* response to the revelation of the
triune God. The church could not have responded in any other way than
the way it did. This normative response is embodied in the shape of the liturgy, which conveys a primary theology. Second, while it is we who worship, worship is human action juxtaposed to divine action, a synergy of divine-human acts. Worship is where the saving activity of Christ is carried on
by members of his body in the power of the Spirit.[57] It is the action of Head
and members in the power of the Spirit. In the ultimate analysis, liturgical
actions are transforming because it is the Spirit who gives life: the Spirit's
action is joined with and confirmed by our action. Robert Taft sums it up
well: "If the Bible is the Word of God in the words of men, the liturgy is the
saving deeds of God in the actions of those men and women who would
live in him."[58] The issue is not whether we are doing it with "right intention
and construals" but whether we are actively doing it. This is not to say that
right intention and construals are unimportant but that spiritual formation
must not be made to depend entirely on how one responds.

In summary, as long as Christians are practicing a normative liturgy, that
is, praying the prayer of the church, one may rightly assume that spiritual
formation is taking place, notwithstanding their inadequate understanding
and motivation. To affirm otherwise would be to deny the reality of grace
and its mysterious workings. Such a theology of practice must form the basis
of our liturgical practices, which are the subject of the next three chapters.

*Part Two*

—

# PRACTICES

# THE
# CATECHUMENATE

**W**e live in a world dominated by the twin global phenomena of technology and consumerism. Technology drives the consumerist culture by creating consumer demands and at the same time by providing the means to satisfy the demands. But technology is changing so rapidly that success in the marketplace depends on the speed with which one adapts to change. It is not uncommon in many societies today for one to be employed, retrenched, retrained and reemployed in a new job at least once in the course of one's working life—if one gets to complete the cycle. Many do not and remain unemployed for long periods. Not only is one expected to learn new skills and switch jobs, one is also expected to work in different places in a globalized market, play multiple roles and engage in "multitasking."

The driving force behind this revolution is information technology. Within a relatively short period of time, IT has radically changed the way people live and, more alarmingly, how they understand themselves. There is no question that "technological man" of the twenty-first century has lost a sense of an enduring self, a stable identity; in its place stands the "plastic" or "distributed self," inhabiting different worlds, playing constantly shifting roles, such that it is difficult to determine what is one's true identity, because technology has blurred the distinction between reality and "virtual reality."[1] The cyberworld is perhaps the most obvious example of an alternative world in which people live out their multiple selves. We see this especially in the Internet chatroom, from which fantasies are sometimes acted out in real life.

This situation is very unlike what life was like even as recently as a generation ago. The mindset of modernity still preserved the notion of a stable self unified around "reason" and sustained by industrial progress. And if we go further back to premodern societies, whether Christian or non-Christian, life was generally governed by a vision of some universal principle, however differently that principle was articulated: God, the *Dao, paramatman,* "heaven" (as in Confucianism). Take the matter of work. In a premodern society a person was likely to live in one place and have one occupation for most of his life. An occupation was a lifelong, life-defining vocation or calling.[2] But under the impact of postmodernity, the stable identity, universal vision and metanarrative of modernity lie shattered. From its ruins emerges the consumer (including the religious consumer) who creates his or her own identity, vision and story out of a plethora of choices that technology has made available and the advertising media want him or her to believe he or she has.

Within this postmodern milieu the evangelical-charismatic church finds itself in deep theological and moral ambiguity. On the one hand, it continues to use the language of Scripture to describe its central concerns. If one goes to an average evangelical church today, one will not fail to notice the intense outpouring of concern for mission and social responsibility. This concern is often articulated with increasing sophistication with massive statistics to back it up (made available through IT). If one enters a charismatic church, the one word that will not escape one's notice is *worship.* Mission and worship are indeed central to the life of the church, as I have already noted. But being caught up with the technological revolution, both the evangelical and charismatic churches' agenda and method have been shaped not so much by the culture of the church as by the culture of consumerism. The mission agenda is often reduced to the numerical growth of the church, and consequently much missions training focuses on how to find the most effective means of growth. The way to achieve growth is to make effective use of the resources that technology, especially information technology, provides. In many charismatic churches worship is reduced to praise.[3] Here again, media technology is put to good use to turn the "praise" event into a highly entertaining experience as well as an occasion for subtle manipulation and coercion.[4] But most of the time these churches are not aware of how the culture of the world is radically reshaping their worldview and value system. In a world dominated by the market economy and driven by the media, the church is readily tempted to think of its role in terms of finding the right "market niche," instead of asking a fundamental question: what does it mean to be a Christian?

Against this postmodern backdrop the church must rethink its response to the call to be the people of God, body of Christ and temple of the Spirit. The basic identity of the church has been explored in chapter one and its primary practice of worship discussed in chapters two to four. But how is the church *practically* to realize what it is called to be? In the ancient church the path led through a process of initiation beginning with the catechumenate, followed by baptism and climaxing in the eucharistic celebration. This long initiation process, lasting up to three years, aimed to help Christians break out of the old pattern of life to embrace the new life in the new community.

It is through incorporation into this community called church that Christians receive their gospel-shaped identity, marked by death and resurrection. Only as the church realizes (or at least seeks to realize) this gospel-shaped identity can it become God's answer to the world; that is to say, the *missio Dei* cannot be understood apart from the ecclesial identity. Aidan Kavanagh has summed it up very succinctly:

> The radical discovery of ourselves as Church is possible only in terms of Jesus dead and rising. Where this passage from death to life is continuously available to us is in the conversion of people actually passing from death to life in him, and by him, and through him among his faithful people. Christian initiation is this passage. It is we ourselves keeping faith, and we ourselves keeping faith is where this world is born anew in life everlasting.
>
> Who does not know initiation does not know the Church. Who does not know the Church does not know the Lord. And who knows neither the Church nor the Lord does not know the world as God meant it to be from before always.[5]

## HISTORY OF THE CATECHUMENATE

The New Testament does not say much about the practice of preparing candidates for initiation into the Christian church. This may be due partly to the fact that in the initial years the church existed within a Jewish milieu and in continuity with the revelation of God in the Old Testament. Jews and Christians had a large shared world. The issue for the early Jewish Christians concerned the identity and mission of Jesus of Nazareth. But when the church's mission was enlarged to include the Gentiles, some form of catechizing became necessary. The Christians probably followed Jewish precedent in catechizing proselytes.[6]

The history of the catechumenate may be divided into two main periods: the pre-Constantinian (first to end of third century) and post-Constantinian (after 313). Before Constantine, when Christianity was a proscribed religion, conversion to the faith involved a costly choice. There were probably not too many "nominal" converts, as we would call them today. Basically, the church was a community that defined itself against a hostile world. In the early part of the second century, catechumenal instruction was probably still flexible, but there is evidence that it was beginning to be formalized. For example we learn from Justin Martyr that before being admitted to baptism one must meet three basic criteria: sorrow for sin, faith in the church as the teacher of truth, and transformation of life.[7] By the time of the *Apostolic Tradition,* thought to be the work of the antipope Hippolytus (217-c. 235), the catechumenal process had become much more elaborate.[8] Before becoming a catechumen, a candidate had to be examined. The testimony of the one who brought him or her to the faith ("sponsor" in today's terms) or that of the potential catechumen's Christian employer was required.[9] The candidate underwent some preliminary examination concerning the motive for wanting to become a Christian, as well as marital state and occupation.[10] Those who did not abandon questionable occupations, such as pimps, sculptors or painters who made idols, gladiators, those wanting to become soldiers, casters of spells, astrologers and soothsayers, were to be rejected.[11] Once accepted, catechumens were expected to hear the Word for up to three years. The length of time was flexible; what was important was their progress in the Christian life.[12] For those "chosen" for baptism (later called *electi*), more "scrutinies" were carried out nearer the time of baptism. The gospel would be taught to them, they had to undergo fasting, and exorcisms were performed on them by the bishop.[13]

The Peace of Constantine in 313 changed the status of Christianity from an illegal religion to a legally tolerated religion and then to the official religion of the Roman Empire. With this change of status, new problems arose. People now wanted to join the church for less than noble reasons. Some entered the catechumenate in order to marry a Christian or to further their political ambitions. The great bishop-theologians of the fourth century, like Cyril of Jerusalem, Ambrose and Augustine, all spoke strongly against entering the catechumenate with ulterior motives. The denunciation of Ambrose, bishop of Milan, is perhaps representative: "And here is one who comes to the Church because he is looking for honors under the Christian emperors; he pretends to request baptism with a simulated respect; he bows, he prostrates; but he does not bend his knees in spirit."[14]

Besides the wrong motivation, there was the practice of delaying one's baptism and prolonging the catechumenate for as long as possible. Two reasons underlay this practice. First, there was no reason to proceed with baptism if entering the catechumenate was sufficient to qualify one for a public position, since a catechumen was considered a Christian. Second, there was a growing popular belief that baptism removed all sins previously committed, and so delaying baptism to the very last would allow one to avoid the hassle of dealing with postbaptismal sins.

The major difference between the pre- and post-Constantinian catechumenate is that whereas in the earlier period catechumens were already converted, in the later period many were not. The catechumenate became a means of conversion rather than of nurturing converts. Bishops of the period had to work hard toward their conversion. Even to those who had submitted their names for baptism "it was still necessary to preach conversion, purity of intention, and transformation of morals!"[15] The Lenten catechumenate was introduced to address this problem; it was a short but intense period of training, consisting of seven weeks of daily catechism, each lasting three hours.[16] But as Michel Dujarier points out, this meant trying to accomplish in a few weeks what in the previous century had taken two to three years.[17] The deteriorating spiritual condition of the church after the fourth century may have been due to the failure of the catechumenate and was one of the factors contributing to the rise of monasticism.

The problem the church encountered after the fourth century has been repeated many times in subsequent church history. Whenever the church's status changes from a persecuted minority to a favored majority, the same problem emerges. There are places in the world today where Christians experience a situation not very different from the pre-Constantinian era, while there are other places where conditions resemble the post-Constantinian age. But whatever the situation, the key to the making of a real Christian is still the catechumenate.

In the Roman Catholic Church, the catechumenate's importance was recognized with the promulgation of the Rite of Christian Initiation of Adults (RCIA) by the Sacred Congregation for Divine Worship in 1972. A cursory reading of the RCIA will show that it seeks to follow the historical process of initiation quite closely.[18] The whole initiation process consists of four "periods" of instruction and three "steps," transitional rites or "liminal moments."[19] First, the period of evangelization is followed by a rite of acceptance into the order of the catechumens; second, the period of the catechumenate proper is followed by election or enrollment of names; third, the period of purification and enlightenment is followed by the rite of the sacrament of initiation; last is the period of postbaptismal catechesis or mystagogy. Acceptance into the catechumenate involves rites of exorcism, renunciation of false worship and the giving of a new name.[20] *Election or enrollment* refers to the approval of the catechumens for baptism after the testimonies of their sponsors are received. The period of purification occurs during the period of Lent, when the "elect" would undergo "scrutinies." The aim is "to uncover, then heal all that is weak, defective, or sinful in the hearts of the elect; to bring out, then strengthen all that is upright, strong and good."[21] During this time, the creed and Lord's Prayer are given over *(traditio)* to the elect, who will commit them to memory. These scrutinies and "presentations" are set within a liturgy on Sundays which includes prayers of exorcism. The message is clear: present-day catechumens, like their ancient counterparts, need to be weaned from the world, the flesh and the devil if they are to live out their faith as Christians.

One of the more remarkable features of the RCIA is that the whole process of initiation is set squarely within the liturgy, so that catechetical instruction, even when not given in the Sunday service, are not far removed from the liturgical context. For example, besides the three ritual "steps," during the period of the catechumenate itself instructions are always carried out together with some liturgical celebration.[22] Initiation in the RCIA is essentially a process of liturgical, and ultimately ecclesial, formation. By contrast, catechism in Protestant churches today tends to be treated as a form of indoctrination without any clear understanding of its relationship to the liturgy.[23] The result is that Christian nurture is separated from the church's liturgical life.

The focus of this study will not be on all the "periods" and "steps," but mainly on the catechumenate proper, baptism and mystagogy, as they provide the basic structure for understanding the theology of initiation that is most wanting in evangelical churches. Most evangelical-charismatic churches are quite adept at evangelization but have a poorly thought-out theology of initiation, including how these initiatory practices are linked to the church's worship. I will therefore be looking at these practices primarily from the perspective of their place within the liturgy.

## NATURE OF THE CATECHUMENATE

The New Testament understands salvation as involving a radical break with the past. In Colossians 1:13-14 we read, "For [God] has rescued us from the dominion of darkness and brought us into the kingdom of the Son he loves, in whom we have redemption, the forgiveness of sins." Salvation is transference from one kingdom to another. The kingdom of God, however, is not an abstract "rule" or dominion, nor is it something merely internal ("in my heart" as in popular evangelicalism); rather, God's kingdom is always manifested in a concrete community. As William Abraham puts it, "There is no kingdom without a community, the church, and there is no church without the presence of the kingdom. God's reign has always had an Israel, an ecclesia, in history."[24] This implies that conversion cannot be thought of simply as a change of heart; it is a change of citizenship. To use an Augustinian imagery, it is a move from the City of Man to the City of God.

The catechumenate seeks to prepare individuals for incorporation into the church, the community in which the gospel finds its concrete expression in worship, life and mission. It attempts to shape individuals to fit into the gospel story and to live as citizens of a new country. It inculcates ecclesial values and clarifies for the new citizen the church's self-identity: What does the church believe and practice? What does it mean to be baptized and to participate in the eucharistic celebration? Essentially, catechesis helps individuals enter the church with a full understanding of what they are in for: they are making the commitment that Christ requires of all his followers.

It is therefore to be expected that the inculcation of Christian moral and spiritual values would constitute a considerable part of catechumenal training. No stones are left unturned. At the end of the long training, catechumens must undergo another round of moral examination: "When those who are to receive baptism are chosen their lives should be examined; whether they lived uprightly as catechumens, whether they honored the widows, whether they visited the sick, whether they were thorough in performing good works."[25] Only those who had adequately satisfied the church's criteria for ecclesial membership were baptized.

## CONTENT OF CATECHISMS

From earliest times Christians preparing for initiation were instructed concerning the Scriptures, especially on important themes like the history of salvation and Christian morals based on the Sermon on the Mount. But over the years three subjects have come to feature regularly in catechetical instruction: the Apostles' Creed, the Ten Commandments and the Lord's Prayer.[26] These three cover three basic areas of Christianity: Christian belief, ethics and spirituality. They are utterly essential to becoming a fully formed Christian.

Most subsequent catechisms—for example, Luther's catechism, the influential Reformed Heidelberg Catechism and the Catechism of the Catholic Church—are organized around these three components. The creed, commandments and prayer are not to be regarded as discrete subjects to be learned by heart but are closely integrated to form a coherent theology and pattern of Christian living.

For example, the Heidelberg Catechism of the Reformed Churches of the Palatinate (1563) begins with the doctrine of sin and human misery (Qs 1-11) followed by the doctrines of redemption and salvation by faith (Qs 12-21). The content of faith is specified in question 22: "What is it, then, for a Christian to believe?" Answer: "All that is promised us in the Gospel, which the articles of our catholic, undoubted Christian faith teach us in sum." The articles of faith are summed up in the Apostles' Creed (Qs 23-58). Questions 59-64 discuss the appropriation of Christ by faith, with question 64 making the transition from creed to sacrament:

> [Question] Since, then, we are made partakers of Christ and all his benefits by faith only, whence comes this faith?
>
> [Answer] The Holy Ghost works it in our hearts by the preaching of the holy Gospel, and confirms it by the use of the holy Sacraments.

Questions 65-85 then deal with the two sacraments, including the issue of discipline in the administration of the Lord's Supper. The redeemed life expresses itself in thankfulness and good works; good works are expressed in living out the commandments (Qs 86, 90-91), while thankfulness is expressed in prayer (Q 116).

In the four-part Catechism of the Catholic Church (CCC), the relationship between creed, commandments and prayer is summed up as follows:

> "Great is the mystery of the faith!" The Church professes this mystery in the Apostles' Creed (Part One) and celebrates it in the sacramental liturgy (Part

Two), so that the life of the faithful may be conformed to Christ in the Holy Spirit to the glory of God the Father [Decalogue] (Part Three). This mystery, then, requires that the faithful believe in it, that they celebrate it, and that they live from it in a vital and personal relationship with the living and true God. This relationship is prayer [Part Four].[27]

While the expositions of the creed, Decalogue, and Lord's Prayer differ among the various Christian traditions, there is a basic pattern underlying their relationship: the creed is the trinitarian faith confessed, the Decalogue is the trinitarian faith lived out in the world, and the Lord's Prayer is the same faith expressed in personal communion with the triune God. The trinitarian faith as professed in the creed is the foundation of the church's moral life and spirituality.

## THE LITURGICAL CONTEXT OF THE CATECHISM

The three basic components of the catechism are recited by all the faithful during worship. When we recite the creed, we are doing more than telling ourselves what we believe; we are engaged in what in speech-act theory is called a performative act.[28] We are making a pledge of self-giving to the God we believe in. As Jean-Jacques von Allmen states, "The credo is much more itself when it is not a doctrinal recitation, but is integrated in the fraternal self-offering of the Church at the moment of communion."[29] In the practice of recitation, the creed functions like a nation's anthem or pledge. When people recite their national pledge or sing their national anthem, they are doing more than repeating the memorized contents of their nation's "core values" or "national ideology"; they are in effect pledging allegiance to the nation. Also, just as singing the national anthem or reciting the national pledge serves to foster a national identity, the church's recitation of the creed, the Ten Commandments and the Lord's Prayer are its way of affirming and internalizing its ecclesial identity. The church in effect is saying, "We are a community marked by belief in the triune God; our practice is governed by God's gracious gift of his law; and this graced life is characterized by personal communion with the triune God."

It is within the liturgical context that the significance of the creed, Decalogue and Lord's Prayer can be most fully appreciated. They are meant to be practiced first in worship before they could be properly lived out in the world. If the creed hangs loose from the life of worship, if it is divorced from the living faith of the church, it becomes hardened dogma, or worse, an ideology. If the Decalogue is divorced from worship, it becomes mere law, a requirement to be followed. The end result could be moralism at best and Pharisaism at worst. If the Lord's Prayer is divorced from worship, it easily becomes an occasion for the practice of private piety.

It is therefore vital that any modern attempt to revive the catechism should link its basic contents as closely as possible to the worshiping community.[30] This is what makes catechetical instruction different from the seminars and training programs that fill up much of the average evangelical church's weekly schedule. In what follows I shall be looking at these three components from the perspective of their location within the liturgy. To recognize their liturgical location does not mean that catechetical instructions must actually be carried out within the worship service; it means, rather, that whenever or wherever catechetical instruction is given, its link to worship must be clearly understood, and some place must be found for the creed, the Ten Commandments and the Lord's Prayer within the liturgical celebration.

*The creed.* The liturgical context of the Apostles' Creed is evident in many ways. The creed first grew out of the early church's baptismal practice. In the ancient church, the creed was first handed over to the catechumens to be learned and memorized before their baptism. It constituted an important part of the process of initiation into the body of Christ. This act is called the handing over of the symbol *(traditio symboli).* The creed is the *symbol* of faith because it is a sign by which believers in Jesus Christ are recognized as such. Ability to recite the creed constitutes an identity maker for the Christians, since only to them is the creed handed over or "traditioned." But more than just acknowledging an identity marker, the baptizand is also saying, in effect, "I risk my life, I stake my existence on the truth of what follows: that is my life and I renounce all else."[31]

It is also a symbol of faith in that it summarizes the principal truths of the Christian faith.[32] The catechumens were expected to memorize it and recite it back *(redditio symboli)* to the bishop at their baptism. At baptism the candidate was asked three questions: "Do you believe in God the Father Almighty . . . ?" "Do you believe in Jesus Christ his Son . . . ?" "Do you believe in the Holy Spirit . . . ?" After each question, having made the response "I believe," the candidate was immersed.[33] The "I believe" signaled a personal act of commitment.

As a regular affirmation at worship, the creed is also a corporate act of commitment: it expresses the faith of the church. As the CCC puts it, "'I believe' is also the Church, our mother, responding to God by faith as she teaches us to say both 'I believe' and 'We believe.'"[34] When the church professes the creed in its worship, it too is testifying to its separate identity from the world. "Beginning with Baptism, the Credo denotes a boundary line between world and church. As this boundary line projects ever anew into worship, the church announces publicly before the world that it is not world but that is has crossed the end-time baptismal boundary."[35]

Faith is more than my own personal belief in the truth of God's revelation. The faith of the church is prior to my personal faith. To speak of "the faith of the church," however, does not mean that the church believes for us; it is not an "implicit faith"—as if we could merely trust the church to do all the believing. Rather, it is to recognize that my own faith does not exist in a vacuum or in isolation from the community that nourishes it. "It is the Church that believes first, and so bears, nourishes, and sustains my faith."[36] As noted in chapter four, the corporate prayer of the church forms us individually; our own prayer arises from the prayer of the church. In the same way, our faith is first and foremost the faith of the church before it becomes "my faith."

In modern liturgies, the recitation of the creed usually occurs after the sermon and thus signals the church's faith response, in which "man completely submits his intellect and his will to God," that is, to God's revelation in the proclamation of the word. This is more than an accent to the truth heard, but expresses a willingness to obey.[37]

*The Decalogue.* The inclusion of the Decalogue in catechetical instructions goes back to Augustine in the fifth century.[38] However, the place of the Decalogue in the life of the church has not always been properly understood. In the Protestant Reformation, theologies of the "uses of the law" *(usus lexis)* set the context for much of the discussion of the Decalogue.[39] Luther sees two "uses" of the law: restraint of evil in the world and conviction of sin in preparation to receiving the grace of God. The idea that the law is meant to convict one of sin (Luther's second "use") has tended to give God's law a rather negative meaning: it sets forth God's righteous demands, to which sinners inevitably fail to conform. This idea is quite biblical in itself (cf. Rom 7:6). What is problematic is a further tendency to set law and gospel in antithesis, as if there were no grace in law: "law" virtually becomes works-righteousness in contrast to grace. Further, this "elenchtic" use of the law tends to give the impression that the law is a kind of checklist of so many items against which penitent souls must measure themselves, especially during the exercise of self-examination. This "penitential piety" was a dominant feature of late medieval and classical Protestant spirituality and has tended to produce a privatized spirituality divorced from the church's corporate life.[40] Today, the Decalogue suffers from a different kind of misunderstanding. For many modern people, the commandments represent a largely outmoded morality. Others find some use for them as a means of analyzing the social conditions of the world. In either case they are understood as essentially a moral code, divorced from the church's life of worship.

Proper use of the Decalogue must begin by setting it within the liturgical context. In many Christian traditions, it is recited as a regular part of worship.[41] But even here, its position in the liturgy reflects different understandings of its uses. In Anglican prayer books it is found before the penitential rites, which seems to reinforce Luther's second use, as means to bring conviction of sin. In Calvin's Genevan Rite (1545), the Decalogue is read *after* the confession and absolution of sin and before the reading of Scripture. This position reflects Calvin's understanding that the law is an expression of gratitude by those who are redeemed by Christ.[42]

The Ten Commandments are more than a summary of God's law. They occupy a unique place in the life of Israel and of the church. First, they were written "with the finger of God," unlike the other laws which were written by Moses (Deut 31:9, 24). Second, they were given in the midst of a theophany, when God spoke face to face with Moses (Deut 5:4, 22). Third, they were God's word spoken directly to Israel (Ex 20:1), whereas the other laws were given indirectly through Moses (cf. Ex 21:1).[43] As CCC puts it, "They belong to God's revelation of himself and his glory."[44]

The Ten Commandments therefore should not be perceived as mere prohibitions and precepts; they are first and foremost an expression of God's grace. This is seen in the fact that they are preceded by a prologue that proclaims Israel's liberty: "I am the LORD your God, who brought you out of Egypt, out of the house of slavery" (Ex 20:2). Israel is reminded that it was a slave in Egypt, but now it is truly free. To live under the commandments is to be free. In the words of the CCC, "The 'ten words' point out the conditions of life freed from the slavery of sin. The Decalogue is a path of life."[45]

What is true of the Decalogue in particular is also true of God's law in general. Far from being a burden, the law is a sign of God's gracious covenant with Israel.[46] The law of the Lord sets Israel apart from other nations. To have God's law is to have God "near" his people (cf. Deut 4:6-8). This is the reason the law is constantly celebrated in the Psalms. Because it stands for God's special relationship with Israel, it is something the godly take delight in and love to meditate on (Ps 1; 119).

The spirit of this biblical idea of law is captured in the Heidelberg Catechism. Rather than discussing the Decalogue in terms of the first and second uses, the catechism sets it in the context of the life redeemed in Christ, within the third part, entitled "On Thankfulness."[47]

[Q 86] Since, then, we are redeemed from our misery by grace through Christ, without any merit of ours, why must we do good works?

[Answer] Because Christ, having redeemed us by his blood, renews us also by his holy Spirit after his own image, that with our whole life we may show ourselves thankful to God for his blessing, and that he may be glorified through us; then, also, that we ourselves may be assured of our faith by the fruits thereof, and by our godly walk may win our neighbors also to Christ.

This seems to comport with Calvin's Genevan Rite. This particular emphasis does not deny the first two uses of the law. Those have their place in the overall scheme of dogmatics, but they should not obscure the biblical context in which God's laws are understood as a sign of covenantal relationship with his people.[48] God's commandments are a gracious provision for which the redeemed must ever be thankful, because they are the means by which the redeemed life finds its concrete expression. Without this understanding, the gracious commandments are reduced to impersonal laws and could easily become either a tool for excessive introspection (penitential piety) or a graceless, moralistic "yoke of slavery" (cf. Gal 5:1).

There is a close parallel between the Decalogue and Jesus' giving of the "new commandment" to his disciples in the Upper Room discourse (Jn 13:34; 15:12). First, the new commandment of Jesus centers on love, just as the Decalogue is the concrete expression of loving God and neighbors (cf. Deut 30:16).[49] This point was noted by Augustine: "As charity comprises the two commandments to which the Lord related the whole Law and the prophets . . . so the Ten Commandments were themselves given on two tablets. Three were written on one tablet and seven on the other."[50] But a more profound truth is that Jesus, by giving the new commandment, was signaling the establishment of the new covenant with the reconstituted people of God. In so doing, he stood in the exact place where Yahweh stood in giving the Decalogue to Israel.

In the light of the Decalogue's strongly covenantal setting, its location in the Genevan Rite, that is, as an expression of the redeemed life, is to be preferred. Again the CCC expresses this well: "Moral existence [as expressed in the Decalogue] is a *response* to the Lord's loving initiative. It is the acknowledgement and homage given to God and a worship of thanksgiving."[51] We might add that this response is itself part of God's gracious revelation. In giving us the Decalogue, God is telling us how our response is properly and concretely expressed.

*The Lord's Prayer.* In the ancient church, the Paternoster, like the Creed, was "handed down" *(traditio)* to catechumens to be memorized and then "handed back" *(redditio),* that is, recited to the bishop at the catechumens' baptism. Its use in baptism, according to the CCC, "signifies new birth into the divine life."

> Since Christian prayer is our speaking to God with the very word of God, those who are "born anew . . . through the living and abiding word of God" learn to invoke their Father by the one Word he always hears. They can henceforth do so, for the seal of the Holy Spirit's anointing is indelibly placed on their hearts, ears, lips, indeed their whole filial being.[52]

The Lord's Prayer is a summary of the prayer of the church. It expresses in direct address to God what the church confesses in its creed. As such it is, as Tertullian calls it, "the summary of the gospel."[53] It is the gospel turned into prayer. Like the creed, it sets forth the corporate life of the church. But unlike the creed, it is never prayed in the singular. It is the prayer of the *church* rather than of the individual. John Chrysostom specifies that our Lord "teaches us to make prayer in common for all our brethren. For he did not say 'my Father' who are in heaven, but 'our' Father, offering petitions for the common body."[54]

To pray is to turn away from oneself and to be fully attentive to the Other. This basic truth about prayer must never be lost to catechumens—nor to any baptized Christian, for that matter. Initiation into the Christian community means that "I" can no longer be the center. The world no longer revolves around me—my desires, my ambitions, my career and (especially for postmodern people) my right to self-fulfillment. Rather, my life revolves around a new Center, Christ, who holds me along with other believers in a relationship that is to be determined solely by him. In short, "I" must see myself as a member of the body of Christ, functioning as his hand, foot, eye or other part (cf. 1 Cor 12). The paradigm shift from being myself to being a member of Christ can come about only through prayer. Learning the Lord's Prayer, therefore, is more than learning a *form* of prayer, or even a structure for formulating one's own prayers.[55] It is learning to pray what is essentially the prayer of the church, and that means learning to become the church.

The addition of the doxology to Matthew's version of the prayer shows that from early times the Lord's Prayer has been used within a liturgical context.[56] In many Christian traditions it is an inextricable part of the liturgy. Even among some free churches its use is encouraged.[57] In some churches, it is used as the conclusion to the "pastoral prayer," an indication that it is a summary of the church's prayer. In other traditions, it is set at the end of the eucharistic prayer just before the Supper. The latter position, according to von Allmen, indicates that the Paternoster belongs properly to the baptized rather than to catechumens: "The Lord's Prayer is much more itself when the first foretaste of its answer is the Eucharist."[58] In that position, both its function as a summary of the church's prayer and its eschatological dimension are highlighted, as the CCC explains: "Placed between the *anaphora* (the Eucharistic prayer) and the communion, the Lord's Prayer sums up on the one hand all the petitions and intercessions expressed in the movement of the *epiclesis* and, on the other, knocks at the door of the Banquet of the kingdom which sacramental communion anticipates."[59]

The Lord's Prayer is largely petitionary, and petitionary prayer shows that the church still exists in the interim, the "not yet," seeking God and praying for the kingdom to come. As Peter Brunner notes, "In the end-time interim of the *ekklesia,* petition is the central content of prayer."[60] Prayer, as noted earlier, is the basic response of worshipers to the coming of the Word. Here it is the response to the gift of Christ in the Eucharist. In remembrance of what Christ has done, the church remembers the world and prays for it to be transformed into God's kingdom.

## THE SOCIAL CONTEXT OF THE CATECHISM

The catechism is one place where contextual issues can and should be properly addressed.[61] The catechism is a flexible tool. The traditional rigid question-and-answer approach based on sheer memorization is hardly appropriate nowadays. A free-flowing exposition that allows for adaptation to different learning situations and contexts characterizes the newer catechisms.[62] It is the place to ground converts both in the Christian tradition and in a Christian perspective of the world in which they live. In fact, the catechism's content should address the situation in which the church finds itself.[63]

The Asian context, for example, is complex. There is the "modern" Asia plugged in to the world market economy with all its attendant material prosperity and moral ambiguities. But there is also the "traditional" Asia with its agrarian lifestyle, extended family, hierarchical structure, animistic consciousness and deep religiosity. In this traditional context, an initiation practice of exorcism during the weeks of scrutiny may involve more than just the performance of a rite. Sometimes the demonic may be encountered in a direct way. Scrutiny may require that candidates renounce explicit association with pagan religious practices. Sometimes the modern and sometimes the traditional predominates, but oftentimes they exist uneasily alongside each other.

Instruction concerning the creed, Ten Commandments and Lord's Prayer too will have to be contexualized to address issues specific to the catechumens' social context. Following are some context-specific questions that the catechumenate may have to address in many Asian societies.

### 1. The creed

- How do we teach the Trinity vis-à-vis the world religions such as Hinduism, Buddhism and Islam?

- Does the Christian understanding of the sacramental community as an *embodied* fellowship challenge the "virtual reality" fostered by the Internet?

- How does the Christian doctrine of the Spirit relate to the traditional Asian animistic instinct?

### 2. The Ten Commandments

- What does the Christian view of life have to say to the secularized world which treats humans as means to an end?

- What does it mean to be Christian in a society dominated by ideals of market and consumerism? What does the gospel have to say to "technological man"?

- What kind of family structure is consistent with the promotion of biblical values?

- What are we to make of the hierarchical structure of the Asian family?

- How is the First Commandment to be observed in a socioreligious context that accepts the existence of many gods and practices magic, divination and ancestral veneration?[64]

### 3. The Lord's Prayer

- How does Christian prayer differ from the idea prevailing in popular religions that it is an "exchange" between a person and the deity?

- How is the petition "Your kingdom come" to be understood in a totalitarian context? What other options are there besides those provided by liberation theology?

- How is the petition for daily bread to be made in a context of mass poverty?

These are weighty issues that the church must help its future members to grapple with, if they are to become full members of the body of Christ. At the end of the catechetical training, and after the catechumens have been satisfactorily "scrutinized" concerning their way of life in accordance with the creed, the Ten Commandments, and the Lord's Prayer, they are ready for baptism.

## BAPTISM-CONFIRMATION

Modern liturgical studies are coming to the conclusion that there was probably no uniform baptismal ritual in the early centuries of Christianity, but many local variations. Baptismal rituals became more standardized only after the peace of Constantine (fourth century). Similarly, confirmation may have grown out of the baptismal rites, which included anointing with oil, and became a more distinct ritual with a fixed meaning much later.[65] What was more or less uniform was the basic pattern of initiation—what Kavanagh calls the "shape" of baptism. The pattern of evangelization followed by catechesis, baptism-confirmation, Eucharist and mystagogy constitutes a whole complex of initiation. "The whole is baptism in its fullness, the making of a Christian."[66] If the catechumenate is the process of weaning the Christian from the world, the flesh and the devil, then baptism constitutes the final break with the three enemies of the soul.

*Baptism.* On the first Pentecost Sunday after Peter's proclamation of the gospel, the crowd asked, "What then shall we do?" Peter's response was, "Repent and be baptized." The world needs to be transformed into church through a radical break with the past (repentance) and incorporation into the body of Christ (baptism). This radical break is differently pictured in the New Testament as deliverance from the domain of darkness and transference into "the kingdom of the Son [God] loves" (Col 1:13) and as transformation from darkness to light (Eph 5:8). The First Epistle of Peter sums it all up: "But you are a chosen people, a royal priesthood, a holy nation, a people belonging to God, that you may declare the praises of him who called you out of darkness into his wonderful light. Once you were not a people, but now you are the people of God; once you had not received mercy, but now you have received mercy" (1 Pet 2:9-10).

Elsewhere the New Testament draws on the story of the flood (1 Pet 2:20-21) and the crossing of the Red Sea (1 Cor 10:2) to portray the passage from death to life. Baptism is a drowning of the entire sinful self, a death and burial—but out of death new life emerges: "just as Christ was raised from the dead through the glory of the Father, we too may live a new life" (Rom 6:4). This is why Cyril of Jerusalem in his mystagogical sermons speaks of the waters of baptism as "at once your grave and your mother."[67]

Baptism is not merely concerned about the sin of the individual, either as cleansing from original sin (as understood by some in the post-Constantinian church) or as a portrayal of the individual's sins already forgiven and the inheritance of eternal life (as understood by many evangelicals today). It is, as Schmemann points out, a cosmic event. We have already seen something of its cosmic dimension in passages like Colossians 1:13. The ancient church's baptismal liturgy conveys nothing less when it asks the one being baptized to renounce the world, the flesh and the devil and signals this renunciation with exorcisms.[68] In some rituals the baptismal candidate would first turn toward the west (the realm of darkness, whence the devil was thought to originate) and curse and spit on the devil. Then he or she would turn to the east to welcome the coming of the Son (Sun) of Righteousness.[69] In these renunciations and exorcisms, the church is making a cosmic claim that God's power has vanquished the enemy. It is a claim "not on souls alone, but on the totality of life, on the whole world."[70] Strong martial language is used, for baptism is part of a cosmic struggle to reclaim humanity and the world for Christ. Thus the church continues its mission of calling people to repentance and baptizing until the body of Christ becomes fully mature (Eph 4:13), that is, the total Christ *(totus Christus)* consisting of members in communion with Christ the Head, rendering praise to the Father.

The cosmic dimension of baptism—this immersion into death and rising to new life in the new creation (cf. 2 Cor 5:17)—does not mean that one's unique personhood is lost. One does not become a nameless member of a herd. It is the old self that is buried, and out of the old emerges the new self. Our true personal identity is revealed in Christ. As members of Christ's body, we are unique persons with very distinctive functions. Each member discovers new relationships with others, based on the Spirit's sovereign distribution of his gifts (cf. 1 Cor 12). The church signals this new identity by giving new believers a new name.[71]

*Confirmation.* The early Christian practice of anointing with oil either before or after the water bath or both suggests that water baptism is closely related to the concept of Spirit baptism.[72] This understanding of water baptism as Spirit baptism is derived from the fact that the mission of Jesus in all four Gospels is uniformly understood to include baptizing believers with the Holy Spirit *in contrast to* John's baptism with water. Christian baptism is unlike John's baptism in that it is Jesus' baptizing with the Spirit. Thus the water ritual can be understood only in relation to the gift of the Spirit. There is of course no mention of anointing with oil in connection with water baptism in the New Testament, so the sudden appearance of the practice in the early church must be attributed to the fact that Christian water baptism was regarded as the sacramental equivalent of Spirit baptism. Although, due to historical circumstances, the rite of anointing with oil later became temporally separated from baptism, this separation does not alter the basic understanding that the gift of the Spirit is an essential component of the rite of initiation.[73] Theologically, this means that it cannot be understood as a "second work of grace" distinct from initiation, as taught in the Wesleyan-Holiness and Pentecostal traditions, but must be understood as part of conversion-initiation.[74]

However, the unity between baptism and confirmation does not mean that there is no distinction of *function* and significance between the two signs. Precisely because they are two signs within one baptismal ritual, two spiritual realities can be distinguished within the single complex of conversion-initiation.[75] Nathan Mitchell notes that a distinction (though not tem-

poral separation) between baptism and anointing with laying on of hands
was widely recognized in the early church. It was based on the understanding that there are two distinct functions of the Spirit that goes back to Irenaeus: first a *formative* function of the Spirit to unite the church into a single body, then a *nutritive* function of the Spirit to refresh all Christians.
Although Irenaeus did not tie these two functions to any initiatory rites,
Cyprian did make the connection. In Cyprian's time, however, unlike in the
ninth century, the distinction did not involve a temporal separation.[76] This
distinction of function was also underscored by Augustine when he spoke
to neophytes:

> You, too, in a certain sense were first ground by the lowly practice of fasting
> and by the sacred rite of exorcism. Next the water of baptism was added, by
> which, as it were, you were moistened in order to be formed into bread. But
> there is yet no bread without fire. What, then, does fire signify? Holy Chrism,
> the oil that supplies the fire, the sacrament of the Holy Spirit. . . . That is how
> the Holy Spirit comes, the sacrament of fire after the sacrament of water, and
> you are made a bread, namely, the body of Christ. And that is how unity is
> signified.[77]

This link between water baptism and Spirit baptism may also shed light
on the strong sacramental realism underlying the ancient church's practice.[78]
Baptism was not a "mere sign" of a prior spiritual work effected by the Holy
Spirit in the human heart; rather, baptism is effective because it is the Spirit
who effects the reality in and by the sign. The sense of spiritual reality associated with the rite is quite pervasive in the early church fathers. An example may be cited from Tertullian: "All waters . . . in virtue of their origin,
do, after invocation of God, attain the sacramental power of sanctification;
for the Spirit immediately supervenes from the heavens, and rests over the
waters, sanctifying them from Himself; and being thus sanctified, they im-
bibe at the same time the power of sanctifying."[79]

Tertullian goes on, at the end of his treatise *On Baptism,* to urge the
newly baptized to pray for spiritual gifts and to expect to receive them. This
seems to accord with Irenaeus's distinction between the two functions of the
Spirit:

> Therefore, blessed ones, whom the grace of God awaits, when you ascend
> from that most sacred font of your new birth, and spread your hands for the
> first time in the house of your mother [the church], together with your breth-
> ren, ask from the Father, as from the Lord, that His own specialties of grace

and distributions of gifts may be supplied you. "Ask," saith He, "and ye shall receive." Well, you have asked, and have received; you have knocked, and it has been opened to you.[80]

For the church fathers there was no separation between the spiritual reality and the sign. The liturgy was no dead ritual but a vibrant reality energized by the Spirit. But it is a truth that the modern mind cannot grasp. It is particularly difficult for evangelicals to appreciate sacramental realities because of an implicit nominalist philosophy which sees signs as mere names or arbitrary pointers rather than as having any necessary connection to the things they signify.[81] As British evangelical Philip Seddon has noted, evangelicals have "a deep-seated suspicion of references to 'mystery' or to anything that is not explicable." Seddon sees this as "the triumph of the Enlightenment at the heart of Evangelical readings of the sacrament."[82] Modern evangelicals find it much easier to grasp the Zwinglian "memorial" theory of the sacraments, since it does not require them to associate transcendence with anything so mundane as water, bread and wine. For many today, it makes better sense if spiritual realities are located within the subjective experience of the person, in the "feelings." If worship stimulates a particularly strong emotional upsurge, that is "real"![83] It is rather ironic that the evangelicalism that claims to be the heir of the opponents of Protestant liberalism in the nineteenth century should find itself unwittingly concurring with the father of liberalism, Friedrich Schleiermacher, who understood the source of religion to be found precisely in human subjectivity: "the feeling of absolute dependence."

## MYSTAGOGY

Besides teaching the creed, Decalogue and Lord's Prayer, the catechumenate in the ancient church trained Christians to participate fully in the worship of the church. The newly baptized were taught the meaning of various liturgical acts and the part they had to play for worship to be effective. The reason for a postbaptismal catechumenate, or mystagogy (that is, instruction in the mysteries of the faith), was that since the culminating act of the liturgy, the Eucharist, had remained closed to the catechumens until they had become full members of the ecclesial community through baptism, liturgical education concerning the sacraments could best be done after their baptism.

It was imperative that the newly baptized or neophytes understand what they had just been through at baptism and what they had received at their first eucharistic celebration. Now that they had been baptized and tasted their first eucharistic meal, they were in a better position to appreciate explanations of these new experiences. This was the reason Cyril, bishop of Jerusalem, gave for his five mystagogical sermons addressed to the newly baptized.[84] The first sermon explains to the neophytes what has happened in their baptism, especially the meaning of turning west to renounce the devil "and all thy works," "and all his pomp," "and all thy service."[85] The "pomp" of the devil includes "theatres, and horse-races, and hunting, and all such vanity," while the "services of the devil" have to do with any rituals or practices associated with idol temples, such as burning of incense, divination, omens, amulets and charms.[86] The second sermon explains the meaning of baptism. It is the "imitation" of Christ's death and rising: "He has freely bestowed upon us, that we, sharing His sufferings by imitation, might gain salvation in reality."[87] In the third sermon, on the chrism, Cyril understands it to mean that "ye have been made Christs, by receiving the antitype of the Holy Ghost." The anointing imitates what Jesus Christ experienced after his baptism: the descent of the Spirit.[88] The nature of the Eucharist is explained in the fourth sermon. The bread and wine are not "bare elements," but "from faith" one is "fully assured . . . that the Body and Blood of Christ have been vouchsafed to thee."[89] In eating and drinking, we are not to trust "the judgment of thy bodily palate" but to receive "the antitypical Body and Blood of Christ."[90] In the final sermon, Cyril explains the different parts of the liturgy, beginning with the kiss of reconciliation ("the sign that our souls are mingled together"), then to the *sursum corda,* sanctus, intercession, the Lord's Prayer, the invitation "Holy things to holy men"; and to conclude he speaks of how the bread and wine are to be received: in a posture symbolizing reverence and awe.[91] Such was the nature of mystagogical catechism. It brought the liturgical education of the newly baptized to its completion.

Underlying mystagogy is a theology of the liturgy. It is an understanding of liturgy, especially the sacraments, as signs mediating the "mysteries" of the faith, the content of salvation in Christ.[92] That is to say, not only does the liturgy initiate one into the knowledge of the mystery, but the liturgical actions embody the mystery (the reality) itself.[93] Typological interpretation played a key role in explaining the relationship between the sign and the reality.[94] Typology presupposes a *necessary* connection between type and antitype, between Old Testament and New, the earthly liturgy and the heavenly liturgy. The type "represents" or "imitates" the antitype. The explanations sometimes involve complex analogies and embellished allegories.[95] An example may be cited from Theodore of Mopsuestia (c. 350-428).[96] In the first part of the Eucharist (the *prothesis*), which represents the sacramental death of Christ, Theodore understands the liturgical actions as corresponding to the angels at the tomb of Christ ("the angelic liturgy"). The altar represents the tomb of Christ; the deacons are the angels; the altar cloth, the wrappings of Christ's body; when the deacons fan the elements, they are signaling the respect shown to an important person at his funeral wake, and so on.[97] But behind these elaborate allegories lies a "sacramental realism": the sacrament is an "image" of the angelic liturgy and participates in the angelic liturgy. Representation and imitation are the chief means to appropriate the reality, but in the final analysis, real transformation of life comes from the redemptive work of Christ effected by the operation of the Spirit.[98]

There are two valuable lessons the modern church could learn from the patristic church in its relentless pursuit of mystagogical instructions. The first is that while we may question its use of fanciful allegories and types, underlying its method is the presupposition that the Scripture is to be treated less as a collection of historical texts than as a unified whole. The modern church has seen the disastrous consequences of the so-called scientific study of the Bible since the Enlightenment. It has led to the fragmentation of theology and the impoverishment of the church's worship. It is largely out of the need to recover a unified theology that modern interpreters are returning to the ancient method of "spiritual exegesis."[99] I shall have more to say about this in the next chapter. Second, in today's church perhaps it is less critical when mystagogical instructions are given; what is vital is that understanding of the liturgy must form a necessary part of the education of those who are seeking to enter the church or already in it. But that is precisely what is missing! Many Christians from the free church tradition have no liturgy to speak of and hence no understanding of what it means. But even where a liturgy is still observed in some mainline Protestant churches, hardly any liturgical education is carried out.[100]

It is important to note that the whole catechumenal process is properly set within a liturgical context. It is more than instruction or indoctrination; it is training through actual participation in the liturgy. As Kavanagh puts it, "One learns how to fast, pray, repent, celebrate, and serve the good of one's neighbor less by being lectured on these matters than by close association with people who do these things with regular ease and flair."[101] This is more than an educational process; it is a process of conversion.[102]

## CONCLUSION

The ancient catechumenate poses two distinct challenges to the evangelical church. First, it challenges the notion that conversion involves simply the initial step of "accepting Christ as my personal Savior." Conversion must be seen as a process rather than merely a crisis event. Missiologist Paul Hiebert has shown that in a context radically different from the West, conversion cannot be readily explained in terms of fixed categories like belief in some essential doctrines or perhaps some defining action like saying the "sinner's prayer"—categories that have been associated with the evangelical doctrine of conversion.[103] The typical evangelical understanding of conversion could be pictured as the crossing of a fixed line, an experience sometimes described as a "crisis conversion." Hiebert argues that conversion is better conceived as a movement toward a center (the Christian faith), but it is a center with a porous rather than fixed boundary. In other words, becoming a Christian means a basic reorientation of life toward the center and a continuing movement into it. As Hiebert says, "Growth is an equally essential part of being a Christian."[104]

While the concept of continuing conversion is increasingly acknowledged, evangelical Protestantism by and large has not come up with a practical response that does full justice to this understanding.[105] In practice, it still tends to operate as if "accepting Christ as Savior" were the climax of conversion, the only thing that really counts, so that all that happens afterward is simply "follow-up" to build up the new convert's faith and prepare him or her for service. Baptism, on this view, is somewhat redundant, more of a formality than an essential element in conversion-initiation. One who has gone through the proper steps of saying the "sinner's prayer" is almost immediately fully integrated into the life of the church. In most free churches, for example, Communion is open to anyone who has "accepted Christ as Savior" whether baptized or not. If certain positions in the church are still barred to them, it is due more to pragmatic than to theological reasons.

The ancient catechumenal process corresponds more closely to the idea of continuing conversion. It is a process of becoming in which the initial response is tested out, clarified and strengthened. Just as true love between a man and woman culminates in marriage, the catechumenal process culminates in baptism, when one renounces the world, vows lifelong commitment to follow Christ and enters into full communion with the church.

Second, through the catechumenate the ancient church inducted new converts into the Christian sacramental universe. The early catechumenate thus challenges evangelicals to rediscover what God's world is really like and to encounter the mystery of grace in the liturgy. Here, however, we run into a serious problem: How do we teach sacramental theology to people who have virtually no experience of encountering God in things? The ancient church would have no such problem, since it inhabited a world that was itself essentially sacramental.[106] This would explain the ancient church's extensive use of typological interpretations, especially in mystagogical instruction. Typology, as noted above, presupposes a close connection between the ordinary world and the spiritual world.

Further, in earlier times, even after the Enlightenment, certain critical life passages such as birth, marriage and death could serve as points of contact for understanding sacramental theology. For instance, one could teach something about the mystery of the sacraments by appealing to the mystery of marriage. Marriage is the sign and seal of two persons' lifelong commitment to each other in love. In marriage, something happens to the couple: before the wedding, they were two separate persons; after the wedding, they are one. In much the same way, one becomes truly and fully a Christian through baptism. But for postmodern people marriage has lost much of its mystery to such practices as ad hoc live-in arrangements, trial marriages, marriages of convenience and same-sex marriage. Once marriage became merely a human construct, it could no longer serve as an appropriate object lesson for teaching sacramental theology.

The sacraments themselves will have to serve as archetypes—in fact, they are the archetypes—to recover the sacramentality of marriage. In the postmodern situation the liturgy will have to be the starting point for inducting new converts into the sacramental universe. The church today will have to find meaningful avenues for connections with transcendent reality. This is what liturgical spirituality seeks to accomplish.[107] But it will not be an easy task in a world that has lost a sense of mystery. Each age has unique challenges. It was no less difficult for the mystagogical bishop-theologians of the fourth century to challenge catechumens who had no compelling cultural reasons to make further spiritual progress toward a fully formed faith in Christ.

# THE SUNDAY
# LITURGY

For Christians from the free church tradition, the idea of "liturgical" worship poses a serious problem. Is not a fixed form of worship inherently opposed to the spiritual freedom that is the hallmark of the free church principle itself? This concern should not be lightly dismissed, as it grew out of a deeply spiritual sense that the Spirit cannot be domesticated. The Spirit works sovereignly, like the wind blowing "wherever it pleases" (Jn 3:8). In the church, the Spirit distributes his gifts to each person "just as he determines" (1 Cor 12:11). We cannot determine on whom the wind of the Spirit will blow and what gifts he will give. Yet freedom of the Spirit is not opposed to form. It is entirely possible for a service to have both.[1]

As noted earlier, it is the work of the triune God revealed in the two sendings of Jesus Christ and the Spirit that gives the Christian liturgy its basic shape. The church's liturgy, far from being an attempt to domesticate the Spirit, is simply an attempt to be faithful to the christologically and pneumatically shaped revelation. The Spirit that hovers over formless matter to bring about an orderly creation (Gen 1:2) descends on the chaos of the old creation at Pentecost to constitute the christologically shaped new creation: the body of Christ, the church. The work of the Spirit always has a form: the Christ pattern. Thus he is also called the Spirit of Christ (Rom 8:9; 1 Pet 1:11). The liturgy is simply a way of structuring worship that is faithful to what the Spirit is doing in the church: forming it into the body of Christ. There is much gospel in the liturgy, especially in the eucharistic prayer; there is also much in the prayer that invokes the presence of the Spirit.[2]

It was probably this understanding of pneumatology that underlies Paul's insistence—precisely when discussing the charisms—that the gifts of the Spirit be used in an orderly way in church worship (1 Cor 14:40). True spiritual worship juxtaposes order to freedom. The freedom of the Spirit implies that many forms of worship are possible. The issue is not even whether there should be a form. Even the most "unstructured" charismatic service has a form—at least it takes on a form after some time.[3] The real issue is whether the form adopted is consistent with the norm of revelation, the gospel of Jesus Christ.

Many Christians of a charismatic bent, however, are not satisfied with just freedom for a variety of forms. What they want to see is freedom within the service for someone to give a word of prophecy or a "message in tongues." A fixed form of worship, it is argued, tends to stifle the Spirit's "surprising works." It leaves no room for unplanned-for changes at any given moment. A few comments are appropriate in response to this. First, there are various types of services outside of Sunday morning in which such freedom could be exercised. Many churches have a weeknight healing service or prayer service but maintain their Sunday liturgy of Word and sacrament. Second, genuinely unpredictable elements even in a charismatic worship service are quite rare. When one has been in charismatic churches long enough, one notices that prophecies and tongues occur at predictable moments. Some form of "planned spontaneous happenings" is at work in these churches, even if it is not explicitly recognized.[4] A message in tongues in the middle of the sermon would be ruled out of order in most charismatic churches. There is an unwritten structure within which such "spontaneous" expressions are allowed to take place. Third, many of the essential elements of Pentecostal faith and practice, such as praying for the sick and the altar call, can be incorporated within a formal liturgy without compromising their integrity.[5] In short, a normative liturgy is large enough to incorporate the charismatic dimensions of worship. But if the normative liturgy is to have formative effect, it needs to be correctly understood, deeply appreciated and consistently practiced.

## WHY SUNDAY?

One way to do this is to examine the separate components of the Sunday liturgy. But why Sunday? Why not the daily liturgy? We begin with the Sunday liturgy because it is the epitome and summit of worship. It is "the original feast day" and "the foundation and nucleus of the whole liturgical year."[6]

The choice of one in seven days is not an arbitrary one. The weekly cycle of worship witnesses to the story of creation in seven days, out of which one day, the seventh, was the day of God's rest (Gen 2:2-3; Ex 20:8-11). The early Christians simply adopted this Jewish pattern, but they also looked beyond it—in fact, critiqued it—when the day of worship was shifted to Sunday, the first day. The idea that the first day of the week is the *Lord's* Day probably goes back to New Testament times and has to do with the resurrection of Jesus Christ.[7] This eschatological event—the inauguration of the new creation—was what led early Christians to call it the Eighth Day. By meeting on the Eighth Day, these Christians understand how life for them is now patterned: the seven-day cycle remains (the old creation is still real), but each week is also a new beginning because the risen Lord is present among them in their liturgical assembly.

This new understanding breaks through the old Jewish understanding of the sabbath. Sunday is not the Christian sabbath.[8] It is the day when the *work* of God through the people of God, the *leitourgia,* is undertaken. But it is similar to the sabbath in one respect: Just as the sabbath rest was the covenant sign for Israel, Sunday worship is the distinguishing sign of the new covenant.[9] The theology of Sunday worship is aptly summed up by Gordon W. Lathrop:

> The observance of the week and the meeting of the eighth day: this juxtaposition, understood in the manner of the biblical rhetoric that uses the old to speak the new, that both destroys and saves the old in speaking the new, is the *ordo* of the church. It provides a patterning for Christian ritual, and at the same time it bears the deepest faith of the church and forms us in that faith.[10]

In short, the reason we study the Sunday liturgy is that the gospel of Jesus Christ is most fully embedded within it. By learning to appreciate the meaning of the different parts of the Sunday liturgy, we can begin to participate in it more actively, and through "active participation" we will be spiritually formed into the gospel-shaped community.

As explained in chapter three, Word and sacrament constitute the basic structure or shape of the liturgy. They are, to use an ancient image, the "two tables at which the bread of life is shared."[11] But Word and sacrament are not the sole content of the liturgy. The whole liturgical celebration includes other elements that set the proper context for Word and sacrament. Peter Brunner, citing Matthew 18:20 and 1 Corinthians 1:2, insists that Word and sacrament "must be carried out in a gathering convening in the name of

Jesus."[12] To this we must add another essential element: the return or dismissal. There is a beginning and an end to the worship, a gathering from the world and dispersal into the world. Word and sacrament are set within the act of gathering and the act of returning, thus giving rise to a fourfold structure. Within this fourfold structure various other elements could be included. Here is an example of an order of service:[13]

*The Entrance*
> Greeting
> Adoration
> Confession
> Absolution

*The Proclamation of the Word*
> Reading of Scripture
>> Old Testament
>> Psalm
>> Epistle
>> Gospel
> Sermon
> Apostles' or Nicene Creed
> Prayers of the people (intercession)
> Sign of reconciliation and peace

*The Eucharist (Holy Communion)*
> Offertory
> The Great Thanksgiving
>> *Sursum corda*
>> Preface prayer (thanksgiving to the Father)
>> Sanctus
>> Recalling God's mighty acts in Christ
>> Words of institution
>> Mystery of faith
>> *Epiclesis*
>> Consecration of the faithful
>> Prayer for the return of the Lord
> The Lord's Prayer

Breaking of bread
Invitation
Eating and drinking

*The Dismissal*
Benediction
Sending forth

## THE ENTRANCE

The assembly or gathering "constitutes the most basic symbol of Christian worship."[14] But even before we arrive at church, the first act of worship is the act of going to church. "Going to church" is what "churchgoers" have to do on Sundays in order to be present at worship. But this is not a perfunctory act or merely a prerequisite for assembly; it has deep theological import. Churchgoers are beginning a journey, on the road, as Schmemann puts it, "to be transformed into the Church of God."[15] They are leaving this world to enter the kingdom of God. The day itself is different. They leave behind their daily work routine; they take a different route: the road to church, or more accurately, the road to becoming church. It is the Lord's day, a day that belongs to the Lord *(dominicus)*. It is also the Eighth Day, the eschatological Day of the Lord. The Old Testament prophets spoke of the coming "day of the LORD" as a day of judgment and of restoration at the end of time. Sunday is the Lord's in that sense. On this day, the people of God are journeying from the old to the new creation.

Worship is the time to heighten and renew the eschatological tension of the church's existence. The people of God are aware of going to taste the fruits of the new creation; in fact, as a people indwelled by the Spirit of the risen Christ, they are the firstfruits of new creation (cf. Rom 8:23; Jas 1:18). They are joining the hosts of heaven to sing praises to the One who sits on the throne (Rev 4). Yet the fact that they are engaged in this gathering on one day of the week is a sign that the heavenly worship is still only partially realized. In the anaphora, the church is lifted up to heaven, yet it must return to the world to serve its Lord in the world by transforming the world into the church.[16] The church cannot let down its guard; its very existence is sustained by the juxtapositions of rest and duty, comfort and judgment, receiving and giving, healing from and enduring pain.[17] In short, it is an eschatological existence.

*Greeting.* When worshipers arrive at church, they are welcomed to the worship. There are different ways in which this welcoming is achieved, just as there are different ways of welcoming guests to one's home. But the first thing to remember is that worshipers are not in church primarily to welcome one another, nor should it be thought that the minister is playing host to the congregation. They are gathered to meet God; God is, in a sense, the host, and we are being welcomed into his presence. This is why the greeting is not "How are you this morning?"—which is often heard in churches that seek to make the service friendly to the visitor. The appropriate greeting is a mutual salutation, "The Lord [or, The peace of the Lord] be with you," and the congregation responds, "And also with you." When the minister says, "The peace of the Lord be with you," and the congregation responds, "And also with you," they are joined together in peace. "The Salutation joins the participants in the action through the gift transmitted through it."[18] The state that defines the community that gathers in the name of Jesus to worship the triune God is peace, that is, reconciliation. If there is no reconciliation between God and people and between people, there can be no true worshiping community.

Sometimes a *call to worship* consisting of an appropriate sentence from Scripture is added to remind the congregation why they are gathered together. They are being constituted as the church, that is, as a corporate body animated by the Spirit of Jesus Christ. "Where two or three come together *in my name,* there am I with them" (Mt 18:20).

*Adoration.* After the *invocation,* in which the minister calls on God to be present among his people, the people (usually standing) declare the praises of God with a hymn of *adoration.* This is an act of proclaiming who God is and also responding to his calling us together. The hymn should therefore possess objectivity. Our full attention must be on God alone. In many traditions the Gloria in Excelsis is sung. Adoration anticipates the eternal praise that the church together with the whole creation renders to God in the new creation. God should not be seen primarily in terms of the benefits *I* can get from him. Unfortunately, this seems to be the accent of much "praise and worship" singing in "contemporary" services. God is lovely, beautiful, holy, powerful—*for me.*[19]

The most common form of adoration is the hymn of praise, but there are other forms of adoration coming at other points of the service, such as the Sanctus and Benedictus in the eucharistic prayer. They contain "nothing but a reflection of God's glory."[20] It is in songs of everlasting praise that the praise of the church militant harmonizes with those of the heavenly hosts (the Preface prayer). Adoration also comes in the form of acclamations scattered throughout the liturgy, such as the Gloria Patri, Hallelujah, "Glory to you, Lord Christ" and "Praise to you, Lord Christ" at the beginning and end of the Gospel lesson. These are performative acts,[21] analogous to acclamations made before royalty ("Long live the king!") or a people's pledge of allegiance to their ruler. In these acts, the church anticipates most closely the time when "the kingdom of this world has become the kingdom of our Lord and of his Christ" (Rev 11:15; cf. Rev 19:1, 3, 4, 6). The appropriate gesture corresponding to the shouts of acclamation is *proskunesis:* bowing down before the divine majesty (Rev 4:10; 7:11; 11:16; 19:4). The disciples of Jesus sometimes took this posture before their Lord (Mt 28:9; Lk 24:52).

*Confession.* In the first thousand years of Christian worship, confession was not part of worship but came before the worship itself.[22] The *confiteor* came only in the eleventh century and consisted of a mutual confession by both priest and people.[23] This is "a very effective weapon against clericalism," as Jean-Jacques von Allmen observes.[24]

The order of adoration and confession is interchanged in different traditions, reflecting different understandings of the "logic" of the divine-human encounter. To begin with confession may reflect an order such as Psalm 24:3-4: "Who may ascend the hill of the LORD? Who may stand in his holy place? He who has clean hands and a pure heart. . . ." This is the order found, for example, in the Roman missal. The penitential rites precede the Gloria. To begin with adoration, on the other hand, reflects the order of Isaiah 6. The revelation of God's glory leads to the realization of one's own unworthiness. Not surprisingly, the Reformed tradition, with its strong sense of the sovereignty of God, favors this order.[25] Here we are confronted with the fact of our lostness before the holy God. The confession occurs in the presence of the divine majesty; it does not arise from self-discovery through self-examination (cf. Is 6; Job 42). The confession leaves nothing hidden before the all-seeing God before whom we have to give account (Heb 4:13). We acknowledge that sins are found "in thought, word, and deed" and are committed in all kinds of situations: "through negligence, through weakness, through our own deliberate fault." The Spirit who convicts the world of sin, righteousness and judgment (Jn 16:3) also begins judgment in the house of God (cf. 1 Pet 4:17). Confession is a poignant reminder that we have not yet arrived.

A proper theology of confession must recognize its close link with the profession of faith. In Scripture, *homologein,* to confess, is both a confession and a profession. That is to say, confession is not just about "bad things" in general that we have done. Sin is particularly in relation to the truth revealed in Jesus Christ: the sin that the Holy Spirit convicts the world of is specifically the sin of unbelief in Jesus (Jn 16:8-9). This truth is embodied in the faith we profess, especially in the Apostles' Creed. Brunner is right, therefore, when he says, "A confession of sin will be possible where there is a vital profession of faith."[26]

Liturgical confession must acknowledge both corporate and personal sins, both sins against God and sins against humanity. One of the common features found in the more recent mainline Protestant liturgies is the strong emphasis given to corporate and social sins, while awareness of personal and "vertical" dimensions of sin—sin against God—is somewhat muted.[27] Here the evangelical doctrine of sin as an act against God's holiness serves as a necessary corrective.[28] Not only must confession acknowledge the "divine majesty" against which the church corporately has sinned, but it must also acknowledge the fact of personal sins. In the liturgy, each person is no longer an individual but a member of the body of Christ, and personal confession is needed *as* members of the body of Christ. This is because the sin of even one member (like Achan's sin) affects the whole body. There is such a symbiotic relation between members of the same body that when one suffers, says Paul, the rest suffer as well (1 Cor 12:26). The Roman Missal appropriately captures Paul's insights by making confession both personal and mutual and links the prayer of the church on earth with the intercession of the church universal: "I confess to almighty God, and to you, my brothers and sisters, that I have sinned through my own fault . . . and I ask blessed Mary, ever virgin, all the angels and saints, and you, my brothers and sisters, to pray for me to the Lord our God."[29]

*Absolution.* Absolution could be understood as "a condensation of the Gospel" just as the Lord's Supper is a condensation of the gospel,[30] since the words of absolution convey the good news of God's forgiveness of sinful creatures. It is both for the individual and for the congregation, just as confession is both a personal and a corporate act. The cross is the basis of forgiveness, but the actual forgiveness comes from God's proclamation: "Your sins are forgiven." When we encounter God, we need to receive God's word of forgiveness as much as we need to confess our sins. Forgiveness is a relational concept. It is necessary that the giving of the word of forgiveness follow from the confession if the relationship is to be reestablished. "Absolution both acknowledges that we do right to confess our sins and takes control of us so that we are renewed for a new beginning in Christ."[31]

## THE PROCLAMATION OF THE WORD

The people of God, assembled in Jesus' name, stand forgiven before God and at peace with their neighbors. They are now ready to hear the Word. There are a number of important characteristics about the proclamation of the Word that we need to consider before looking at the separate components. First, proclamation is more than the sermon. An essential part of the liturgy of the Word is the reading of Scriptures. In fact, reading should determine the subject of the sermon rather than vice versa. This will ensure that the sermon is truly an exposition of the gospel, since the readings themselves are based on the gospel events set within the Christian calendar. Besides reading and the sermon, the Word is proclaimed in the absolution, the greeting and the blessing, the psalmody, and indirect forms of the Word such as hymns, confession of faith, doxologies and collects.[32]

Second, as noted above, proclamation is a sacramental event just as the sacrament is a proclamation. It is human action joined with the action of the Spirit. In the act of proclamation, human words are united with the divine Word.

> This poor and wretched word of proclamation is, thanks to God's gracious condescension, pervaded and permeated with God's saving presence, which is materialized in His Son Jesus for all eternity. The outpoured Holy Spirit unites, *realiter,* with this human word as the epiphany of God's incarnation-presence in Jesus. In this Pneuma-pervaded Word, the One who is the Bread of Life can Himself be received and eaten (John 6), so that, in the reception of this Word, Christ's righteousness becomes our righteousness, Christ's divine life becomes our life, Christ's union with the Father becomes our union with the Father, until in the resurrection from the dead also the medium of the Word will be eliminated, and we shall see Him face to face and be with Him in immediate communion.[33]

The Word proclaimed is truly the Word of God. As the Second Helvetic Confession (1566) puts it, "The preaching of the word of God is the word of God."[34] This is the closest that Protestants get to a doctrine of transubstantiation. Human words do "become" God's Word in the event of preaching—

in much the same way as Christ who was the Word "became" flesh without ceasing to be God. If this is so, why is it so difficult to believe that created things like bread and wine could "become" the body and blood of Christ in the event of the eucharistic celebration (without ceasing to be bread and wine)? Preaching and eucharistic celebration share the same logical function. In the Protestant doctrine of preaching a kind of transubstantiation occurs. Could not the traditional doctrine of transubstantiation be understood in a similar way? The fact is that God uses ordinary things to convey spiritual blessings, even if we have no adequate explanation of *how* it is done. If evangelicals are to return to the norm of Word and sacrament in their worship, their strong sacramental doctrine of preaching must be extended to include the Eucharist and baptism.

Third, the sole content of the proclamation *(kerygma)* in all its forms is the gospel of Jesus Christ. The gospel may have many different ramifications in and through time; that is to say, there can be many contextual theologies. But these theologies are true only to the extent that they are faithful to the apostolic witness concerning the life, death and resurrection of Jesus Christ. There are many witnesses to the gospel (Matthew, Mark, Luke, John, Paul, Peter and others), but only one gospel.[35] This can be seen in the many accounts of preaching in Acts. They always revolve around Jesus' death and resurrection (Acts 2:23-24; 4:10; 10:39; etc.). In fact, it was the discerning and consolidation of the christological content of various apostolic documents through the practice of liturgical reading that led eventually to the canonization of some of these texts and the exclusion of others.[36] The central message of "Christ and him crucified" (1 Cor 1:23) was further elaborated upon and eventually became more or less a fixed body of truths known as the rule of faith, which came to be embodied in the baptismal confession we now call the Apostles' Creed.

What this process implies is that the sermon, as the exposition of Scripture, should not just explain isolated texts without tying them to the whole of Scripture, which in the understanding of the church bears witness to Jesus Christ. One of the problems with so-called expository preaching today is that texts can become isolated depending on the type of critical theory with which the exegete approaches the text. One can get so involved with the exegetical details that one loses sight of the gospel. Exposition, rather, should be of the text in relation to the whole; and in seeking to expound Scripture as a whole, the preacher must also come to terms with the dogmas of the church, which are but the true ramifications of the gospel. This is why every preacher should be well versed in Christian doctrine and dogmatic theology, if he or she is to preach biblically.

The way in which the Bible is preached and read liturgically implies that the Bible is to be treated as one book. As noted above, the practice of liturgical reading brings the different books of the Bible together. The whole Bible is God's Word. This is what the church proclaims when any part of the Bible is read publicly: "This is the Word of God." This unity, however, is often undermined by a historical-critical method that treats the Bible as a motley collection of disparate documents. While we must not minimize the rich contribution of the critical study of the Bible to the church's understanding of the texts of Scripture, we must also recognize its limitation. The acclamation "This is the Word of God" takes us beyond a view of the Bible as merely a collection of historical texts. It is also a confession that the Bible is one book, one Word of God, the rule (canon) for faith and practice.

The church at worship has always understood the Bible in this manner, and evangelicals are no exception. However, their preference for the literal as opposed to the typological or allegorical interpretation of Scripture shows that they are, at bottom, seeking after the same kind of "objective truth" that the critical reading of the Bible has supposedly discovered.[37] They hail literal interpretation as the great rediscovery of the sixteenth-century Reformation. They see this as the triumph of the Antiochene school of interpretation over the Alexandrian allegorical method. Two things must be said in response to these historical idealizations. First, the whole notion of the literal interpretation of the school of Antioch as opposed to the allegorical school of Alexandria must be questioned. Liturgical scholarship, especially the study of postbaptismal mystagogical instructions, has shown that there is little basis, if at all, for making such a distinction between the two schools.[38]

Second—and this is by far the more important issue, as it has to do with the church's liturgical use of Scripture—it is not the case that allegorists rejected the literal meaning. Even before the birth of the historical-critical method, the church always believed that a literal interpretation of the Bible, while valid, is not adequate. Thomas Aquinas, for example, believed that while there is a literal-historical meaning intended by the *authors,* these literal meanings are pointers to a fuller meaning intended by the Author of Scripture taken as a whole—God. In other words, patristic and medieval exegetes were looking for meanings that presuppose the Bible as a unified book.[39] The unity of the Bible grows out of the church's liturgical use based on its understanding that God is the final Author and Christ the chief content of Scripture. Jesus is its center, the fulfillment of salvation history, "the object and mediator of revelation." The Bible is canonical or authoritative precisely in that sense. From this understanding a "spiritual exegesis" arose.[40]

> Spiritual exegesis, which is supposed by the whole liturgy, is an exegesis dominated by two principles. The first principle is that the Bible is the Word of God, not a dead word, imprisoned in the past, but a living word addressed immediately to the man of today taking part in the celebration of the liturgy. The second principle is that the Old Testament is illumined by the New, just as the New only discloses its profundity once it is illumined by the Old.[41]

The Bible cannot be properly understood apart from the worshiping community, which shaped the canon through its liturgical reading and which in turn was shaped by the canon.[42] This symbiotic relationship between the church and its Scriptures has helped the modern church to appreciate once again the value of typology and allegory.[43]

*Reading of Scripture.* Reading is one form of proclamation of the Word and holds a distinctive place within the liturgy. "The apostolic witness whose indissoluble connection with the prophetic witness of the Old Covenant we constantly bear in mind has a right to address the congregation directly without the interposition of expounding comment."[44] In reading we are letting the "historical form of the church-founding Word," that is, the apostolic witness that brought the church into being, to become "immediately the present, edifying Word."[45] In reading we are hearing the apostolic witness afresh. It is as if "the apostle of Jesus Christ himself appears . . . *hic et nunc* at the heart of the community, to feed it with that living Word."[46]

> When the Sacred Scriptures are read in the Church, God himself speaks to his people, and Christ, present in his own word, proclaims the Gospel.
>
> Therefore we must listen with reverence to the readings from God's word, for they make up an element of greatest importance in the Liturgy.[47]

Reading is a communal act. The early Christians adopted the Jewish practice of reading the Scriptures aloud in their public assembly (cf. 1 Tim 4:13).[48] In many churches today, several parts of the Scriptures are read, and between the readings of Old Testament, psalm, epistle and Gospel are acclamations and responses: "This is the Word of God," the lector affirms, and the congregation responds with "Thanks be to God."[49] The Gospel's central-

ity in the liturgy is highlighted in a number of ways. In some traditions, it is
preceded by the procession of the Bible, a kiss of the Gospel book,[50] standing up and singing the Hallelujah, followed by the proclamation "A reading
from the Gospel according to St. [name of Gospel]." The congregation responds with "Glory to you, O Christ!" or something similar. The Hallelujah
is an acclamation "by which the assembly of the faithful welcomes and
greets the Lord who is about to speak to them in the Gospel."[51] Christ is truly
alive and present among them; they are about to hear his good news, and
so with joy they cry out, "Hallelujah!" At the end of the reading of the Gospel
the lector proclaims, "This is the gospel of Christ," and the congregation responds with "Praise to you, O Christ!" The affirmations and responses un-
derscore the truth that in reading the Bible we are not engaged in mere historical recollection. We are saying that God is speaking to us today; it is the
Living Word that addresses us in our present condition.

  *Sermon*. What is said of the sacramental character of proclamation in general is especially true of the sermon in particular. It constitutes "a free, wit-
nessing, pneumatic speech," different from reading yet not divorced from
it.[52] The sermon must not take a life of its own but must be consonant with
the reading. It should clarify, explain and comment on the reading, in short,
do whatever is necessary to make the reading of Scriptures clear. "Although
in the readings from Sacred Scripture God's word is addressed to all people
of every era and is understandable to them, nevertheless, a fuller understanding and a greater effectiveness of the word is fostered by a living commentary on the word, that is, the homily, as part of the liturgical action."[53]

  But preaching is more than exposition; it is a performative act.

> To hear the Christian story retold is not to gather new ideas about the gospel;
> it is to hear God's speaking afresh to us, reassuring us of his covenantal faith-
> fulness. It is like a lover proclaiming to the beloved: "I love you!" When lovers
> proclaim these words they are not simply supplying information; the words
> perform a certain function: they seal a relationship; they reveal the speakers'
> intention; they have transforming power.[54]

  Putting it theologically, preaching is a Spirit-inspired speech. It is Spirit
inspired in that the Spirit is invoked in preaching, just as the Spirit is invoked
at the Supper. It has to be a word "reborn by the Holy Spirit in the preacher."
A greater existential involvement is required by preaching than by reading.
In preaching, the preacher is bearing witness to the truth he or she proclaims and staking his or her life on it. "A sermon is an exposition of the

apostolic Word in the form of testimony." It is the words of the apostles attested by a person as "a Word apprehended, believed, and experienced in its saving power." It builds a bridge between the "there and then" of the salvation event in Jesus and the "here and now" of God's continuing saving activity by the Spirit.[55]

The preaching of the gospel of Jesus Christ is also the preaching of the eschatologically oriented kingdom of God, since Jesus is the embodiment or "eschatological representative" of the future of history.[56] In him we see the reign of God realized: God's will fulfilled through his obedience, culminating in the victory of God through the cross. This is more than just the good news that "Jesus died for my sins." It is not the good news of triumphalism, of health and wealth or cozy fellowship and self-fulfillment. Rather, it is the good news with the cross at its center, where the fellowship is with Jesus the Crucified and through him with the "least of the brethren."[57] This dimension of the gospel must not be lost sight of; otherwise preaching could easily become a means to maintain the comfortable status quo.

*The Creed (Apostles' or Nicene).* For thoughts on this element of worship, see chapter five's section "The Creed."

*Prayers of the people.* The prayer of general intercession, as it is sometimes called, focuses on matters that are basic to the life of the church in the world. Four areas of concern are usually covered:

1. the needs of the church

2. civil authorities and the salvation of the world

3. those burdened by any kind of difficulty

4. the local community[58]

These concerns, as Lebon has noted, are "vast horizons, commensurate with the size of God's heart."[59] They keep before us the perennial needs of the church and the world. They give us the "big picture" but should not be diluted into generalities. They provide the framework for the church to address specific issues that it is currently facing locally and globally. It is the prayer of the entire church but is usually led by one person, with the congregation making response ("Lord, in your mercy, hear our prayer") after each petition has been prayed.

Care should be exercised in composing the intercessions. Two practical issues must be borne in mind. First, if the prayers are not taken from a prayer book, they are best composed beforehand, as few are capable of praying extemporaneously without falling into "vain repetitions" and irritating mannerisms in a struggle for words. Second, the intercessor must always bear in mind that she or he is not praying as an individual but as the representative of the whole community of the faithful. The intercessor is praying the prayer of the church. Therefore the plural "we" should be used at all times. Privatized worship is a persistent problem, especially in a church where people are accustomed to understanding worship as primarily the engagement between the individual and God.

*Sign of reconciliation and peace.* Its location in the liturgy differs in different traditions,[60] but it always occurs before the eucharistic meal and thus serves as a reminder that the children of God must be reconciled to one another before they can partake of the Supper. This is in keeping with the spirit of Matthew 5:23-24: "Therefore, if you are offering your gift at the altar and there remember that your brother has something against you, leave your gift there in front of the altar. First go and be reconciled to your brother; then come and offer your gift."

The Peace, as it is usually called, carries out or corporately appropriates what is objectively given in the mutual salutation at the beginning (see "Greeting"). This fact is implied in one form of the declaration before the exchange of peace takes place:

> Christ is our peace.
> He has reconciled us to God in one body by the cross.
> We meet in his name and share his peace.[61]

Another reminds the people:

> We are the Body of Christ.
> In the one Spirit we were all baptized into one body.
> Let us then pursue all that makes for peace
> and builds up our common life.[62]

Our baptism into the one body carries with it the responsibility to be at peace with one another. Appropriate gestures or signs of peace are then exchanged.

## THE EUCHARIST (HOLY COMMUNION)

I noted in chapter three that the liturgy is eucharistically oriented and that the essential nature of the Eucharist is summed up in two key terms: *communion* and *sacrifice*. The whole worship of the church could be said to be eucharistic, since it is the Eucharist that gives the liturgy its basic direction and constitutes its culmination. Here I shall explore the theology underlying the eucharistic prayer.

The importance of the Eucharist for the life of the church is based ultimately on the New Testament witness that it was instituted by Jesus Christ himself. What Jesus did on the night he was betrayed was "an institutive act."[63] It was probably such an understanding that accounted for the particularly poignant way in which the disciples' meals with Jesus were recalled: the incident on the Emmaus Road in which Jesus was recognized through the breaking of bread; the miraculous catch of fish and Jesus' invitation to a meal (Jn 21:11-14); his eating a piece of broiled fish as confirmation of who he was (Lk 24:37-43).

The rite of Holy Communion that the church observes is not a result of some historical event that eventually produces a commemorative event. It is not the creation of the community but the creation of Jesus Christ himself. He instituted it because he actualized or fulfilled the reality that the bread and wine symbolize. He took ordinary bread and wine and lifted them from ordinary use after he prayed a prayer of thanksgiving. In the same way, the words of institution and the *epiclesis* in subsequent celebrations provide the crucial link between ordinary bread and wine and spiritual food and drink.

*Offertory.* Robert Jenson describes the offertory before the Great Thanksgiving as "an audacious act."[64] We offer to God the fruits of creation, and God makes these ordinary gifts the body and blood of Christ for us. Before the rise of the money economy, people would bring their gifts in kind to church. Parts of these would be used for the Lord's Supper; the rest would be distributed to the poor. In the modern church, servers bring in the bread and wine as offerings of the firstfruits of creation.[65] This is an act of thanksgiving and symbolizes the offering up of our selves. "The offering of the bread and wine is a sign of what human labor has done to the gifts of God— making wheat into bread and grapes into wine. Thus we offer our whole selves and our whole lives to him."[66] It is therefore appropriate for the collection to be taken at this point.

*The Great Thanksgiving.* It begins with the dynamic of proclamation and response: "The Lord be with you." "And also with you." I noted earlier that God's presence and peace are necessary conditions for true worship to take place. The mutual salutation here also shows the critical importance of true prayer: it is the Lord's presence among us, with the minister as well as congregation, that makes the Great Thanksgiving Prayer possible.[67]

Following the salutation, the minister calls on the people to "lift up your hearts" *(sursum corda)*. The congregation responds with "We lift them up to the Lord." The minister continues, "Let us give thanks to the Lord our God," and the response follows: "It is right to give him thanks and praise." In this dialogue the liturgical journey reaches another critical point. The *sursum corda* signals the church's ascension to heaven. We could say that the whole Eucharist is defined by the *anaphora,* the lifting up to heaven, where the chief occupation of saints is thanksgiving and praise of God's glorious grace (cf. Eph 1:6). "Eucharist (thanksgiving) is the state of perfect man. Eucharist is the life of paradise. Eucharist is the only full and real response of man to God's creation, redemption and gift of heaven."[68]

The whole thanksgiving is addressed to the Father, and much of it consists of recalling the works of the triune God *(anamnēsis)*. The first part, called the Preface, recalls the Father's works of creation of the world and humanity and the establishment of his covenant through the law and the prophets. It is so called because the works of the Father recounted here open "the door into the kingdom." The kingdom has come with Christ, the perfect "Eucharistic being," who renders perfect praise and thanksgiving to the Father by his life and work.[69]

> You are worthy of our thanks and praise,
> Lord God of truth,
> For by the breath of your mouth
> You have spoken your word,
> And all things have come into being.
> You fashioned us in your image
> and placed us in the garden of your delight.
> Though we chose the path of rebellion
> you would not abandon your own.
> Again and again you drew us into your covenant of grace.
> You gave your people the law and taught us by your prophets
> to look for your reign of justice, mercy and peace.[70]

The Preface culminates in the Sanctus, in which the saints on earth join with the hosts of heaven in their unending songs of praise, "Holy, holy, holy . . ." The setting is unmistakably heaven (Is 6:3; Rev 4:8).

The thanksgiving continues by recalling the works of Jesus Christ: his life and works on earth, his death, resurrection, ascension and sending the Spirit at Pentecost. This *anamnēsis* culminates with the "words of institution," in which we "remember" his offering of himself for us—his body and blood as spiritual food. The church in response to "these your mighty acts in Jesus Christ" offers itself "as holy and living sacrifice, in union with Christ's offering for us," and proclaims the mystery of the faith: "Christ has died, Christ is risen, Christ will come again." The Eucharist "proclaims" in word and sign the death, resurrection and return of the Lord and thereby makes the mystery of the gospel an ever-present reality. As Brunner puts it, "By virtue of the proclamation-character of the Meal instituted by Jesus, the one and only 'establishment' of the New Covenant becomes an ever saving presence in this Meal."[71]

The prayer continues for the Father to send his Spirit on the church and on the gifts: on the church so that it might become the perfect sacrifice, the body of Christ for the world, and on the gifts that they may become spiritual food for the church.

> Pour out your Holy Spirit as we bring before you these gifts of your creation; may they be for us the body and blood of your dear Son.
>
> As we eat and drink these holy things in your presence, form us in the likeness of Christ, and build us into a living temple to your glory.[72]

In *Common Worship,* Prayer F, the *epiclesis* is followed by a prayer to "bless the earth, heal the sick, let the oppressed go free and fill your Church with power from on high." The church feeds on Christ in order that it might be the extension of Christ to the world. It is the firstfruits of the new creation and as such offers itself back to God. The goal is that through the mission of the church the world will be transformed into the body of Christ ("that we may be for the world the body of Christ").[73] This is why the *epiclesis* concludes with a prayer anticipating the coming of the new creation: "Gather your people from the ends of the earth to feast with . . . all your saints at the table in your kingdom, where the new creation is brought to perfection in Jesus Christ our Lord."[74]

The Great Thanksgiving prayer ends with a doxology: "By whom, and with whom and in whom, in the unity of the Holy Spirit, all honour and glory be yours, almighty Father, for ever and ever" (Prayer F). The final goal of all creation is always the glory of God: "that God may be all in all" (cf. 1 Cor 15:28). The prayer provides a majestic vision that takes in the triune God's eternal purpose actualized in the coming of Christ and the creation of the church by the power of the Spirit, and finding its final perfection in the new creation epitomized in the heavenly banquet.

*The Lord's Prayer.* See "The Lord's Prayer" section in chapter five.

*Breaking of bread.* At the breaking of bread the minister declares, "We break this bread to share in the body of Christ." The congregation responds, "Though we are many we are one body, because we all share in one bread."[75] In the Eucharist the church manifests its essential being as the one body of Christ. The sharing of one bread and cup is a poignant way of manifesting its unity. The early Christians maintained the sense of unity of the church by gathering at one place in each town, and even when it was necessary to have more than one congregation meeting in large cities and towns, each congregation would send a piece of the consecrated bread to other congregations in the city as a sign of their unity.[76]

*Invitation.* "Holy things for holy people." This is a solemn reminder that the Eucharist is no ordinary meal. It is consecrated, made holy, for people who are made holy by the power of the Holy Spirit. It is also an implicit warning that holy things are *meant for* holy people. Nonetheless it is an invitation.

The response of God's people is the prayer of humble access:

> We do not presume to come to this your table, O merciful Lord, trusting in our own righteousness, but in your manifold and great mercies.[77]

Or,

> Lord, I am not worthy to receive you,
> but only say the word and I shall be healed.[78]

Humility is the only appropriate attitude possible before the holy God.[79] We are not worthy, nor are we holy, but God alone can make us worthy and holy to receive the "holy things."[80]

*Eating and drinking.* Justin Martyr taught that just as ordinary food for which we give thanks nourishes our bodies, so the body and blood of Christ nourish our souls.[81] But how are we to understand the relationship between bread and wine and body and blood? Some would insist that there is a "real" identification between the physical and spiritual food.[82] Others speak of the body and blood of Christ in the "form," "sign" or "figure" of bread and wine.[83] Differences also exist over whether the "conversion" of bread and wine occurs by the invocation of the Holy Spirit or by recitation of the words of institution of Christ.[84] Scripture teaches that ordinary food is consecrated by the Word of God and prayer (1 Tim 4:4-5).[85] There is therefore no reason to choose between the two. Perhaps the question is not at what point the "change" takes place; rather, as Schmemann puts it, the more important point is that "the whole liturgy is *sacramental,* that is, one transforming act and one ascending movement." [86]

Even though we do not have an answer to the how or when of the mystery of real presence, it is possible to make sense theologically of how our life, all creation, food and drink are ultimately linked to the body and blood of Christ. Schmemann has summed up their relationship beautifully:

> In this world Christ is crucified, His body broken, and His blood shed. And we must go out of this world, we must ascend to heaven in Christ in order to become partakers of the world to come.
>
> But this is not an "other" world, different from the one God has created and given to us. It is our same world, *already* perfected in Christ, but *not yet* in us. It is our same world, redeemed and restored, in which Christ "fills all things with Himself." And since God has created the world as food for us and has given us food as means of communion with Him, of life in Him, the new food of the new life which we receive from God in His kingdom *is Christ Himself.* He is our bread—because from the very beginning all our hunger was a hunger for Him and all our bread was but a symbol of Him, a symbol that had to become reality.
>
> He became man and lived in this world. He ate and drank, and this means that the world of which he partook, the very food of our world became His body, His life. But His life was totally, absolutely *eucharistic*—all of it was transformed into communion with God and all of it ascended into heaven. And now He shares this glorified life with us.[87]

The mystery of the eucharistic presence can be understood ultimately in terms of the mysteries of the incarnation in which divine nature is joined with human nature, of the ascension through which the creature is taken up into the Godhead, and of the parousia when the church will also rise bodily to join with all the saints in the heavenly banquet (cf. 1 Thess 4:17). These are the "mysteries of the faith" that we celebrate in the Eucharistic Prayer and affirm in the creed: Christ has died (incarnation), Christ is risen (resurrection and ascension), Christ will come again (parousia). The whole liturgy is a celebration and an actualization of the gospel.

## THE DISMISSAL

*Benediction.* The benediction spoken at the end of the service is the final word to the people of God before they leave their "Mount of Transfiguration" to return to the world to serve. It is pronounced on those who are *in via* (on the way) but have had a foretaste of the blessings of the new creation. Jesus himself pronounced his blessing on his disciples before he left the earth (Lk 24:50). The work of Jesus is to transmit the blessing of Abraham to the Gentiles (Acts 3:25; Rom 15:8-9); and he gives his disciples the power to bless (Jn 14:12). The church, after feeding on Christ, returns to the world to bless the world with the same blessing. The words of benediction are not just a "wish" but a "gift"; they are not "optative" but "indicative."[88]

The blessing, however, is not a magical formula.[89] The difference is this: in the benediction we are proclaiming the action of the triune God. It is God's personal engagement with his people. It is the Lord who personally comes to bless. We are not using a formula that mechanically induces a blessing. We are not in charge; we do not have the power to control. The gift can only be received by faith, that is, in an attitude of openness to and humble dependence on the triune God "from whom all blessings flow."

*Sending forth.* The liturgical journey begins with Christians' leaving the world and ends with a return to it. The fact that this journey into the kingdom of God always includes a return into the world highlights the present eschatological tension. We ascend the Mount of Transfiguration so that we may descend to face the painful reality of this world. Thus Jürgen Moltmann can say, "Where people begin to live in the kingdom of the Son of man, inhuman relationships and inhuman behaviour become painfully obvious."[90] After we have completed our journey, we know a little better what it means to live in this interim state. True worship heightens rather than resolves the tension, and this is because in the liturgy the eucharistic presence of Jesus through the power of the Spirit is actualized again and again, in proclamation and in eucharistic celebration.[91]

## CONCLUSION

There is a rich and deep primary theology in the liturgy of Word and sacrament. But for many evangelicals who have virtually no experience of liturgical worship, the primary theology needs to be explicated and reflected upon before it can be fully entered into. Hopefully, a study of the different parts of the liturgy will encourage greater active participation.

# ACTIVE
# PARTICIPATION

Understanding the liturgy, the focus of the two preceding chapters, is a necessary step for ecclesial formation. But effective formation is more than understanding; it also presupposes some degree of engagement with the liturgy. One of the key phrases in the Constitution on the Sacred Liturgy of Vatican II is "active participation."[1] This phrase contains many rich ramifications, but if it is to be properly understood, it needs to be set within the broader context of liturgical spirituality.

## THE NATURE OF LITURGICAL SPIRITUALITY

Liturgical spirituality has to do with the relationship between liturgy and Christian living. How does the liturgy form us into the body of Christ? The question may be approached from two perspectives. First, liturgical formation can be considered from the perspective of what the liturgy is and does. Different facets of the liturgy provide resources for shaping our ecclesial life. Susan White, for example, speaks of six ways in which the liturgy forms the Christian community: (1) The prayers of the liturgy are models for and help shape our own personal prayers. (2) The liturgy sets the pattern for spiritual discipline, much like the way the culture in which we were born molds us through a gradual and subliminal process. (3) The liturgy provides "an arena for an encounter with God" that is life changing. (4) The liturgy supplies "signs, symbols and rituals by which to express the relationship with God." (5) The liturgy challenges us to consider our relationship with the world outside and forces us to consider the need for reconciliation with one another in the body. It reminds us of the mission of the church, especially at the end of each service. (6) It is a source of sustenance in times of crisis. The prayers we have learned by heart in the liturgy may be what we remember when everything else is forgotten in times of crisis.[2]

Along a similar line of thought, Richard Eyer points out how the liturgy brings wholeness and healing to worshipers. For example, confession-absolution releases us from guilt; liturgical prayer, by its corporateness, heals our loneliness and fosters true solitude.[3] Further, we could examine the transforming effect of the liturgy through its exalted language, poetry and songs. The liturgy is a "school" using these tools to train worshipers in the way of Christ.[4]

> The purpose of the liturgy is not to express our thoughts and feelings but to develop them, and like any good school the liturgy expands our horizon, liberating us from captivity to the moment and to the familiar. . . . Because the liturgy does not always express what we think or feel it has the potential to transform those who share in it.[5]

Theologically, we could say that the liturgy and Christian living are ontologically one. The liturgy itself is the primary expression of Christian living, and Christian living is actualized primarily in the liturgy (see chapter two). In the words of Joyce Zimmerman:

> *The deep, dynamic structure of liturgy is identical to the deep, dynamic structure of Christian living.* Liturgy and life are essentially related because they share a generic dynamic structure that gives access to an ever-deepening experience of their common referent: the Paschal Mystery. Herein lies the key to our understanding of liturgical spirituality. What we celebrate in liturgy is none other than what we live as Christians committed to entering into the ongoing redemptive work of the Risen Christ. What we live is the content of what we celebrate.[6]

Liturgy and everyday Christian living "are but two expressions of the one gift of God's paschal Presence to us."[7] If, as pointed out in chapter one, to be a Christian is to be in the body of Christ, then there is no Christian living apart from living out what is celebrated in the liturgy, since the liturgy is where the body of Christ is primarily manifested and actualized. The objective celebration of the liturgy can therefore provide a way to critique our own inadequate Christian living. It is perhaps more in its challenges to us than in reinforcing positive religious feelings that true spiritual formation through the liturgy takes place. For if the liturgy only makes us feel good and never challenges us, perhaps the liturgy is not shaping us but we are simply making use of it for our own ends. Keeping the critical function of the liturgy in view will have a significant effect on the way we approach liturgical celebration, as Zimmerman points out:

> When we celebrate liturgy and experience emptiness or boredom, we might see this as a critique of our life. Pastorally, we generally assume there is a problem with the ritual itself or the way we celebrate liturgy (and often there is). But there is another possible explanation: If the thrust of our Christian living is not response to the Paschal Mystery, then no matter what we do to the ritual, its depth meaning will still escape us. We worship neither to be entertained nor to feel good but to be transformed into the Body of Christ.[8]

In summary, liturgical spirituality begins with the fact of our being Christians, that is, baptized into the body of Christ; and by enacting the gospel, that is, the paschal mystery, the liturgy constantly challenges us concerning the living out of our baptismal faith within the body. This challenge should lead to new appropriation of and a deeper penetration into the paschal mystery that the liturgy celebrates.[9] All these understandings help us see what it is about the liturgy that makes it formative. They reveal the *objective pole* of liturgical spirituality.

Second, liturgical spirituality can also be approached from the perspective of the participants who perform the liturgy. This is its *subjective pole*.[10] Here "subjective pole" does *not* refer to how we might be able to make use of the liturgy to promote spiritual growth, such as using "praise and worship" to induce a certain religious mood. We do not *use* the liturgy; rather, the nature of the liturgy itself must determine what the appropriate response should be. What worshipers *do* must be consistent with what the liturgy *is*.

Liturgical spirituality in its fullest meaning brings the objective and subjective poles of the liturgy together. There needs to be a creative tension between the two.[11] In a vibrant liturgical spirituality, the prayers of the church are at the same time personally appropriated and made one's own. Here we could explore different modes by which the liturgy is personally appropriated.[12] What is being aimed at is the integration of the two poles. This is what the liturgist W. Jardine Grisbrooke had in mind when he challenges Anglican ordinands to grow in ever-deepening levels of engagement with the liturgy until it "cuts grooves in the mind" and instead of doing the liturgy (and perhaps falling into activism), one engages the liturgy contemplatively and lets it take hold of one's life.[13] Liturgical spirituality, in the view of Grisbrooke, should become so definitive in the life of the priest that it makes any additional "private" prayer superfluous.[14] When we begin to appropriate the prayers of the church into our life, we begin to function as a member of the body of Christ—that is, always in relation to others. Such a life is distinguished by mutual acceptance, mission and hospitality (cf. Rom 14:1; 15:7).[15]

If liturgy is to be done at all, it has to be done well. The issue becomes clearer if it is put negatively. The liturgy is objectively formative and affects us in untold ways, sometimes despite our poor efforts. But what if, after being in church for most of one's life, one finds that nothing much has *happened?* That discovery may be quite revelatory in itself, but such an "awakening" is more likely to result in one's leaving rather than remaining in church.

What if liturgy fails to form? This question posed by the "new ecclesiology" (see chapter four) needs to be addressed more fully. I mentioned earlier that the liturgy is a synergy. It is divine action working through human action. The indicative of God's action needs to be joined with the imperative of human action. This is what it means to say that grace is both prevenient and concomitant, operating and cooperating. But exactly what is the human part in the synergy?

The answer to this question can be formulated in two parts. One part is to begin with some understanding of the what and why of the liturgy. This is about not only the theology of the liturgy as a whole but the meaning of its constituent parts: What does each part of the liturgy mean? Why do we do what we do? Answering these questions (which I have tried to do in chapter six) will give us a reason to do it well. Without *meaningful* participation, a liturgical practice is quickly turned into mere ritualism. An example may help here. A student of mine who had recently joined a Presbyterian church wondered about the practice of a server's giving the bread and wine directly to each communicant, rather than having the bread and wine pass from person to person as was done in his previous church, a free church. The Presbyterian procedure seemed unnecessary, inefficient and time consuming. But after it was explained that God's grace must be received directly and not through an intermediary,[16] the student's level of meaningful participation increased.

## THE NATURE OF ACTIVE PARTICIPATION
The second part of the answer is to examine *how* the liturgy is to be done.

And this brings us to the heart of liturgical spirituality. Spirituality, in the final analysis, must come down to the part that we must play. Here is where "active participation" comes in. But what is active participation? The moment we try to answer the question, we are immediately confronted with issues that are too numerous and complex to be addressed in a single chapter. There are different degrees of participation.[17] Participation is affected by one's understanding, attitude and discipline. How leaders perform affects the ways the congregation responds and vice versa. A ritual that is meaningful for one person may not have the same meaning or the same degree of meaningfulness for another. A particular mode of participation (e.g., a spontaneous or unstructured form of worship) may elicit different responses from different persons, or from the same person at different times in his or her life. A liturgy that conveys a sense of sameness or a lack of variety is not likely to elicit active participation; on the other hand, the problem may have more to do with the attitude of the worshiper than with the liturgy itself. What for one is drab sameness may be for another welcome familiarity. The complexity of trying to determine what constitutes active participation should make us wary of simplistic solutions to the worship crisis affecting the church. Still, application of certain broad principles could help foster active participation in the liturgy.

The Congregation for Divine Worship, in its document *Redemptionis Sacramentum,* has well described how active participation can be nurtured.

> For promoting and elucidating active participation, the recent renewal of the liturgical books according to the mind of the Council fostered acclamations of the people, responses, psalmody, antiphons, and canticles, as well as actions or movements and gestures, and called for sacred silence to be maintained at the proper times, while providing rubrics for the parts of the faithful as well. In addition, ample flexibility is given for appropriate creativity aimed at allowing each celebration to be adapted to the needs of the participants, to their comprehension, their interior preparation and their gifts, according to the established liturgical norms. In the songs, the melodies, the choice of prayers and readings, the giving of the homily, the preparation of the prayer of the faithful, the occasional explanatory remarks, and the decoration of the Church building according to the various seasons, there is ample possibility for introducing into each celebration a certain variety by which the riches of the liturgical tradition will also be more clearly evident, and so, in keeping with pastoral requirements, the celebration will be carefully imbued with those particular features that will foster the recollection of the participants. Still, it

should be remembered that the power of the liturgical celebrations does not consist in frequently altering the rites, but in probing more deeply the word of God and the mystery being celebrated.[18]

The statement lays out a number of important principles. First, it recognizes that there are many parts of the liturgy that give rise to active participation, ranging from "acclamations" to "silence." Second, it acknowledges the need to adapt the liturgy to a congregation's needs, comprehension, interior preparation and gifts. In other words, active participation is possible if the people understand what is going on, are inwardly prepared and are able to use their gifts in the worship service. Third, it sees a variety of expressions (songs, melodies, prayers, readings, homily, intercession and church decorations) as opportunities for fostering the "recollection of the participants." At the same time, fourth, there must also be stability if the congregation is to probe "more deeply the word of God and the mystery being celebrated." The last two principles suggest the need to juxtapose the old and the new in a vibrant liturgy. I will have occasion to comment on some of these principles later.

*Leaders and people.* The first condition for active participation is to recognize that the liturgical assembly is constituted by the gathering of the church consisting of leaders *and* people.[19] Worship necessarily involves a dualism or, to use Gordon W. Lathrop's favored term, a "juxtaposition": those who stand to proclaim *in persona Christi* and those who respond to the proclamation. Leaders and people participate actively in their different roles and capacities. What leaders and people do correspond to the essential revelation-response dynamic of worship.[20] The work of proclaiming the Word, broadly understood, and the work of responding to the Word are necessary to one another. In the liturgical assembly one is not complete without the other. We may even go further and say that the relationship involves mutual dependence. There is no church without the interplay of leaders and people.[21] This mutuality is well expressed in an eighth-century liturgical document explaining the role of the bishop in the assembly: "The bishop addressing the people, blesses them, saying: 'The Lord be with you always.' The blessing is returned, 'And with your spirit.' He receives a blessing from the mouths of all the people so that he may be more worthy to bless them in return."[22]

Active participation, then, is the responsibility of both leader and people. There needs to be as much active participation on the part of the minister who declares, "The peace of the Lord be always with you," as on the part of the congregation that responds, "And also with you." The preacher who proclaims the Word engagingly is more likely to be met with an equally engaging response from the people.

*Redemptionis Sacramentum,* following Constitutions on the Sacred Liturgy, recognizes that there are in fact many opportunities within the liturgy for active participation of the people: "acclamations, . . . responses, psalmody, antiphons, . . . canticles, . . . movements and gestures, and . . . silence." "The acclamations and responses of the faithful to the priest's greetings and prayers constitute that level of active participation that the gathered faithful are to contribute to every form of the Mass, so that the action of the entire community may be clearly expressed and fostered."[23]

One of the most frequently heard complaints in Protestant churches is that leaders do all the "real" work while the people are reduced to passive observers. Worship looks that way because of the way services are structured in most free churches. There are actually not many possibilities of variation in a typical Sunday service if the main focus is the preaching of the Word; modern liturgical worship actually allows for far more congregational expressions and in many more ways.[24] A solution often attempted in nonliturgical churches is to get as many people as possible involved on the platform. But this marks a misunderstanding of the nature of participation and reinforces the misconception that only leaders do the real work. If worship manifests the dynamic of revelation-response and this dynamic is realized in the dialectic between ministers and people, then participation must involve the whole church acting in different capacities *as* leaders *and* people. There must be participation of those who proclaim and those who respond to the proclamations, and the responses constitute no less an active participation. "Amen," "And also with you," "Hallelujah!" as well as active listening, praying with the intercessor, and receiving bread and wine—all these can be actively engaged in when worshipers understand their place as the people of God in the assembly. Failure to understand this dialectic in worship is the reason some churches have resorted to the rock-concert model of worship, with the "praise and worship" component giving everyone a sense of being "actively involved." What people are not aware of is that this form of participation may not be "active" at all, especially when a certain type of music is being used as a tool for subtle manipulation.[25]

The nature of the liturgy as revelation-response and as a dynamic act involving leader and people in their different roles implies that active participation is a cooperative act in the way Alasdair MacIntyre understands it.[26] Just as "goods" intrinsic to the community are formed and extended through cooperative practices, a corporate spirituality emerges through cooperative participation in the liturgy. Both leaders and people need to play their respective parts well. Although God may still bless despite poor execution of the liturgy (since grace sometimes comes to us preveniently, *sine nobis*), that should not be an excuse for detached performance and halfhearted participation. If synergy is the normal way of God's working, then we may expect God to work in a liturgical assembly where all are fully engaged in their respective roles as ministers and congregants.

*Doing it well.* Active participation also means that the *way* things are done is just as important as what is being done. Our participation must be in a manner that is consistent with the dynamic nature of the liturgy itself. Doing the liturgy is not a matter of dutifully carrying out a set of instructions in red (the rubric); it is more like acting out a drama. The language of the liturgy is not the language of scientific description or a do-it-yourself manual. It addresses God directly; it declares, exclaims and proclaims. As Robert Jenson aptly states:

> Insofar as the gospel is a verbal event, it is fundamentally by the *motion* of its utterance, by clear and springing rhythm, lifting music, precise rhetoric, that we are specifically grasped by the Spirit. What we mostly can speak *about* is the world that is. It is by the ways in which speech itself moves that the eschatological tension of what is with what is not yet comes to utterance.[27]

The reality is, in a sense, carried by the language of the liturgy. There is power in the spoken word and in the gestures and movements,[28] but if we do the liturgy poorly, whether in speech, gestures and movements, we undermine our belief in the power of the liturgy to form and transform us. Jenson warns:

> If the language of our gospel-address is broken and unnatural in its speech rhythms, if we read texts that set us glumly aback just as we are well launched into declamation, if "free" prayer simply means clumsy and repetitious prayer, this is not merely an aesthetic misfortune; it is quenching of the Spirit. If music provides no way for the congregation to move singingly together, it is quenching the Spirit. If our speech has no grandeur, it is quenching of the Spirit.[29]

Dietrich Bonhoeffer suggests that the public reading of Scripture should be done the way one would read to others a letter from a friend.

> I would not read the letter as though I had written it myself. The distance be-

tween us would be clearly apparent as it was read. And yet I would also be unable to read the letter of my friend to others as if it were of no concern to me. I would read it with personal interest and regard. Proper reading of Scripture is not a technical exercise that can be learned; it is something that grows or diminishes according to one's own spiritual frame of mind. The crude, ponderous rendition of the Bible by many a Christian grown old in experience often far surpasses the most highly polished reading of a minister.[30]

*Disciplined participation.* For the liturgy to be done well, certain disciplines are needed. *General Instruction of the Roman Missal* instructs that texts should "be spoken in a loud and clear voice" and in a manner suited to the dynamics of the liturgy.

> In texts that are to be spoken in a loud and clear voice, whether by the priest or the deacon, or by the lector, or by all, the tone of voice should correspond to the genre of the text itself, that is, depending upon whether it is a reading, a prayer, a commentary, an acclamation, or a sung text; the tone should also be suited to the form of celebration and to the solemnity of the gathering. Consideration should also be given to the idiom of different languages and the culture of different peoples.[31]

It is not just the leaders who are to participate actively; the role of the responders is no less critical. *General Instruction of the Roman Missal* instructs responders to "listen with attention."[32] Attentiveness means that "mind and voice must be in harmony," thus demonstrating "intent on cooperating with God's grace."[33] Attentiveness is one of many disciplines needed to foster active participation. What is acted out by the celebrant should be attentively observed, what is spoken should be attentively listened to. Liturgy is not something done for the people by the minister; it is done by all in their different capacities. Just as there is power in the spoken word, there is also power in attentiveness, as Philip H. Pfatteicher observes:

> If then one listens attentively to the liturgy with ears and heart and mind and indeed even with the eyes, one can learn new and exciting things. Doors open on new questions, new ideas, new insights. What seemed hopelessly obsolete becomes suddenly contemporary. What was familiar and dull may one day, as one goes through it yet again, even by rote, mechanically and unfeelingly, suddenly open before one's eyes to reveal an unsuspected layer of meaning for that person at that moment in that person's life. A word or phrase or image may suddenly attack, perhaps jumping us from behind, perhaps opening the mind slowly and inexorably.[34]

Besides attention, right intention and attitude are also needed. Sometimes worshipers may not fully understand or, for various reasons, may fail to be attentive. But if there is good intention, the act is not entirely in vain. As Chrysostom wisely observes, "And even if you do not understand the meaning of the words, for the time being teach your mouth to say them, for the tongue is sanctified by the words alone whenever its says them with good will."[35]

Another necessary discipline is silence. It is a necessary correlate to sound and action. Just as there are rests in music, just as sabbath correlates with work in the seven-day cycle, silence within the liturgy enables everyone to better attend to its deeper meaning. Silence puts us in a receptive mode—a prerequisite to responding well. It brings us face to face with mystery, the awesomeness of God, the God who cannot be named. "Words of prayer and devotion bring us to the edge of eternity, and there they dissolve [into silence]."[36] Silence has different functions in different parts of the liturgy. When it is done before the prayer of confession, it is meant to help participants recollect themselves. When observed immediately after the reading and preaching, it is meant for them to meditate on what was just read and heard.[37] Silence before the service is not only appropriate but a prerequisite for what is to come, yet in many a church it is more often enjoined than carried out.

*The role of music.* Singing, chanting and other musical forms are other important means of fostering active participation. Almost all cultures in the world have their own music; they recognize its power to transport and transform. And the liturgy at its best has the qualities of good singing. Pfatteicher points out a number of ways in which music teaches us about ourselves and the liturgy. For example, songs, like individuals, are unrepeatable and unique. The same song may be sung many times, but each singing is unique and unrepeatable, an action within a set of circumstances that cannot be exactly replicated. It renews and refreshes even though it is the same song. "A song has a forward-driving energy." Once it is begun, it must go on until it ends. A song draws listeners not so much to listen *to* the singer as to participate *with* the singer.[38] All these are possible if the singing is done well.

Singing, like prayer, is not just one component of worship but a basic mode through which the liturgy is carried out. Certain prayers and different forms of proclamation, especially the reading, greeting and benediction, are well expressed in some musical form such as singing and chanting. Praise, thanksgiving and proclamation of the wonderful works of God are better sung than said. The singing of the psalms, for instance, has the same theological function as reading: the direct proclamation of the Word. But the cadence of music gives it an additional dimension. This mode has power and beauty exceeding those of ordinary spoken words. The early Christians understood this very well. According to Basil, "The Holy Spirit sees how much difficulty mankind has in loving virtue, and how we prefer the lure of pleasure to the straight and narrow path. What does he do? He adds the grace of music to the truth of doctrine. Charmed by what we hear, we pluck the fruit of the words without realizing it."[39]

In many "contemporary" services, music is largely confined to a part of the service called "praise and worship" before the preaching of the Word. This has resulted not only in a severely limited function for singing but also a constricted concept of worship. Worship has come to mean only singing songs of praise. Both song and worship have suffered impoverishment, just as Word and sacrament have shrunk.[40]

Perhaps the most crucial question the modern church needs to address is how music helps to retell and reenact the Christian story and enhance the traditioning process. Much of modern Christian music in the church fails precisely at this point. For example, music (including songs and dance) can be an effective way of strengthening the church's communal consciousness and collective memory, yet all too often in the "contemporary" service, modeled on the entertainment world, singing is turned into a means of individual self-expression. A solo or choir piece seems to be aimed at turning on the crowd rather than understood as an offering rendered to God on behalf of the congregation, eliciting the congregation's participation. Again, the didactic function of hymn singing has been recognized throughout church history,[41] but this vital dimension of singing has been undermined by poor compositions, lyrics with questionable theology and words that convey largely individualistic religious experiences. If music is to fulfill its intended purpose in worship, it has to be understood as an important medium through which the various components of worship retell the Christian story. If singing fails to communicate the church's metanarrative or to reinforce the church's basic identity as the covenant people of God, then worship has fallen short of being a "divine office." The real reason we worship is that we are a people shaped by the Christian story. If this is so, can we simply entrust our worship to worship leaders who have no such understanding?

Special mention must be made of the place of psalmody. *General Instruction of the Liturgy of the Hours* devotes considerable attention to the use of the psalms in the liturgy of the hours. The church from ancient times has made the psalms its own prayers because it recognizes from New Testament precedents that in the "full sense" *(sensus plenus)* they refer to Jesus Christ. They are truly the prayer of Jesus and also of his church.[42] As song, a psalm aims "to move the heart of those singing it or listening to it and also of those accompanying it 'on the lyre and harp.'"[43] The psalms express a wide variety of moods and feelings; they convey "pain and hope, the unhappiness and trust of people of every age and country, and sing above all of faith in God, of revelation, and of redemption."[44] Individually we may not be able to identify with all of a given psalm's moods and feelings, but we can be sure that somewhere in the body of Christ there are members who can. Therefore we pray the psalms in the spirit of Romans 12:15: "Rejoice with those who rejoice; mourn with those who mourn."[45] In singing the psalms, we become aware of being a part of the church catholic.

If there is to be a return to liturgical worship, the Protestant churches probably need to return to the psalms. There was a time in the Reformed tradition when the only permissible singing in church was the singing of psalms; nowadays, however, Protestants have learned to sing everything else—from sacred country music to sacred rock—except the psalms!

## LITURGICAL RHYTHMS

Methodist theologian Don E. Saliers insists that true worship should evoke the "senses" of awe, delight, truthfulness and hope.[46] These particular senses (or "religious affections," to use a phrase from Jonathan Edwards)[47] are signs of true worship. The question for liturgical spirituality is how these senses are evoked.

Saliers notes that our experience of, say, awe is possible when we are able to connect worship with the awe we experience in daily living, such as when we encounter the beauty of creation, sense the vastness of the universe, face the reality of mortality at a funeral service, experience the joy of a newborn baby or encounter God's healing in a healing service.[48] There are moments in ordinary living when we experience "signals of transcendence,"[49] and these moments help us make the connection between daily living and the liturgy.[50]

Liturgical formation, however, should not be made to depend solely on occasional experiences of transcendence. Earlier I observed in connection with mystagogical instruction that postmodern people have lost their sense of mystery, even in liminal events like marriage. For them, signals of transcendence will only get weaker and fewer. Liturgical formation therefore needs to be pursued systematically if it is to forge a regular pattern of living—what in spiritual theology is called asceticism.[51]

This is not to deny that sometimes a single service may evoke a powerful religious affection that may decisively alter the course of one's life. More often, however, the effect comes over a period of time as we participate regularly in the liturgy. This is not unlike our experience of eating. Many of us have experienced the immediate satisfaction of an exceptionally good meal, while having to struggle through the regimen of a healthy diet with no apparent effect. Yet it is the regular practice of a balanced diet that will bring long-term benefits. The same could be said of worship. To use a different analogy, "liturgy and liturgical change is like reforestation: we do not immediately gather profit."[52] The kind of worship that gives worshipers an immediate "high" may not even be good for their spiritual development in the long term; what truly forms worshipers is regular attendance in a church that practices a normative liturgy. This patterned way of living reveals another feature of active participation: to participate actively in the liturgy is to become so involved that we are absorbed into its rhythm. Liturgical rhythm is a kind of music by which the truth of the gospel is inculcated over time.

The rhythm of the liturgy comes through in many ways. Gestures and movements, silence and music are all part of a larger pattern and serve to enhance the worshipers' involvement. As *General Instruction of the Roman Missal* observes, gestures and movements "ought to contribute to making the entire celebration resplendent with beauty and noble simplicity, so that the true and full meaning of the different parts of the celebration is evident and that the participation of all is fostered." For example, a "common posture . . . is a sign of the unity of the member of the Christian community" which "both expresses and fosters the intention and spiritual attitude of the participants."[53]

Liturgical rhythm is also found in the way the worship service is composed. There are two basic components, the fixed or "ordinary" elements, like the Lord's Prayer, creed and offering, and the "propers," which vary from day to day and week to week (readings, hymns, prayers for various occasions, sermon and others). "Ordinaries" anchor us in the familiar, while "propers" direct us to the new. The whole liturgy with its interplay of fixed and variable elements may be compared to play. The nature of play is that it consists of neither purely predictable nor purely random movements. Within play, the rules of the game are strictly observed, yet there is an infinite number of moves, and this makes each game different and exciting.

The rhythm of worship is what maintains the spirituality of the liturgy. Rhythm not only occurs within the liturgy; the liturgy itself is set within a daily and weekly rhythm in which catechizing, baptizing, confirming, hearing, praying, eating and drinking are all maintained within the larger pattern of the Christian calendar. It is a repetitive process, yet not a mere repetition: it is a journey toward an intended end, the *telos*.[54]

*Rhythm of daily prayers: Liturgy of the hours.* The early Christians' observance of daily prayer was no doubt prompted by the injunctions of Jesus and the apostles to engage in unceasing prayer (Lk 18:1; 1 Thess 5:17; Heb 13:15). According to Acts 2:42, "They devoted themselves to the apostles' teaching and to the fellowship, to the breaking of bread and to prayer." They probably followed Jewish practices of praying at certain times of the day (cf. Acts 3:1; 10:9; 16:25).[55] There are also numerous references to their praying in "one accord" (Acts 1:14; 4:24; 12:5, 12). These two characteristics—fixed times and corporate prayer—gave rise to the "liturgy of the hours," whose aim was to "sanctify the day and the whole range of human activity."[56]

Although early Christian communities probably did not have a fixed number of times of daily prayer, nor a universally accepted format,[57] one of the most widely accepted patterns of daily prayer used by Christians today involves morning and evening prayers. They are "the two hinges on which the daily Office turns."[58] This twofold pattern is very much tied to the natural cycle of the day. In ancient societies, much of life was governed by the daily rising and setting of the sun. Work and rest, waking and sleeping were organized around this pattern.

The invention of electricity has changed all that. We no longer depend on natural light for our work. In modern cities it is sometimes difficult to tell day from night. Life seems to go on endlessly, without rest, without sleep. For people involved in the round-the-clock service industries, working in any of three shifts, morning and evening no longer govern their way of life. Yet the basic alternation between work and rest, waking and sleeping serves as a reminder of a life that was once intimately connected with nature, with the evening-morning rhythm of creation (Gen 1). Modern people may seem to have transcended nature, but they still need the work-rest, waking-sleeping cycle and so have not entirely left behind the creation rhythm.[59]

Evangelical Christians are no exception when it comes to daily prayers. The "quiet time" is considered essential to nurturing the Christian life. Unfortunately, there is a tendency to treat daily prayers as "private devotions," divorced from the corporate prayer of the church, although this was not the case in the past.[60] Daily prayers need to be theologically informed if they are to be spiritually sustaining. They were originally part and parcel of the church's liturgical life.[61] We are spiritually nourished by being in the church—a branch of the vine, a member of the body. To divorce private prayer from liturgical prayer is to cut the branch from the vine. We need to see our own quiet times as joined with the corporate prayer of the church.[62] They are not just "my private prayers" but belong to the whole church. Ultimately they are effectual because they are the prayers of Christ.

> Christ Jesus, high priest of the new and eternal covenant, taking human nature, introduced into this earthly exile that hymn which is sung throughout all ages in the halls of heaven. He joins the entire community of mankind to Himself, associating it with His own singing of this canticle of divine praise.
>
> For He continues His priestly work through the agency of His Church, which is ceaselessly engaged in praising the Lord and interceding for the salvation of the whole world. This she does not only by celebrating the Eucharist, but also in other ways, especially by praying the divine office.[63]

The church at prayer is praying "the very prayer which Christ Himself, together with His body, addresses to the Father."[64] We must never lose sight of this basic theological fact; otherwise prayer becomes privatized and isolated from corporate life in Christ.

Personal devotional habits, then, should be understood as a necessary preparation for better participation in common prayer. Lack of preparation before coming to the assembly is one major reason the liturgy is not done well. I noted in the last chapter that for more than a millennium, confession was not part of public worship, and that is because it was regarded as a preparation for worship—what believers should be doing before coming to church. Daily prayers are meant to better prepare people to "realize the church" on Sunday. *Redemptionis Sacramentum* notes that various devotional habits are "extremely helpful" for liturgical worship:

> For encouraging, promoting and nourishing this interior understanding of liturgical participation, the continuous and widespread celebration of the Lit-

urgy of the Hours, the use of the sacramentals and exercises of Christian popular piety are extremely helpful. These latter exercises—which "while not belonging to the Liturgy in the strict sense, possess nonetheless a particular importance and dignity"—are to be regarded as having a certain connection with the liturgical context. . . . Furthermore, since these practices of piety lead the Christian people both to the reception of the sacraments—especially the Eucharist—and "to meditation on the mysteries of our Redemption and the imitation of the excellent heavenly examples of the Saints, they are therefore not without salutary effects for our participation in liturgical worship."[65]

The liturgy of the hours, consisting mostly of praise, intercessions and the Word, helps to orient the Christian's daily living toward God by highlighting its essentially eschatological nature. It reminds Christians that they are on a journey rather than merely engaged in a repetitive ritual. It brings together the paradoxical themes of resurrection and death, hope and perils, joy and repentance. In morning prayer (Lauds), the main focus is the resurrection of Christ. The new day begins with hope and praise.

> Leader: O Lord, open our lips,
> People: And our mouth shall proclaim your praise.[66]

Then the Venite (Ps 95) or Jubilate (Ps 100) is chanted. The Scripture lessons for the day are read, followed by the Gospel canticle: the Benedictus (the Song of Zechariah, Lk 1:68-79) or the Magnificat (Song of Mary, Lk 1:46-55). The last part of morning prayer consists of prayers of intercession or "suffrages" (Latin *suffragium,* prayer of intercession) and a collect, the best known of which is probably the collect for grace:

> Almighty and everlasting Father, we thank you that you have brought us safely to the beginning of this day. Keep us from falling into sin or running into danger; order us in all our doings; and guide us to do always what is right in your eyes; through Jesus Christ our Lord. Amen.[67]

While morning prayer looks forward with renewed hope, evening prayer (Vespers) is a time for solemn recollection, repentance and committing oneself to God's care. A traditional invitatory sets the mood of evening prayer:

> Leader: O God, make speed to save us.
> People: O Lord, make haste to help us.[68]

If morning prayer focuses on hope and new life, evening prayer focuses on the hope that belongs to the Christian at the end of life. It is not about darkness and death per se, but about light that has come into the darkness. Thus it is called the service of light *(Lucernarium)*. In ancient evening prayers, an important feature was the lighting of lamps or candles symbolizing the coming of light to dispel darkness, a theme going back to creation (Gen 1:1) and the new creation (cf. Jn 1:5). And as the lamps are lighted, the ancient song "O Gladsome Light" (Phos Hilaron) was sung:

> O gracious Light,
> pure brightness of the everlasting Father in heaven,
> O Jesus Christ, holy and blessed!
>
> Now as we come to the setting of the sun,
> and our eyes behold the vesper light,
> we sing your praises, O God: Father, Son and Holy Spirit.
>
> You are worthy at all times to be praised by happy voices,
> O Son of God, O Giver of life,
> and to be glorified through all the worlds.[69]

The hymn is an "occasional meditation."[70] The fading of natural light and the kindling of lamps bring to mind the coming of Christ, the light of the world (Jn 8:12), who reflects the glory of the Father (cf. Heb 1:3) and is even now dispelling the darkness, prompting a response of praise to the holy Trinity "by happy voices."

It should be noted that in the Jewish reckoning the day begins at sunset, and so the evening is also a time when we look forward to a new day even as the world is being enfolded in darkness. Appropriately, one of the Gospel canticles for evening prayer is the Song of Simeon (Nunc Dimittis): "Lord, now let your servant go in peace . . ." Simeon was ready to depart because "my own eyes have seen the salvation which you have prepared in the sight of every people."[71] As one of the collects that ends evening prayer shows, there are "perils and dangers" as night comes, but the Light has come to "lighten our darkness":

> Lighten our darkness,
> Lord, we pray;
> and in your mercy defend us
> from all perils and dangers of this night;
> for the love of your only Son,
> our Saviour Jesus Christ. Amen.[72]

As we enter deeply into the rhythm of morning and evening prayer, we are reminded that the Christian life is not governed by the vicissitudes of optimism or pessimism that characterize the way of this world. Rather, Christian life is lived in hope in the midst of death. The morning and evening cycle furnishes the appropriate symbols of death and rebirth, but the basis of this perspective of life is the historic death and resurrection of Jesus Christ.

*Rhythm of the Christian calendar.* The Christian calendar is variously called the church year, the church calendar and the liturgical year. Its origins in the Northern Hemisphere explain its close correspondence with the natural seasons. Easter coincides with spring, a time that sees nature renewed. For Christians in the tropics, however, this association with the cycle of nature is not so obvious; for them it is primarily a journey or pilgrimage tied to the gospel events. The gospel is the central focus of the Christian calendar, as the Constitution on the Sacred Liturgy explains: "Within the cycle of a year . . . [the church] unfolds the whole mystery of Christ, not only from His incarnation and birth until His ascension, but also as reflected in the day of Pentecost, and the expectation of a blessed, hoped-for return of the Lord."[73]

Originally, the calendar was anchored on the three main feasts of Epiphany, Pascha or Easter, and Pentecost, but by the fourth century other events were being distinguished within these main feasts. Easter, for example, came to encompass several events in Holy Week leading up to Easter Sunday. Seasons of preparation, such Advent before Christmas and Lent before Easter, were added. Thus what we have today is a cycle of feasts beginning with Advent (the coming of Christ) and culminating in Easter (the resurrection of Christ), with Pentecost concluding the Easter season seven weeks later.[74] Between Pentecost and the next Advent is a long period called "ordinary time."[75] This is the time of the church, the time in which the church is to live out its calling in the world, fulfilling the mission of God until the next season of Advent and Christmas, which "functions as the proclamation of the parousia."[76]

In the liturgical year the church rehearses and actualizes the gospel story, which is the history of the triune God in the church. When we order our lives around the church year, we ensure that no part of the gospel goes missing and that we are furthering the gospel story until the parousia, since the church is part of that story.[77] Because it is the gospel that is being enacted, it offers a complete set of themes for Christian living:[78] we died and are buried with Christ; we are raised with him to life; we are filled with his Spirit; we advance the mission of God by the power of the Spirit; and we await Christ's return. This cycle helps us discover what is really important: the great events of God's mighty acts in Christ that we proclaim and for which we give thanks in our worship. The church that observes the church year and the lectionary that goes along with it is less likely to find itself a victim of the urgent or the fashionable. (Although it should be added that it does not always guarantee that preaching will be gospel-centered as texts could still be hijacked to serve ideological interests, as often happens in liberal Protestant churches.)

The daily, weekly and yearly cycles bear an integral relationship to each other. The liturgy of the hours reinforces and prepares for the Sunday liturgy.[79] At the same time, the liturgical year provides a framework in which the weekly liturgy is given its distinctive shape and meaning. Each Sunday liturgy is not merely a repetition of the same ritual but is shaped by the particular time of the church year in the lectionary and "propers," so that the church is made aware of its eschatological journey. The eschatological tension of "already and not yet" is evident also in the daily and weekly cycles.[80] But in the church year it is especially highlighted in the two high points consisting of the two cycles of feasts (Epiphany and Easter) and one low point of "ordinary time." According to Zimmerman, while we experience the rhythm of ebb and flow in the daily (day and night) and weekly (weekdays and Sunday) cycles, it is in the ebb and flow of the yearly cycle that this tension is felt most acutely. This is because in the church year each gospel event and the interplay between festive and ordinary time are sufficiently distanced from each other to be given their distinct foci.[81]

## LITURGICAL PROFICIENCY

Real formation is going on when we are no longer consciously figuring out what the liturgy means but are fully attentive to it. This is active participation in the fullest sense. We are most fully participating and letting the liturgy form us when we are not consciously thinking about the liturgy, just as we are driving most proficiently when we are not thinking about driving. It is like art appreciation. We are truly appreciating a work of art when we let it communicate to us rather than have its "meaning" explained to us. Of course it needs to be said that some reflection or explanation of the liturgy may help to make the initial contact with the liturgy less stressful. This is particularly the case for Christians who wish to find out for themselves what liturgical worship is like—just as learning from an art critic might provide a use-

ful introduction to art appreciation. In the early church, this reflection/
explanation was done through the catechumenate. But to be fully formed
by the liturgy, one needs to go beyond words and explanations and enter
imaginatively into it by articulating its language, listening to its music, and
acting out its signs, gestures and movements. *Anamnēsis,* the act of remembering so central to the Eucharist, is an act of the imagination.

In a world where truth is measured in terms of engineering precision,
churchgoers are not likely to be greatly endowed with the gift of imagination. Perhaps, as Henry Horn suggests, they need to learn from preliterate
cultures how to appreciate concrete symbols once again.[82] Above all, they
need to learn the language of the liturgy and not be too quick to dismiss it
when it cannot be readily understood.[83] In worship we make the discovery
that the truth we encounter is not an abstract thought to be analyzed but a
living Person. This process takes time and patience, just as getting to know
a person requires much patience and sacrifice. It is liturgical worship with
its carefully crafted language, sights, sounds and movements that could best
assist us in that personal encounter.

## CONCLUSION

In the postmodern world the church has to struggle with the fact that it is
only one of many communities that Christians inhabit, and for many churchgoers it is not even one of the more significant ones. How is the church to
regain its position as a community whose way of life has a decisive bearing
on individual Christians? This is probably the greatest challenge facing the
church in the twenty-first century. I have argued for the need of a clear theological understanding of what the church is, and this understanding needs
to be coupled with a strong liturgical practice as the foundation of all other
ecclesial practices. But we should have no illusions about achieving quick
success if this line of approach is followed. Forming such a community is
going to be slow and painstaking.

The temptation is to seek quick results and look for ways to market the
church as a more attractive option among a plethora of options. But if truth
and integrity are the hallmarks of the church whose Head is the Truth, then
we have to do what is necessary with perseverance and excellence and
leave the results to God (1 Cor 3:7). This requires a certain spiritual attitude
to sustain the conviction that the God who calls out a people for himself will
ultimately bring such a community into being.

# NOTES

## Introduction

[1]Robert Webber notes a "dizzying array of options" within the movement broadly denominated "evangelical" but identifies three distinctive movements within it: "pragmatic" evangelicalism, "traditional" evangelicalism and "younger" evangelicalism. The problem I am addressing here is associated with the "pragmatic" evangelicals, whose severest critics have often been the "traditional" evangelicals. But as I shall point out later, "traditional" answers fall short as well because of an inadequate ecclesiology. It remains to be seen whether the emerging "younger evangelicals" will eventually carry the day. See Robert E. Webber, *The Younger Evangelicals: Facing the Challenges of the New World* (Grand Rapids: Baker, 2002).

[2]David Wells, *No Place for Truth* (Grand Rapids: Eerdmans, 1993), p. 130.

[3]Ibid., pp. 172-75.

[4]Ibid., p. 231.

[5]Edward Farley, *Theologia: The Fragmentation and Unity of Theological Education* (Philadelphia: Fortress, 1983).

[6]Wells, *No Place for Truth,* p. 237.

[7]Mark Noll, *The Scandal of the Evangelical Mind* (Grand Rapids: Eerdmans, 1995).

[8]Ibid., p. 61.

[9]Ibid., pp. 66-68.

[10]David Bebbington, *Evangelicalism in Modern Britain: A History from the 1730s to the 1980s* (London: Unwin Hyman, 1989), pp. 54-60.

[11]Ibid., pp. 167-80.

[12]Noll, *Scandal,* p. 249.

[13]Ibid., p. 243.

[14]Ibid., p. 253.

[15]David Wells, *God in the Wasteland: The Reality of Truth in a World of Fading Dreams* (Grand Rapids: Eerdmans, 1994), pp. 115-17.

[16]See Wells, *No Place for Truth,* p. 25. Cf. D. H. Williams's assessment of Wells's proposed solution (D. H. Williams, *Retrieving the Tradition and Renewing Evangelicalism: A Primer for Suspicious Protestants* [Grand Rapids: Eerdmans, 1999], p. 25).

[17]Wells, *God in the Wasteland,* p. 214.

[18]Wells, *No Place for Truth,* p. 292.

[19]Wells, *God in the Wasteland,* p. 223.

[20]Ibid., p. 226.

[21]Alasdair MacIntyre, *After Virtue: A Study in Moral Theory* (Notre Dame, Ind.: University of Notre Dame Press, 1981), pp. 169-89.

[22]Interestingly, although Donald Bloesch was one of the signatories of the Chicago Call, his first systematic theology does not even contain a locus on the church. See his *Essentials of Evangelical Theology,* 2 vols. (San Francisco: Harper & Row, 1978). This point is also noted by Stanley J. Grenz in *Renewing the Center: Evangelical Theology in a Post-theological Era* (Grand Rapids: Baker, 2000), p. 290.

[23]Donald Bloesch, *The Church: Sacraments, Worship, Ministry, Mission* (Downers Grove, Ill.: InterVarsity Press, 2002).

[24]Ibid., p. 174.

[25]Ibid., p. 173.

[26]Faith and Order Commission of the World Council of Churches, *Baptism, Eucharist and Ministry* (Geneva: World Council of Churches, 1982).

[27]Bloesch, *The Church*, p. 177.

[28]Ibid., p. 133.

[29]See Gerald R. Cragg, *From Puritanism to the Age of Reason: A Study in Changes in Religious Thought Within the Church of England, 1660-1700* (Cambridge: Cambridge University Press, 1966).

[30]Bloesch, *The Church*, p. 119.

[31]Cf. Reinhard Hütter, *Suffering Divine Things: Theology as Church Practice*, trans. Doug Stott (Grand Rapids: Eerdmans, 2000), where theology is "pathos" in the sense that it is not our own active construction but always done in response to the active construction *(poiesis)* of the Holy Spirit.

[32]Bloesch, *The Church*, pp. 143-44.

[33]This issue will be dealt with in the following chapter.

[34]Bloesch, *The Church*, pp. 47-48.

[35]Grenz, *Renewing the Center*, pp. 288-89.

[36]Ibid., pp. 293-94.

[37]Ibid., pp. 293-99.

[38]Ibid., pp. 321-24.

[39]Stanley J. Grenz, *Revisioning Evangelical Theology: A Fresh Agenda for the Twenty-first Century* (Downers Grove, Ill.: InterVarsity Press, 1993), p. 187.

[40]Roger E. Olson, "Free Church Ecclesiology and Evangelical Spirituality: A Unique Compatibility," in *Evangelical Ecclesiology: Reality or Illusion?* ed. John G. Stackhouse Jr. (Grand Rapids: Baker, 2003), pp. 161-78.

[41]The situation appears to be somewhat different in England. Ian M. Randall's study of evangelical spirituality between the world wars has shown that with a few exceptions, evangelical spiritualities developed from their own church traditions. See *Evangelical Experiences: A Study in the Spirituality of English Evangelicalism, 1918-1939* (Carlisle, U.K.: Paternoster, 1999), pp. 5-6.

[42]This is not the case, however, with evangelicals who remained within the Church of England. David Bebbington notes that they had by and large maintained close relationship with high churchmanship for much of the nineteenth century and that those who opposed it were a small minority. If anything, it shows that being evangelical is not incompatible with being liturgical. See his *Evangelicalism in Modern Britain*, pp. 94-99, 146-49.

[43]Thomas Howard, *Evangelical Is Not Enough: Worship of God in Liturgy and Sacrament* (San Francisco: Ignatius, 1984).

[44]This is one major reason that most mainline Protestant denominations in Singapore, that is, churches that still maintain historic links with their mainline counterparts in the West, opt for "contemporary" services. The problem appears to be present in the West as well, although, I suspect, not as pervasive, if the works of writers like Marva Dawn (Lutheran) and Ronald Byars (Reformed) are anything to go by. See Marva Dawn, *Reaching Out Without Dumbing Down: A Theology of Worship for the Turn-of-Century Culture* (Grand Rapids: Eerdmans, 1995), and Ronald P. Byars, *The Future of Protestant Worship: Beyond the Worship Wars* (Lou-

isville, Ky.: Westminster John Knox Press, 2002).

[45]Christopher Cocksworth, *Evangelical Eucharistic Thought in the Church of England* (Cambridge: Cambridge University Press, 1993), pp. 105, 150-52.

[46]This is what I have sought to show in "Evangelical Theology in an Asian Context," in *The Cambridge Companion to Evangelical Theology* (Cambridge: Cambridge University Press, forthcoming).

## Chapter 1: The Ontology of the Church

[1]See R. Kendall Soulen, *The God of Israel and Christian Theology* (Minneapolis: Fortress, 1996), pp. 12-17.

[2]H. Richard Niebuhr, *Christ and Culture* (New York: Harper & Brothers, 1951), pp. 30-32. For a critique of the Niebuhrian view, see David S. Yeago, "Messiah's People: The Culture of the Church in the Midst of the Nations," *Pro Ecclesia* 6, no. 1 (Spring 1997): 146-71.

[3]Daniel W. Hardy, "Created and Redeemed Sociality," in *On Being the Church: Essays on the Christian Community*, ed. Colin E. Gunton and Daniel W. Hardy (Edinburgh: T & T Clark, 1989), pp. 31-35, 40.

[4]Especially by those advocating a nonsupersessionist understanding of the relationship between Israel and church. Besides Soulen, see also Scott Bader-Saye, *Church and Israel After Christendom: The Politics of Election* (Boulder, Colo.: Westviews, 1999), and Douglas Harink, *Paul Among the Postliberals* (Grand Rapids: Brazos, 2003), esp. pp. 151-84.

[5]One might raise questions over the extent of nonsupersessionism. Is there *any* sense at all in which the church can be said to supersede Israel? The problem of Soulen's view is that he sees no real development in God's covenantal relationship with Israel. In his reading, the story of Jesus Christ does not constitute the central point of departure of the canonical plot, since Jesus' role is largely instrumental for rather than constitutive of the kingdom of God. His reading of the canonical narrative is determined almost exclusively by Old Testament monotheism rather than by the narrative of the triune God. Yet it is in Jesus, who is not just the instrument of the kingdom but the very embodiment of the kingdom of God, that we discover the narrative of the triune God in which God's covenant relationship with both Jews and Gentiles is brought to a new level. This new level of relationship will inevitably affect the way God relates to the Jews. Some form of supersessionism is unavoidable. That is the burden of the book of Hebrews.

Be that as it may, nonsupersessionism provides a better account of the canonical narrative compared to the "standard" narrative by giving priority to the covenant people rather than to creation. For a similar critique of Soulen from another perspective, see George R. Sumner, *The First and the Last: The Claim of Jesus Christ and the Claims of Other Religious Traditions* (Grand Rapids: Eerdmans, 2004), p. 38n.

[6]This understanding of the church is parallel to the way in which Jesus Christ the Incarnate Son could be said to preexist from eternity with the Father. Robert W. Jenson speaks of "the movement to incarnation, as itself a pattern of God's triune life" (*The Works of God*, vol. 2 of *Systematic Theology* [New York: Oxford University Press, 1999], p. 141). Such a view is based on the idea that "God *is* the act of his decision. . . . The Incarnation happens in eternity as the foundation of its happening in time, in eternity as the act of decision that God is, and in time as the carrying-out of what God decides" (p. 140).

[7]Robert W. Jenson, "The Church's Responsibility for the World," in *The Two Cities of God: The Church's Responsibility for the Earthly City*, ed. Carl E. Braaten and Robert W. Jenson (Grand Rapids: Eerdmans, 1997), p. 4.

[8]Yeago, "Messiah's People," pp. 146-50.

[9]See Sergius Bulgakov, *The Bride of the Lamb,* trans. Boris Jakim (Grand Rapids: Eerdmans, 2002), pp. 253-55.

[10]Jenson, *Works of God,* p. 167.

[11]Cf. Colin E. Gunton, "The Church on Earth: The Roots of Community," in *On Being the Church: Essays on the Christian Community,* ed. Colin E. Gunton and Daniel W. Hardy (Edinburgh: T & T Clark, 1989), pp. 75-79. Gunton sees the need to ground the church's ontology in its relationship to the Trinity, but the relationship is rather weakly conceived, as the following statement makes clear: "Too much is therefore not being claimed for the theology of the Church. . . . The hope is to have created the framework by which a link may be drawn between the being of God and that which is from time to time realized by the Spirit. It is a kind of analogy of echo: the Church is what it is by virtue of being called to be a temporal echo of the eternal community that God is" (p. 75). Gunton's ecclesiology does not sufficiently stress the identity between the church and the Trinity, whereas the ecclesiology of Jenson, drawing from the Catholic and Orthodox traditions, recognizes both identity and distinction. See Carl E. Braaten, *Mother Church: Ecclesiology and Ecumenism* (Minneapolis: Fortress, 1998), for an ecclesiology similar to Jenson's.

[12]There is nothing very new in this approach; more than fifty years ago Lesslie Newbigin in his landmark study of the church uses the same images. See *The Household of God: Lectures in the Nature of the Church* (London: SCM Press, 1953).

[13]Jenson, *Works of God,* pp. 189-95.

[14]See note 1 above.

[15]Harink, *Paul Among the Postliberals,* p. 162, italics author's.

[16]See note 8 above.

[17]Lesslie Newbigin, *The Gospel in a Pluralist Society* (Grand Rapids: Eerdmans, 1989), p. 87.

[18]Harink, *Paul Among the Postliberals,* pp. 175-76.

[19]Ibid., p. 161.

[20]See note 6 above.

[21]Harink, *Paul Among the Postliberals,* p. 174.

[22]Jenson, *Works of God,* p. 194.

[23]On the other hand, seeing the church as a historical people has led some to treat the church as largely a sociological entity. This is true not only of liberal Protestants but also of Catholic "progressives." See Dennis M. Doyle, *Communion Ecclesiology* (Maryknoll, N.Y.: Orbis, 2000), pp. 121-26.

[24]For a discussion of the "core practices" of the church, see Reinhard Hütter, "The Church," in *Knowing the Triune God: The Word of the Spirit in the Practices of the Church,* ed. James J. Buckley and David S. Yeago (Grand Rapids: Eerdmans, 2001), pp. 23-47.

[25]"Whenever we see the Word of God purely preached and heard, and the sacraments administered according to Christ's institution, there . . . a church of God exists" (John Calvin, *Institutes* 4.1.9).

[26]Martin Luther, "On the Councils of the Church," in *Luther's Works* (Philadelphia: Fortress, 1966), 41:150-66.

[27]See Gilbert C. Meilaender, *Faith and Faithfulness: Basic Themes in Christian Ethics* (Notre Dame, Ind.: University of Notre Dame Press, 1991).

[28]Stanley Hauerwas and William Willimon, *Resident Aliens: Life in the Christian Colony* (Nashville: Abingdon, 1989); Stanley Hauerwas, *A Community of Character: Toward a Constructive Christian Social Ethic* (Notre Dame, Ind.: University of Notre Dame Press, 1981).

[29]Yeago, "Messiah's People," pp. 170-71.

[30]Anders Nygren, *Christ and His Church*, trans. Alan Carlsten (London: SPCK, 1957), p. 96.

[31]Gustaf Aulén, *The Faith of the Christian Church*, trans. Eric H. Wahlstrom and G. Everett Arden (Philadelphia: Muhlenberg, 1948), p. 332, emphasis author's.

[32]Geoffrey Preston, *Faces of the Church: Meditations on a Mystery and Its Images* (Grand Rapids: Eerdmans, 1997), p. 89, emphasis author's.

[33]Jenson, *Works of God*, p. 213.

[34]John D. Zizioulas, *Being as Communion* (Crestwood, N.Y.: St. Vladimir's Seminary Press, 1985), pp. 110-22. Cf. Nygren, *Christ and His Church*, esp. pp. 89-107; Aulén, *Faith of the Christian Church*, esp. pp. 329-35.

[35]Jenson, *Works of God*, p. 213.

[36]I have noted earlier Bloesch's fear that too close an identification between the church and Christ might undermine the doctrine of *solus Christus* (Christ alone). See Bloesch, *The Church*, pp. 47-48.

[37]See the book's introduction.

[38]The phrase "plausibility structure" was coined by the sociologist Peter Berger and refers to the structure of belief a particular society accepts, which determines what is plausible or implausible. It is the lens by which we see and make sense of everything else. See Peter L. Berger and Thomas Luckmann, *The Social Construction of Reality: A Treatise in the Sociology of Knowledge* (London: Penguin, 1967).

[39]Quoted in Jean-Marie Tillard, *Flesh of the Church, Flesh of Christ: At the Source of the Ecclesiology of Communion*, trans. Madeleine Beaumont (1992; reprint, Collegeville, Minn.: Liturgical, 2001), p. 40. Similar ideas can be found in John of Damascus and Cyril of Jerusalem. See Jenson, *Works of God*, pp. 211-12, and Tillard, *Flesh of the Church*, pp. 75-77.

[40]I suspect that for many evangelicals, identifying ecclesial communion as eucharistic communion will seem un-Protestant and a sign of Romanizing influence. But Jenson notes that it "has become a standard item of ecumenical consensus" and refers to the Anglican-Orthodox Dialogue in support (Jenson, *Works of God*, p. 212). Further, the spiritual reality of feeding on the eucharistic body and blood of Christ should not be confused with the Catholic doctrine of transubstantiation. Transubstantiation is one of many theories of *how* the bread and wine might convey spiritual realities, whereas a sacramental view that bread and wine are symbols conveying the thing signified does not seek to explain how the spiritual reality is conveyed. There is increasing recognition of the latter view among evangelical scholars today—e.g., Bloesch, *The Church*, pp. 147-77; Clark Pinnock, *Flame of Love: A Theology of the Holy Spirit* (Downers Grove, Ill.: InterVarsity Press, 1996), pp. 120-29; and Christopher Cocksworth, *Evangelical Eucharistic Thought in the Church of England* (Cambridge: Cambridge University Press, 1993). Bloesch is Reformed, Pinnock is Baptist, and Cocksworth is Anglican.

[41]Tillard, *Flesh of the Church*, p. 24. Tillard notes that the tendency in the West is "to see the church as a society of baptized persons held together by obedience to the word, rather than as the communion united by the eucharistic body" (p. 139). This could not be said of the East, which sees the church as first and foremost *sobornost* (communion) or a priesthood of believers and only secondarily as the relationship between the orders of clergy and laity.

[42]Bulgakov, *The Bride of the Lamb*, p. 281.

[43]Quoted by D. H. Williams, *Retrieving the Tradition and Renewing Evangelicalism: A Primer for Suspicious Protestants* (Grand Rapids: Eerdmans, 1999), p. 22.

[44]Roger Lundin has pointed out that in repudiating the need for an intervening tradition for the interpretation of Scripture, evangelicals show themselves to be heirs of Friedrich

Schleiermacher, whose search for a fixed and certain meaning in the text goes back to René Descartes' grounding of certainty in the autonomous self. Roger Lundin, "Interpreting Orphans: Hermeneutics in the Cartesian Tradition," in Roger Lundin, Anthony C. Thiselton and Clarence Walhout, *The Promise of Hermeneutics* (Grand Rapids: Eerdmans, 1999), pp. 34-41.

[45]In other words, scriptural authority is identified with a closed text. For a critique of this view of Scripture from a Pentecostal perspective, see James K. A. Smith, "The Closing of the Book: Pentecostals, Evangelicals and the Sacred Writings," *Journal of Pentecostal Theology* 11 (1997): 49-71.

[46]Alasdair MacIntyre, *Whose Justice? Which Rationality?* (Notre Dame, Ind.: University of Notre Dame Press, 1988), p. 12.

[47]Williams, *Retrieving the Tradition,* p. 27.

[48]In point of fact, whether its regulative role is accepted or rejected, tradition is often implicitly relied upon to explain Scripture. For example, the way some Protestant exegetes try to avoid the sacerdotal interpretation of Romans 15:15-16 shows the critical role that the Protestant tradition plays. The "generally accepted view" that Paul is exercising a priestly ministry is rejected by C. E. B. Cranfield, who thinks rather that Paul was thinking of his ministry as a Levite, one subordinate to the priest (in this case, Christ). See *Romans,* International Critical Commentary (Edinburgh: T & T Clark, 1975), 2:755-57. Ernst Käsemann, on the other hand, while recognizing the priestly ministry of Paul in this passage, would still insist that Paul here "is not stressing the cultic dimension as such" (*Commentary on Romans,* trans. Geoffrey W. Bromiley [Grand Rapids: Eerdmans, 1994], p. 393).

[49]Hütter, "The Church," p. 34.

[50]Luther, "On the Councils," p. 166.

[51]Jenson, *Works of God,* p. 198.

[52]One consequence of this view is the important role that tradition plays in the unfolding of Scriptures, that is, the continuing development of doctrine. Some evangelicals are coming to this point of view. For example, John R. Franke sees church tradition as providing "a hermeneutical trajectory for theology." This openness to the future is made possible by the presence of the Spirit. "Scripture, Tradition and Authority, Reconstructing the Evangelical Conception of *Sola Scriptura,*" in *Evangelicals and Scripture: Tradition, Authority and Hermeneutics,* ed. Vincent Bacote, Laura C. Miguélez and Dennis L. Okholm (Downers Grove, Ill.: InterVarsity Press, 2004), pp. 206-10.

[53]*Lumen Gentium* 48.

[54]Jenson, *Works of God,* pp. 154-55.

[55]Ibid., pp. 156-57.

[56]Ibid., p. 158.

[57]Ibid., p. 160.

[58]Ibid., p. 179, emphasis added.

[59]"The people of God," as noted earlier, is a pre-Pentecost event that includes the election of Israel.

[60]Peter Brunner, *Worship in the Name of Jesus,* trans. M. H. Bertram (St. Louis: Concordia, 1968), p. 77.

[61]The inclusiveness of the first church is underscored by Luke's mentioning the presence of women (Acts 1:14).

[62]Preston, *Faces of the Church,* p. 11.

[63]E.g., David Yonggi Cho, pastor of the world's largest church in Seoul, South Korea, speaks of

"fellowship *with* the Holy Spirit" as a new revelation: *More Secrets for a Successful Faith Life,* vol. 2 of *The Fourth Dimension* (Plainfield, N.J.: Bridge, 1983), pp. 9-11. See Simon Chan, "The Pneumatology of David Yonggi Cho," in *David Yonggi Cho: A Close Look at His Theology and Ministry,* ed. Wonsuk Ma, William Menzies and Hyeon-song Bae (Baguio, Philippines: Asia Pacific Theological Seminary Press, 2004), pp. 95-119.

[64]Zizioulas, *Being as Communion,* pp. 110-22. See my article "Mother Church: Toward a Pentecostal Ecclesiology," *Pneuma,* Fall 2000, pp. 177-208, for the ramifications of this concept.

[65]Thus through the Spirit, the church is both identified with Christ (the *totus Christus*) and distinguished from Christ.

[66]See Carl E. Braaten, "The Role of Dogma in Church and Theology," pp. 23-54, and Stylianos Harkianakis, "Dogma and Authority in the Church," pp. 55-78, in *The Task of Theology Today,* ed. Victor Pfitzner and Hilary Regan (Grand Rapids: Eerdmans, 1998); Simon Chan, "The Church and the Development of Doctrine," *Journal of Pentecostal Theology* 13, no. 1 (October 2004): 57-77.

[67]Jenson, *Works of God,* p. 179.

[68]Cf. Reinhold Hütter, *Suffering Divine Things: Theology as Church Practice* (Grand Rapids: Eerdmans, 2000), pp. 125-26.

[69]For an account of the gospel as public truth, see Lesslie Newbigin, *Truth to Tell: The Gospel as Public Truth* (Grand Rapids: Eerdmans / Geneva: World Council of Churches, 1991), esp. pp. 41-64.

[70]Cf. *Confessing the One Faith* (Geneva: World Council of Churches, 1991), pp. 194, 216.

[71]See Boris Bobrinskoy, "The Church and the Holy Spirit in 20th C Russia," *Ecumenical Review,* July 2000, pp. 1-17.

[72]Jenson, *Works of God,* pp. 178-79.

[73]Douglas Farrow, *Ascension and Ecclesia: On the Significance of the Doctrine of the Ascension for Ecclesiology and Christian Cosmology* (Edinburgh: T & T Clark, 1999).

[74]In the liturgy, the *epiclesis* is that part of the eucharistic prayer of invoking the action of the Holy Spirit on the bread and wine: "By your Holy Spirit let these gifts of your creation be to us the body and blood of our Lord Jesus Christ" (Eucharistic Prayer F in *Common Worship of the Church of England,* available at <http://www.cofe.anglican.org/worship/liturgy/commonworship/texts/hc/prayerf.html>).

[75]Paul Hiebert, *Anthropological Reflections on Missiological Issues* (Grand Rapids: Baker, 1994), pp. 189-201.

[76]Third Wavers are mostly evangelicals who turned charismatic. The most prominent leader of the Third Wave was probably John Wimber. Other well-known leaders are Charles Kraft and Peter Wagner, who coined the phrase "Third Wave."

[77]A noted example is Jack Deere, a former Dallas Theological Seminary professor, who was converted from cessationism to being an ardent advocate of "signs and wonders."

[78]M. Scott Peck, *People of the Lie: The Hope for Healing Human Evil* (New York: Simon & Schuster, 1983).

[79]Peck's answer to "group evil," however, is to seek to change individuals in the group, especially the leader (ibid., p. 252). We could, in fact, see the transformation of leaders as the key to renewing the church, provided the leaders are understood as standing *in persona Christi,* that is, as representing the very person of Christ as Head in relation to his body. Our theology of leadership grows out of our theology of the church.

[80]Jenson, *Works of God,* p. 213.

[81]Newbigin, *Gospel in a Pluralist Society,* p. 227. Along a similar line of thought, Darrell L.

Guder argues that mission must be understood primarily as the continuing conversion of the church to become a community that bears witness to the gospel. See *The Continuing Conversion of the Church* (Grand Rapids: Eerdmans, 2000), esp. pp. 62-70.

[82]*Lumen Gentium* 48.

[83]Matthew Fox, *Original Blessing* (Santa Fe, N.M.: Bear, 1983).

## Chapter 2: The Worship of the Church

[1]For an update on the "wars," see Terry W. York, *America's Worship Wars* (Peabody, Mass.: Hendrickson, 2003).

[2]Louis Bouyer, *Liturgical Piety* (Notre Dame, Ind.: University of Notre Dame Press, 1955), pp. 25-27; Kevin W. Irwin, *Liturgy, Prayer and Spirituality* (New York: Paulist, 1984), pp. 25-26.

[3]Jean-Jacques von Allmen, *Worship: Its Theology and Practice* (London: Lutterworth, 1966), p. 63.

[4]Quoted by Joseph Ratzinger, *A New Song for the Lord: Faith in Christ and Liturgy Today*, trans. Martha M. Matesich (New York: Crossroad, 1996), pp. 59-60.

[5]von Allmen, *Worship*, pp. 63-66.

[6]C. K. Barrett, *A Commentary on the Epistle to the Romans* (London: Adam & Charles Black, 1957), p. 275.

[7]The phenomenon of a church becoming very much like the consumerist world is captured in John Drane's book *The McDonaldization of the Church: Spirituality, Creativity and the Future of the Church* (London: Darton, Longman & Todd, 2000).

[8]Alexander Schmemann, *Introduction to Liturgical Theology* (1966; reprint, Crestwood, N.Y.: St. Vladimir's Seminary Press, 1996), pp. 29, 31.

[9]von Allmen, *Worship*, p. 44.

[10]Josef A. Jungmann's classic study *The Place of Christ in Liturgical Prayers*, trans. A. Peeler (1965; reprint, London: Geoffrey Chapman, 1989), shows a number of different trinitarian patterns in the early church, all differentiating the works of the three Persons. It was largely in reaction to Arianism and in the interest of underscoring the equality between the three Persons that the different prepositions assigned to the three Persons of the Trinity were changed to a coordinated doxology: to the Father, and the Son and the Holy Spirit (pp. 220-21).

[11]Anscar J. Chupungco, ed., *Handbook of Liturgical Studies: Introduction to the Liturgy* (Collegeville, Minn.: Liturgical, 1997), 1:6-7.

[12]Edward Kilmartin, *Systematic Theology of Liturgy*, vol. 1 of *Christian Liturgy: Theology and Practice* (Kansas City, Mo.: Sheed and Ward, 1988), p. 14.

[13]Quoted in ibid., p. 74.

[14]Schmemann, *Introduction to Liturgical Theology*, p. 16.

[15]Alexander Schmemann, *Liturgy and Tradition: Theological Reflections of Alexander Schmemann*, ed. Thomas Fisch (Crestwood, N.Y.: St Vladimir's Seminary Press, 1990), p. 39.

[16]The actual phrase from Prosper is *legem credendi lex statuat supplicandi:* "let the rule of supplicating establish the rule of believing." The phrase occurs in a work defending the Augustinian concept of grace against the semi-Pelagians. Prosper argues that it is according to apostolic tradition throughout the world in every church to pray for faith to be given to unbelievers, thus showing that salvation is by the grace of God. Jacques Migne, *Patrologia Latina* 51, col. 209.

[17]The two main chapters of Geoffrey Wainwright's *Doxology* deal respectively with this dialectic: *Doxology, the Praise of God in Worship, Doctrine and Life: A Systematic Theology* (New

York: Oxford University Press, 1980), chaps. 7-8. See especially pp. 249-50.

[18]Aidan Kavanagh, *On Liturgical Theology* (New York: Pueblo, 1984), pp. 7-8. See especially chap. 5.

[19]Wainwright, *Doxology,* pp. 46-62.

[20]Ibid., pp. 223-24, 238-40.

[21]The best-known study of the stable shape of the liturgy is probably Gregory Dix's *The Shape of the Liturgy,* 2nd ed. (Glasglow: Dacre, 1945). Schmemann prefers the word *ordo*. See his *Introduction to Liturgical Theology*. The notion of the liturgy's "deep structure" is borrowed from the structuralist Claude Lévi-Strauss by Robert Taft, "The Structural Analysis of Liturgical Units: An Essay in Methodology," *Worship* 52 (1978): 314-29.

[22]Kavanagh, *On Liturgical Theology,* pp. 146-47.

[23]Ibid., p. 93.

[24]This is one of the issues raised by Geoffrey Wainwright in his review of Kavanagh's *On Liturgical Theology* in *Worship* 61, no. 2 (March 1987): 183-86.

[25]Cf. Kavanagh, *On Liturgical Theology,* pp. 80-83.

[26]Schmemann, *Introduction to Liturgical Theology,* p. 17.

[27]Calvin's doctrine of the Eucharist is usually interpreted in spiritualistic terms, but according to the nineteenth-century Reformed theologian John W. Nevin, his doctrine of the "real presence" is much closer to the Catholic tradition. See *The Mystical Presence: A Vindication of the Reformed or Calvinistic Doctrine of the Holy Eucharist* (1846; reprint, Hamden, Conn.: Archon, 1963).

[28]Schmemann, *Liturgy and Tradition,* p. 54.

[29]This comes through forcefully in Schmemann's exchange with two liturgiologists, Bernard Botte and W. Jardine Grisbrooke. The exchange illustrates the marked difference between East and West. The Western theologians could not conceive of a theology that is not in some way "reflective"—some kind of talk *about* talk to God—whereas for Schmemann, theology in the liturgy is first and foremost talk *to* God that is true. See ibid., chap. 3; cf. his *Introduction to Liturgical Theology,* pp. 16-19. The problem Schmemann discusses here is very similar to the problem of theology in Edward Farley, *Theologia: The Fragmentation and Unity of Theological Education* (Philadelphia: Fortress, 1983).

[30]The *Alternative Service Book* (1980) of the Church of England.

[31]Quoted by Frank Senn, *Christian Liturgy: Catholic and Evangelical* (Minneapolis: Fortress, 1997), p. 272.

[32]This is especially pronounced in "charismatic" churches. We see this tendency coming through repeatedly in David Yonggi Cho's "prosperity" teaching. See his *The Fourth Dimension: The Key to Putting Your Faith to Work for a Successful Life* (Plainfield, N.J.: Logos, 1979), pp. 97-100.

[33]Philip H. Pfatteicher, *Liturgical Spirituality* (Valley Forge, Penn.: Trinity Press International, 1997), p. 12.

[34]Ibid., p. 14.

[35]Romano Guardini, *The Spirit of the Liturgy,* trans. Ada Lane (London: Sheed and Ward, 1937), pp. 95-96.

[36]Ibid., p. 99.

[37]Frank Senn, *New Creation: A Liturgical Worldview* (Minneapolis: Fortress, 2000), p. 63.

[38]William Willimon, *The Service of God: How Worship and Ethics are Related* (Nashville: Abingdon, 1983), pp. 42-43.

[39]Ibid., p. 37.

[40]See Alasdair MacIntyre, *After Virtue: A Study in Moral Theory* (Notre Dame, Ind.: University of Notre Dame Press, 1981), pp. 175-78.

[41]Willimon, *Service of God*, pp. 44ff.

[42]Johann Huizinga, *Homo Ludens: A Study of the Play Element in Culture* (Boston: Beacon, 1955), pp. 46-75.

[43]Constitution on the Sacred Liturgy 30.

[44]Alexander Schmemann, *For the Life of the World: Sacraments and Orthodoxy* (Crestwood, N.Y.: St. Vladimir's Seminary Press, 2000), p. 32.

[45]See Irwin, *Liturgy, Prayer and Spirituality,* chap. 2.

[46]Gordon W. Lathrop, *Holy Things: A Liturgical Theology* (Minneapolis: Fortress, 1993), pp. 117-20. This paradox is part of a larger pattern of the Christian liturgy which reveals the church's essentially eschatological existence. See chapters three and six below.

[47]William C. Placher, *The Domestication of Transcendence: How Modern Thinking About God Went Wrong* (Louisville, Ky.: Westminster John Knox, 1996).

[48]C. S. Lewis, *The Lion, the Witch and the Wardrobe* (New York: HarperCollins, 1994), p. 182.

[49]Kilmartin, *Systematic Theology of Liturgy,* p. 98.

[50]Ibid., p. 102.

[51]Ibid., pp. 100-101.

[52]Ibid., p. 131.

[53]Ibid., pp. 172, 173.

[54]Kilmartin seems to have this point in mind when he says, "The personal mission of the Spirit explains why the Church is united to Christ and, at the same time, is not identified with Christ. In other words, the Spirit, whom Christ possesses in fullness, is shared with the Church. The Spirit is the bond of union between Christ and the Church, and simultaneously, the source of the distance between the Head and Body" (ibid., p. 218). The basis of the difference between the earthly and heavenly liturgies is the ascension of Christ. The ascension reveals as much about the *absent* Christ as about the presence of Christ. Within the "ascension-parousia differential" Christ is present as *totus Christus,* i.e., as Head-and-members. He is given to the church in bread and wine so that the church might become the body of Christ. We may therefore speak of his presence in the church as the eucharistic presence. Failure to make the distinction has resulted in the conflation of salvation history and world history with disastrous consequences. See Douglas Farrow, *Ascension and Ecclesia* (Grand Rapids: Eerdmans, 1999), esp. chap. 5.

[55]J. D. Crichton, "A Theology of Worship," in *A Study of Liturgy,* rev. ed., ed. Cheslyn Jones et al. (London: SPCK, 1992), pp. 3-31.

[56]For a fuller discussion of the synergy of the liturgy, see Jean Corbon, *The Wellspring of Worship,* trans. Matthew J. O'Connell (New York: Paulist, 1988).

[57]Ibid., pp. 73-74.

[58]Ibid., p. 21.

[59]Ibid., pp. 21-23.

[60]Kilmartin, *Systematic Theology of Liturgy,* p. 183.

[61]Synergy does not mean that humans can contribute a share in the advancement of God's work. The Christian life is not the outcome of part grace and part human effort. It is solely by grace working through human will. Cf. Philippians 2:12-13: "Work out your salvation . . . for it is God who works in you to will and to act according to his good purpose." See chapter four, below, for a fuller account of the relationship between the church and the mystery of grace.

## Chapter 3: The Shape of the Liturgy

[1]This chapter's title is borrowed from Gregory Dix's classic study. But it should become obvious that the focus of my discussion is on the basic structure of the liturgy, namely Word and sacrament, rather than the shape of specific eucharistic prayers thought to be derived from a fixed Jewish pattern in the first century. For an evaluation of this view, see Paul F. Bradshaw, *The Search for the Origins of Christian Worship: Sources and Methods for the Study of Early Liturgy* (New York: Oxford University Press, 1992), pp. 137-43.

[2]See, e.g., the landmark document of the Faith and Order Commission of the WCC, *Baptism, Eucharist and Ministry* (1982; reprint, Geneva: World Council of Churches, 2001), p. ix. Cf. Frank Senn, *New Creation: A Liturgical Worldview* (Minneapolis: Fortress, 2000), pp. 48-49.

[3]Senn, *New Creation*, p. xi.

[4]John Calvin *Institutes of the Christian Religion* 4.1.9.

[5]Senn, *New Creation*, p. 7.

[6]Justin Martyr *Apology* 1.67.

[7]Gregory Dix, *The Shape of the Liturgy*, 2nd ed. (Glasglow: Dacre, 1945), p. 37. See also Herman Wegman, *Christian Worship in the East and West: A Study Guide to Liturgical History*, trans. Gordon W. Lathrop (New York: Pueblo, 1985), pp. 21-24. Paul Bradshaw, however, notes that while a separate synaxis may have its precedent set in the Jewish synagogue liturgy, there are indications in the New Testament itself of a liturgy of the Word coming before the eucharistic meal in a single service (e.g., Lk 24:13-35; Acts 20:7-12; 1 Cor 14:26; cf. 1 Cor 11). See his *Early Christian Worship: A Basic Introduction to Ideas and Practices* (London: SPCK, 1996), pp. 42-43.

[8]Jean-Jacques von Allmen, *Worship: Its Theology and Practice* (London: Lutterworth, 1966), p. 146.

[9]A growing appreciation of the "liturgy of the Word" can be seen after Vatican II. As Catholic Gerard Austin puts it, "The word of God not only forms and shapes our liturgical piety; at times it stands in judgment of it." "Spirit Through Word," in *Called to Prayer: Liturgical Spirituality Today* (Collegeville, Minn.: Liturgical, 1986), p. 21.

[10]Reformed theologian Donald Bloesch sometimes falls into this way of speaking about Word and sacrament. Word and sacraments are set in a contrastive relationship, as when he characterizes the Protestant Reformation as "Word-centered rather than altar-centered" (p. 143) and the sacrament as "subordinate" to the Word (p. 146). Bloesch, faithful to the Reformed tradition, seeks to make the proclamation of the Word *the* high point of worship while seeing the sacrament as "a high point" (p. 133). See *The Church: Sacraments, Worship, Ministry, Mission* (Downers Grove, Ill.: InterVarsity Press, 2002).

[11]von Allmen, *Worship*, p. 287.

[12]Ibid., p. 288.

[13]Philip Seddon, *Gospel and Sacrament: Reclaiming a Holistic Evangelical Spirituality*, Grove Spirituality Series 89 (Bramcote, Nottingham, U.K.: Grove, 2004), p. 7.

[14]John Stott, *Basic Christianity* (London: Inter-Varsity Fellowship, 1958), p. 142.

[15]Leonard J. Vander Zee, *Christ, Baptism and the Lord's Supper: Recovering the Sacraments for Evangelical Worship* (Downers Grove, Ill.: InterVarsity Press, 2004), p. 231.

[16]Ibid., p. 232.

[17]J. D. Crichton, "A Theology of Worship," in *A Study of Liturgy*, rev. ed., ed. Cheslyn Jones et al. (London: SPCK, 1992), p. 23.

[18]Louis Bouyer, *Liturgical Piety* (Notre Dame, Ind.: University of Notre Dame Press, 1955), p. 29.

[19]Gilbert C. Meilaender, *Faith and Faithfulness: Basic Themes in Christian Ethics* (Notre Dame, Ind.: University of Notre Dame Press, 1991), p. 5.

[20]See chapter five, below.

[21]Cf. Meilaender: "The constant encouragement of self-reflection undermines the ability to act habitually and confidently. The pause of reflection that is always needed before one acts can paralyze" (*Faith and Faithfulness,* p. 6).

[22]This is what Richard Lovelace calls "the sanctification gap." See *Dynamics of Spiritual Life: An Evangelical Theology of Renewal* (Downers Grove, Ill.: InterVarsity Press, 1979), pp. 229-37.

[23]The practice of some free churches, such as the Brethren assemblies, to reverse the order suggests that Eucharist is just the visual form of the Word and thus it makes no great difference whether it comes before or after the preaching.

[24]Third Instruction on the Correct Implementation of the Constitution on the Sacred Liturgy (1970), 2b. Cf. Constitution on the Sacred Liturgy, 56: "The liturgy of the word and the eucharistic liturgy are so closely connected with each other that they form but one single act of worship." In *Vatican II: The Conciliar and Post Conciliar Documents,* rev. ed., ed. Austin Flannery (Dublin: Dominican, 1988).

[25]Jean-Marie Tillard, *Flesh of the Church, Flesh of Christ: At the Source of the Ecclesiology of Communion,* trans. Madeleine Beaumont (1992; reprint, Collegeville, Minn.: Liturgical, 2001), p. 131.

[26]Jean-Jacques von Allmen, *Preaching and Congregation,* trans. B. L. Nicholas (London: Lutterworth, 1962), p. 34.

[27]Ibid., p. 32.

[28]Constitution on the Sacred Liturgy 56.

[29]See chapter six, below, on mystagogy.

[30]von Allmen, *Preaching and Congregation,* p. 7.

[31]Ibid., p. 12. The sacramental nature of preaching is very much underscored in the Eastern tradition. "The Word," according to Schmemann, "is as sacramental as the sacrament is 'evangelical'" (Alexander Schmemann, *For the Life of the World: Sacrament and Orthodoxy* [Crestwood, N.Y.: St. Vladimir's Seminary Press, 2000], p. 33).

[32]Edward Schillebeeckx, *Christ the Sacrament of the Encounter with God* (New York: Sheed and Ward, 1963), pp. 13-45.

[33]Geoffrey Wainwright, *Doxology, the Praise of God in Worship, Doctrine and Life: A Systematic Theology* (New York: Oxford University Press, 1980), pp. 70-79.

[34]Ibid., p. 70.

[35]Geoffrey Preston, *Faces of the Church: Meditations on a Mystery and Its Images* (Grand Rapids: Eerdmans, 1997), p. 107.

[36] Cf. Jean Corbon, *The Wellspring of Worship,* trans. Matthew J. O'Connell (New York: Paulist, 1988), pp. 99, 108.

[37]Ibid., p. 110; Preston, *Faces of the Church,* p. 134.

[38]For Protestants, the sacraments are baptism (some include confirmation) and Eucharist, while the others—marriage, orders, confession and anointing—could be called sacramentals. See John Macquarrie, *A Guide to the Sacraments* (London: SCM Press, 1997).

[39]Schmemann, *Liturgy and Tradition,* p. 80.

[40]Preston, *Faces of the Church,* p. 137.

[41]Schmemann, *For the Life of the World,* pp. 27-28.

[42]Senn, *New Creation,* p. 7.

[43]Peter Brunner, *Worship in the Name of Jesus,* trans. M. H. Bertram (St. Louis: Concordia, 1968), p. 86.

[44]Cf. von Allmen, *Preaching and Congregation,* p. 42.

[45]Wainwright, *Doxology,* p. 32; Alexander Schmemann, *The Eucharist: Sacrament of the Kingdom* (Crestwood, N.Y.: St. Vladimir Seminary, 1988), p. 12.

[46]Cf. Frank Senn, *Christian Liturgy: Catholic and Evangelical* (Minneapolis: Fortress, 1997), p. 499.

[47]This comes through clearly in the Dogmatic Constitution on the Church of Vatican II, commonly known as *Lumen Gentium.* The hierarchical nature of the church (chap. 3) is balanced by the concept of the church as people of God (chap. 2) and the pilgrim church (chap. 7). See especially *Lumen Gentium* 7.

[48]For an excellent study of various interpretations of communion ecclesiology (mostly within Catholicism) see Dennis M. Doyle, *Communion Ecclesiology* (Maryknoll, N.Y.: Orbis, 2000).

[49]Tillard, *Flesh of the Church,* p. 6.

[50]Ibid., author's italics.

[51]John Chrysostom *Baptismal Homily* 2.13, quoted in ibid., p. 68.

[52]Tillard, *Flesh of the Church,* p. 47.

[53]*Alternative Service Book* (1980). The *Book of Common Prayer* of 1549 includes "Spirit and word": "Hear us, O merciful Father, we beseech thee; and with thy Holy Spirit and word, vouchsafe to bless and sanctify these thy gifts, and creatures of bread and wine, that they may be unto us the body and blood of thy most dearly beloved Son Jesus Christ."

[54]Dix, *Shape of the Liturgy,* pp. 36-47.

[55]Irenaeus *Against Heresies* 4.17.5.

[56]Ibid. 4.18.5-6.

[57]Schmemann, *For the Life of the World,* p. 14.

[58]Tillard, *Flesh of the Church,* p. 86.

[59]Justin Martyr *The First Apology* 67.

[60]The 1549 prayer book was largely the work of the archbishop of Canterbury, Thomas Cranmer.

[61]Tillard, *Flesh of the Church,* p. 84.

[62]Rite B, *Alternative Service Book.*

[63]See chapter one, above.

[64]See, e.g., Gordon Fee, *Commentary on the First Epistle to the Corinthians* (Grand Rapids: Eerdmans, 1987), pp. 562-64.

[65]Robert Webber refers to them as "the younger evangelicals." See *The Younger Evangelicals: Facing the Challenges of the New World* (Grand Rapids: Baker, 2002). They are often found in "convergence" churches that blend charismatic, evangelical and liturgical-sacramental elements in the worship. See Wayne Boosahda and Randy Sly, "The Convergence Movement," in *The Complete Library of Christian Worship,* ed. Robert Webber (Nashville: StarSong, 1994), 2:134-40. A better-known example of a convergence church is the Charismatic Episcopal Church. See its website, <http://www.iccec.org/whowerare/index.html#organizational>.

[66]See Tillard, *Flesh of the Church,* pp. 88-90.

[67]Ibid., p. 89.

[68]Geoffrey Wainwright, *Worship with One Accord* (New York: Oxford University Press, 1997), pp. 20, 19-32.

[69]Alexander Schmemann, *Introduction to Liturgical Theology* (1966; reprint, Crestwood, N.Y.: St. Vladimir's Seminary Press, 1996), pp. 64-75.

[70]Ibid., p. 43.

[71]Schmemann, *For the Life of the World,* p. 37.

[72]Schmemann, *Introduction to Liturgical Theology,* p. 45. Here Schmemann faults Odo Casell for reducing worship to *mysterium,* that is, making worship entirely sacramental and failing to distinguish between eucharistic and noneucharistic worship.

[73]The already–not yet tension of the church should not be conceived as an existence that differs from the old creation and the new creation only in terms of degree, so that progression could be made from one age to another by gradual accretion. The church age is different in kind from the old creation and from the new creation, precisely because it represents a different phase of the work of the triune God in the history of salvation: the age of the Spirit in the church.

[74]Schmemann, *Introduction to Liturgical Theology,* pp. 73-74.

[75]Gordon W. Lathrop, *Holy Things: A Liturgical Theology* (Minneapolis: Fortress, 1993), esp. chap. 2.

[76]E.g., the morning and evening prayers in the Anglican service books.

[77]Joyce Ann Zimmerman, *Liturgy as Living Faith: A Liturgical Spirituality* (Scranton, Penn.: University of Scranton Press, 1993), pp. 92-98.

[78]In the Genesis account of creation the day is reckoned from evening to morning.

[79]The phrase is taken from Milton's description of hell in *Paradise Lost.*

[80]Schmemann, *For the Life of the World,* p. 52.

[81]Ibid., p. 54, emphasis of last phrase added.

[82]The word *orientation* itself suggests the idea of turning eastward. Joseph Ratzinger notes that this eastward orientation was so persistent that when St. Peter's Basilica was built facing west, it resulted in the priest (who faced east) and people facing each other instead of facing one direction. This new configuration was later taken to mean that the Lord's Supper is a face-to-face fellowship meal. Thus a new theology was devised to explain what began as a historical accident. What we see here is a dubious example of *lex orandi est lex credendi!* See Joseph Ratzinger, *The Spirit of the Liturgy,* trans. John Saward (San Francisco: Ignatius, 2000), pp. 74-84.

[83]Liturgy is itself a spiritual exercise, not something we observe the ministers *say* but something the entire congregation *does.* See Dix, *Shape of the Liturgy,* pp. 13-15.

[84]See above, p. 48.

[85]Schmemann, *Liturgy and Tradition,* p. 41.

[86]Ibid., pp. 41-42.

[87]von Allmen, *Worship,* p. 77.

[88]Jean-Jacques von Allmen, *The Lord's Supper* (Cambridge: James Clarke, 2002), pp. 109-10.

[89]Ibid., p. 111.

[90]Schememann, *For the Life of the World,* pp. 26-46.

[91]Ibid., p. 27.

[92]Ibid., p. 37.

[93]Ibid., p. 46.

[94]Cf. von Allmen, *The Lord's Supper,* p. 111. A word is in order here concerning John Wesley's understanding of the Eucharist as a "converting ordinance." The idea has sometimes been used today to argue for unrestricted access to the Communion table. It should be noted, however, that in Wesley's day practically everyone was already baptized. Further, the idea makes sense only if conversion is understood as a continuing event. That Wesley may have such an idea is seen in his reference to Jesus' disciples at the Last Supper as proof. According to Wesley, the disciples at that point were "not believers" "in the full sense of the word" since they "had not yet 'received the Holy Ghost.'" See *The Works of John Wesley: Journal and Diaries,*

vol. 19, ed. W. Reginald Ward and Richard P. Heitzenrater (Nashville: Abingdon, 1990), dated June 27, 1740.

[95]Schememann, *For the Life of the World*, p. 36.

[96]von Allmen, *The Lord's Supper*, p. 49.

[97]Ibid., p. 50.

[98]See chapter one, above.

### Chapter 4: The Liturgy as Ecclesial Practice

[1]Several books on this subject have been published in recent years, including Nancey Murphy, Brad J. Kallenberg and Mark Thiessen Nation, eds., *Virtues and Practices in the Christian Tradition: Christian Ethics After MacIntyre* (Harrisburg, Penn.: Trinity Press International, 1997); Dorothy C. Bass, ed., *Practicing Our Faith: A Way of Life for a Searching People* (San Francisco: Jossey-Bass, 1997); Craig Dykstra, *Growing in the Life of Faith: Education and Christian Practices* (Louisville, Ky.: Geneva, 1999); Dorothy C. Bass, *Receiving the Day: Christian Practices for Opening the Gift of Time* (San Francisco: Jossey-Bass, 2000); James J. Buckley and David S. Yeago, eds., *Knowing the Triune God: The Work of the Spirit in the Practices of the Church* (Grand Rapids: Eerdmans, 2001); Miroslav Volf and Dorothy C. Bass, eds., *Practicing Theology: Beliefs and Practices in Christian Life* (Grand Rapids: Eerdmans, 2002). The two most influential figures behind these discussions are Alasdair MacIntyre (*After Virtue: A Study in Moral Theory*, 2nd ed. [Notre Dame, Ind.: University of Notre Dame Press, 1984]) and Pierre Bourdieu (*Outline of a Theory of Practice*, trans. Richard Nice [1977; reprint, Cambridge: Cambridge University Press, 2003]). They represent, respectively, the traditional and postmodern view of community.

[2]The expression "new ecclesiology" is used by Nicholas Healy to designate a range of ecclesiological options that have developed from the postmodern milieu. It could therefore be called postmodern ecclesiology. Nicholas M. Healy, "Practices and the New Ecclesiology: Misplaced Concreteness?" *International Journal of Systematic Theology* 5, no. 3 (November 2003): 287-308.

[3]Nicholas M. Healy, *Church, World and the Christian Life: Practical-Prophetic Ecclesiology* (Cambridge: Cambridge University Press, 2000), chap. 2.

[4]As seen, e.g., in Avery Dulles, *Models of the Church* (1978; reprint, New York: Image, 2002).

[5]Healy, *Church, World*, p. 16.

[6]Ibid., p. 4.

[7]Ibid., pp. 19-21.

[8]Stanley J. Grenz, *Renewing the Center: Evangelical Theology in a Post-theological Era* (Grand Rapids: Baker, 2000), p. 308.

[9]E.g., Gilbert Bond has shown that a practice done well with "insiders" within the church does not always translate into good practices involving "outsiders." "Liturgy, Ministry and Stranger," in *Practicing Theology: Beliefs and Practices in Christian Life*, ed. Miroslav Volf and Dorothy C. Bass (Grand Rapids: Eerdmans, 2002), pp. 149-55.

[10]Kathryn Tanner, "Theological Reflection and Christian Practices," in *Practicing Theology: Beliefs and Practices in Christian Life*, ed. Miroslav Volf and Dorothy C. Bass (Grand Rapids: Eerdmans, 2002), p. 229.

[11]Healy, "Practices and the New Ecclesiology," p. 295.

[12]Ibid., pp. 298-99.

[13]Reinhold Hütter identifies Luther's seven "sacraments" as the church's core practices, namely, the preached word, baptism, the Lord's Supper, church discipline, ordination, public worship,

discipleship in suffering. See *Suffering Divine Things: Theology as Church Practice* (Grand Rapids: Eerdmans, 2000), p. 129. Hütter characterizes the core practices as the soteriologically oriented works *(poiesis)* of the Spirit in which the human being is a "recipient" and "always remains in the mode of pathos" (p. 132). This is to be distinguished from practice in MacIntyre's sense, where the "goods" inherent in the practice are produced by human action (p. 130). In the light of this distinction, it would appear that some of the "core practices" like discipline and discipleship are more like practices in the MacIntyrean sense; they do not properly belong to the *esse* of the church. It is noteworthy that historically the magisterial Reformers disputed over whether discipline was to be regarded as a mark of the church. Whereas Martin Bucer saw it as a mark of the true church, John Calvin regarded it as belonging to the *bene esse* of the church rather than to the church's very definition. See François Wendel, *Calvin: Origins and Development of His Religious Thought*, trans. Philip Mairet (New York: Harper & Row, 1963), pp. 300-301.

[14]The church, as John D. Zizioulas puts it, is instituted by Christ and constituted by the Spirit: *Being as Communion* (Crestwood, N.Y.: St Vladimir's Seminary Press, 1985), p. 140. Pentecost is the constitutive event. But the Pentecost event could be further qualified by saying that the Spirit constitutes the church as a worshiping community in which Word and sacraments are the determinative means.

[15]John Calvin *Institutes of the Christian Religion* 4.1.9. Thus Calvin in the same passage distinguishes between "individual men and churches" on the one hand, who are to be evaluated according to their personal appropriation of the truth, and "the whole multitude itself" on the other, who must be regarded as truly the church as long as it has the administration of Word and sacraments.

[16]We see something of the objective nature of the sacrament powerfully portrayed in Graham Greene's novel *The Power and the Glory*. The main character is a priest of dubious character who transcends personal weaknesses to answer his calling to dispense the sacrament.

[17]This is because a practice like hospitality could be performed by, say, Buddhists from a distinctly Buddhist framework of belief, in which case it would have to be qualified as a Buddhist practice. It will not do to call a good practice in another religion a "Christian" virtue any more than it is proper to call a good Buddhist an "anonymous Christian."

[18]Healy, "Practices and the New Ecclesiology," p. 293.

[19]Here Healy is quite clearly adopting Pierre Bourdieu's theory of practice that sees cultural practices as characterized by struggle and conflict within their cultural milieu and therefore possessing multiple meanings rather than having a unified meaning. See Pierre Bourdieu, *Outline of a Theory of Practice*, trans. Richard Nice (1977; reprint, Cambridge: Cambridge University Press, 2003). For an application of this postmodern concept of culture to theology, see Kathryn Tanner, *Theories of Culture: A New Agenda for Theology* (Minneapolis: Fortress, 1997).

[20]Cf. Miroslav Volf's statement that "core Christian beliefs are *by definition normatively inscribed in sacraments* but not in 'practices.' Hence sacraments ritually enact normative patterns for practices." "Theology for a Way of Life," in *Practicing Theology: Beliefs and Practices in Christian Life*, ed. Miroslav Volf and Dorothy C. Bass (Grand Rapids: Eerdmans, 2002), p. 248, author's emphasis.

[21]That is to say, the fixed meaning is the official interpretation of the church. This implies a church with a unified center, as opposed to a decentered church or one with many centers generating competing meanings, for instance, a meaning from the "underside." Cf. Tanner, *Theories of Culture*, pp. 46-57.

[22]Cf. Healy, "Practices and the New Ecclesiology," p. 295.

[23]L. Gregory Jones, "Beliefs, Desires, Practices and the Ends of Theological Education," in *Practicing Theology: Beliefs and Practices in Christian Life,* ed. Miroslav Volf and Dorothy C. Bass (Grand Rapids: Eerdmans, 2002), p. 185.

[24]See, e.g., Hans Urs von Balthasar, *Prayer,* trans. A. V. Littledale (London: SPCK, 1973), p. 12.

[25]The terms were coined by Anton Baumstark (*Comparative Liturgy,* trans. F. L. Cross [London: Mowbrays, 1958], pp. 111-29) and since then have been adopted by others. See Paul F. Bradshaw, *Two Ways of Praying: Introducing Liturgical Spirituality* (London: SPCK, 1995).

[26]Bradshaw, *Two Ways of Praying,* pp. 13-25. See also Paul F. Bradshaw, *The Search for the Origins of Christian Worship: Sources and Methods for the Study of Early Liturgy* (New York: Oxford University Press, 1992), pp. 187-89.

[27]Quoted in Richard Byars, *The Future of Protestant Worship: Beyond the Worship Wars* (Louisville, Ky.: Westminster John Knox, 2002), p. 47.

[28]Gregory Dix, *The Shape of the Liturgy,* 2nd ed. (Glasglow: Dacre, 1945), pp. 1-11.

[29]Bradshaw, *Two Ways of Praying,* p. 55.

[30]Alexander Schmemann, *Liturgy and Tradition: Theological Reflections of Alexander Schmemann,* ed. Thomas Fisch (Crestwood, N.Y.: St. Vladimir's Seminary Press, 1990), pp. 16-17. Cf. Hütter, *Suffering Divine Things,* pp. 131-33.

[31]Alexander Schmemann, *Introduction to Liturgical Theology* (1966; Crestwood, N.Y.: St. Vladimir's Seminary Press, 1996), p. 31.

[32]See chapter two, above, pp. 48-52.

[33]The idea that Word culminates in the sacrament does not feature strongly in Protestantism but has been argued by the Reformed liturgiologist Jean-Jacques von Allmen in *Preaching and Congregation,* trans. B. L. Nicholas (London: Lutterworth, 1962), pp. 32-34.

[34]Craig Dykstra and Dorothy C. Bass, "Times of Yearning, Practices of Faith," in *Practicing Our Faith: A Way of Life for a Searching People,* ed. Dorothy C. Bass (San Francisco: Jossey-Bass, 1997), p. 9.

[35]See Jean-Marie Tillard, *Flesh of the Church, Flesh of Christ: At the Source of the Ecclesiology of Communion,* trans. Madeleine Beaumont (1992; reprint, Collegeville, Minn.: Liturgical, 2001), pp. 68-72.

[36]The *Canons of Hippolytus* shows that one of the basic responsibilities of the bishop is to visit the sick (canon 24). In the early church, care for those who are unable to attend is shown by the deacon's taking them a portion of the consecrated bread and wine (Justin Martyr *Apology* 1.67).

[37]This is one of the central affirmations of the Constitution on the Sacred Liturgy 2 (Vatican II).

[38]Karl Rahner, "Mystery," in *Sacramentum Mundi* (New York: Herder and Herder, 1969), 4:133-36.

[39]See, e.g., Kathryn Tanner, *Jesus, Humanity and the Trinity: A Brief Systematic Theology* (Minneapolis: Fortress, 2001), pp. 1-33.

[40]William Placher has argued that the classical doctrine of divine transcendence focuses on the mystery of God rather than God's distance from the world. Transcendence is not set *in contrast to* immanence. The basic problem for the post-Enlightenment church (at least in the West) is the "domestication of transcendence" within some supposedly larger philosophical category. See William C. Placher, *The Domestication of Transcendence: How Modern Thinking About God Went Wrong* (Louisville, Ky.: Westminster John Knox, 1996).

[41]Ibid., pp. 46-49.

[42]Rahner, "Mystery," pp. 134-35.

[43]Ibid., p. 135.

[44]For a summary of the various workings of grace, see Thomas Oden, *The Transforming Power of Grace* (Nashville: Abingdon, 1993).

[45]Quoted in ibid., p. 98.

[46]For a study of the place of humility in spiritual formation, see Michael Casey, *A Guide to Living in the Truth: Saint Benedict's Teaching on Humility* (Liguori, Mo.: Liguori, 2001). Casey notes that Benedict does not call humility a virtue (p. 42). Rather, as the seventh chapter of the Rule of St. Benedict makes clear, humility is the summary of all virtues, the ladder with twelve steps each marking a virtue the monk must cultivate in order to reach perfect love.

[47]Calvin *Institutes of the Christian Religion* 2.2.11.

[48]Augustine, *Letters of Saint Augustine*, ed. John Leinenweber (Liguori, Mo.: Triumph, 1992), p. 101. Augustine goes on to say that just as "expression" is the first rule of rhetoric, the first precept of religion is humility. Cf. Calvin *Institutes of the Christian Religion* 2.2.11.

[49]Evagrius of Pontus, "On Prayer: One Hundred and Fifty-three Texts," in *Philokalia* (London: Faber and Faber, 1979), 1:55-71. One might question the choice of Evagrius, whose Origenist leanings put his own orthodoxy not entirely above reproach. I am using Evagrius, however, simply to illustrate the monastic understanding of prayer as practice, leaving aside his peculiar emphasis on prayer as an act of the intellect. On Evagrian spirituality, see John D. Zizioulas, "The Early Christian Community," in *Christian Spirituality: Origins to the Twelfth Century,* ed. Bernard McGinn, John Meyendorff and Jean Leclercq (London: SCM Press, 1985), pp. 35-43.

[50]An exception is Sarah Coakley's essay "Deepening Practices: Perspectives from Ascetical and Mystical Theology," n *Practicing Theology: Beliefs and Practices in Christian Life,* ed. Miroslav Volf and Dorothy C. Bass (Grand Rapids: Eerdmans, 2002), pp. 78-93.

[51]Constitution on the Sacred Liturgy 30. This will be more fully discussed in chapter seven.

[52]Martin Thornton, *Christian Proficiency* (London: SPCK, 1964), p. 19.

[53]I have used the category of friendship rather than love to highlight the mutuality of the relationship between the Christian and God. The assumption here is that God's love has elicited a positive response from us. Love can be quite unilateral: God loves us while we are yet sinners. There is no guarantee that divine love will always elicit a positive response. A person could reject God's love. But when we return love, it becomes a relationship of friendship.

[54]Cf. Evagrius's idea that friendship with God is expressed through prayer ("On Prayer" 77).

[55]Susan J. White, *The Spirit of Worship: The Liturgical Tradition* (Maryknoll, N.Y.: Orbis, 1999), p. 15.

[56]Geoffrey Wainwright, *Worship with One Accord* (New York: Oxford University Press, 1997), p. 46.

[57]For an excellent summary of the formative effects of the liturgy, see Robert Taft, "What Does Liturgy Do? Toward a Soteriology of Liturgical Celebration: Some Theses," *Worship* 66, no. 3 (May 1992): 194-211.

[58]Ibid., p. 201. Cf. Joseph Ratzinger, *The Spirit of the Liturgy,* trans. John Saward (San Francisco: Ignatius, 2000), with reference to the eucharistic prayer: "There is only one action, which is at the same time his and ours—ours because we have become 'one body and one spirit' with him" (p. 174). One wonders, however, why Ratzinger should distinguish the synergistic action of the Eucharist from what he terms "external actions" like reading, singing and liturgy of the Word, which he considers "secondary actions" (pp. 174-75). Aren't the latter part and parcel of the liturgy of Word and sacrament? See Schmemann's critique of Odo Casell on this point (Schmemann, *Introduction to Liturgical Theology*, p. 45).

## Chapter 5: The Catechumenate

[1]David Pullinger, *Information Technology and Cyberspace: An Extra-connected Community?* (Cleveland: Pilgrim, 2001), pp. 91-93.

[2]This is how John Calvin and the Puritan tradition have understood calling. Every Christian has two callings: the calling to salvation (*Institutes of the Christian Religion* 3.24.8) and the calling to be faithful to the work that God has appointed for him or her to do. This second calling is "a sort of sentry post" which we can only leave at the God's bidding (*Institutes* 3.11.6).

[3]Protestant worship has its own form of reductionism as well. See Ronald P. Byars, *The Future of Protestant Worship: Beyond the Worship Wars* (Louisville, Ky.: Westminster John Knox, 2002), pp. 68-74.

[4]See the study of Martyn Percy concerning the use of songs of the Vineyard Fellowship in *Words, Wonders and Power: Understanding Contemporary Christian Fundamentalism and Revivalism* (London: SPCK, 1996), pp. 68-80.

[5]Aidan Kavanagh, "Christian Initiation: Tactics and Strategy," in *Made, Not Born: New Perspectives on Christian Initiation and the Catechumenate* (Notre Dame, Ind.: University of Notre Dame Press, 1976), pp. 5-6.

[6]For a brief history of the catechumenate see Michel Dujarier, *A History of the Catechumenate: The First Six Centuries,* trans. Edward J. Haasl (New York: Sadlier, 1979).

[7]Ibid., pp. 38-39.

[8]For the question of authorship and dating, see Hippolytus, *On the Apostolic Tradition,* with introduction and commentary by Alistair Stewart-Sykes, Popular Patristics (Crestwood, N.Y.: St. Vladimir's Seminary Press, 2001). Stewart-Sykes favors a third-century date and Hippolytus as the probable redactor. The *Apostolic Tradition* is believed to be the source of the fourth-century *Canons of Hippolytus* (probably between 336 and 340). See *The Canons of Hippolytus,* ed. Paul F. Bradshaw, trans. Carol Bebawi (Bramcote, Nottingham, U.K.: Grove, 1987), pp. 5-10.

[9]Hippolytus, *On the Apostolic Tradition,* pp. 97-98.

[10]Ibid., p. 98.

[11]Ibid., pp. 99-100.

[12]Ibid., p. 103.

[13]Ibid., pp. 105-6.

[14]Quoted by Dujarier, *History of the Catechumenate,* p. 80.

[15]Dujarier, *History of the Catechumenate,* p. 95.

[16]As reported by the pilgrim Egeria in her visit to the church in Jerusalem: *Egeria Travels,* trans. John Wilkinson (London: SPCK, 1971), p. 145.

[17]Dujarier, *History of the Catechumenate,* p. 98.

[18]See *Rite of Christian Initiation of Adults: Study Edition* (Collegeville, Minn.: Liturgical, 1988). Aidan Kavanagh calls the RCIA "a most traditional norm of baptismal polity." See Aidan Kavanagh, *The Shape of Baptism: The Rite of Christian Initiation* (1978; reprint, Collegeville, Minn.: Liturgical, 1991), p. 121.

[19]Thomas H. Morris, *The RCIA: Transforming the Church,* rev. ed. (Mahwah, N.J.: Paulist, 1997), p. 14.

[20]*Rite of Christian Initiation of Adults,* nos. 70-73.

[21]Ibid., no. 141.

[22]Ibid., nos. 81-89.

[23]An example from a conservative Reformed perspective can be seen in Donald Van Dyken, *Rediscovering Catechism: The Art of Equipping Covenant Children* (Phillipsburg, N.J.: P & R,

2000). The liturgical isolation of the Protestant catechism is reflected in the traditional practice of assigning parents to catechize their children at home. While this practice has its laudable points, it tends to assume a view of catechism as indoctrination rather than liturgical formation.

[24]William J. Abraham, "On Making Disciples of the Lord Jesus Christ," in *Marks of the Body of Christ*, ed. Carl E. Braaten and Robert W. Jenson (Grand Rapids: Eerdmans, 1999), p. 159.

[25]Hippolytus *On the Apostolic Traditions* 105-6.

[26]On the content of the catechism, see Robert M. Grant, "Development of the Christian Catechumenate," in *Made, Not Born: New Perspectives on Christian Initiation and the Catechumenate* (Notre Dame, Ind.: University of Notre Dame Press, 1976), pp. 40-46. The Anglican report *On the Way: Towards an Integrated Approach to Christian Initiation* (London: Church Publishing House, 1998) notes the difficulty of using the Decalogue in the liturgy and proposes the use of Jesus' summary of the law (loving God and neighbor) and the Beatitudes, following the Orthodox tradition. The reason for the use of the latter is that it evokes life in the kingdom of God (4.68).

[27]Catechism of the Catholic Church, no. 2588.

[28]See John R. Searle, *Speech-Acts: An Essay in the Philosophy of Language* (Cambridge: Cambridge University Press, 1969). For an application of speech-act theory to theology, see Nicholas Wolterstorff, *Divine Discourse: Philosophical Reflections on the Claim That God Speaks* (Cambridge: Cambridge University Press, 1995).

[29]Jean-Jacques von Allmen, *Worship: Its Theology and Practice* (London: Lutterworth, 1966), p. 293.

[30]See Anscar Chupungco, *Liturgical Inculturation: Sacramentals, Religiosity and Catechesis* (Collegeville, Minn.: Liturgical, 1992), pp. 134-74. He cites John Paul II's *Catechesi Tradendae* as saying that "the catechesis that prepares for the sacraments is an eminent kind, and every form of catechesis necessarily leads to the sacraments of faith" (p. 137). Cf. the following from Pope John Paul II: "Catechesis is intrinsically linked with the whole of liturgical and sacramental activity, for it is in the sacraments, especially in the Eucharist, that Jesus Christ works in fullness for the transformation of human beings" (*Catechesi Tradendae* 23.1, in *The Postsynodal Apostolic Exhortation of John Paul II*, ed. J. Michael Miller (Huntington, Ind.: Our Sunday Visitor, 1998).

[31]von Allmen, *Worship*, p. 166.

[32]Catechism of the Catholic Church, no. 188.

[33]Hippolytus *On the Apostolic Tradition* 21. For details of baptismal liturgies, see E. C. Whitaker, *Documents of the Baptismal Liturgy*, rev. and exp. Maxwell E. Johnson (Collegeville, Minn.: Pueblo, 2003). Modern liturgical scholarship has highlighted the variety of patterns of baptismal rituals, which probably explains the many versions of the Apostles' Creed. See Paul F. Bradshaw, *The Search for the Origins of Christian Worship: Sources and Methods for the Study of Early Liturgy* (Oxford: Oxford University Press, 1992).

[34]Catechism of the Catholic Church, nos. 166-67.

[35]Peter Brunner, *Worship in the Name of Jesus*, trans. M. H. Bertram (St. Louis: Concordia, 1968), p. 206.

[36]Catechism of the Catholic Church, no. 168.

[37]Ibid., nos. 142-44.

[38]Ibid., no. 2066.

[39]For a brief discussion of the different uses of the law in classical Protestantism, see Otto Weber, *Foundations of Dogmatics*, trans. Darrell L. Guder (Grand Rapids: Eerdmans, 1983), 2:380-99.

[40]For a critique of this form of piety, see Wolfhart Pannenberg, *Christian Spirituality and Sacramental Community* (London: Darton, Longman, and Todd, 1983), pp. 13-30.

[41]E.g., in the Reformed and Anglican traditions (see below) but, interestingly, not in the Lutheran. The reason for Luther's omission may be his understanding of the nature of confession. In his Small Catechism under the question "What sin should we confess?" Luther distinguishes two kinds of confession. "Before God" we must confess "all manner of sins, even of those which we do not ourselves perceive," whereas before our confessor we must confess specific sins that we recall with the help of the Decalogue. It appears, then, that for Luther liturgical confession is concerned with the general sinful condition of worshipers, and therefore the recitation of the Decalogue, which is meant to help one recall specific sins, would not be appropriate.

[42]Anglican moral theologian Oliver O'Donovan has suggested that an ethical portion (not the Decalogue but perhaps one of the lists of virtues from the Epistles) could be read after Communion "to spread before us the glory of a fully human life into which we are now free to enter." *Liturgy and Ethics,* Grove Ethical Studies 89 (Bramcote, Nottingham, U.K.: Grove, 1993), p. 9.

[43]Margaret Killingray and Jo Bailey Wells, *Using the Ten Commandments,* Grove Biblical Series 17 (Cambridge, U.K.: Grove, 2000), p. 7.

[44]Catechism of the Catholic Church, nos. 2056-57.

[45]Ibid., no. 2057.

[46]Killingray and Wells, *Using the Ten Commandments.*

[47]Weber notes that the Heidelberg Catechism is virtually the exception from this understanding of the place of the commandments (*Foundations of Dogmatics,* 2:391-92).

[48]We could say that the *usus lexis* in dogmatics represents a broader understanding of law. It is an attempt to relate the covenantal idea of law to the social context and to incorporate other Pauline understandings of law as creating awareness of sin (cf. Rom 7:6) and as preparation for the gospel (Gal 3:24).

[49]The interchangeability of the Decalogue and the new commandment is reflected in certain liturgical orders where either one or the other may be read. See, e.g., the *Book of Common Prayer* (1979), Order of Holy Communion Rite A, no. 24.

[50]Quoted in Catechism of the Catholic Church, no. 2067.

[51]Ibid., no. 2062.

[52]Ibid., no. 2769.

[53]Tertullian *De oratione* 1, quoted in ibid., no. 2761.

[54]Noted in Catechism of the Catholic Church, no. 2768.

[55]The way the public prayer of the church is put to private use can be seen in many late medieval and early Protestant devotional primers. See Helen C. White, *English Devotional Literature (Prose), 1600-1640* (Madison: University of Wisconsin Press, 1931).

[56]Catechism of the Catholic Church, no. 2760.

[57]As seen, e.g., in *Baptist Praise and Worship* (Oxford: Oxford University Press, 1991), produced by the Baptist churches of the United Kingdom. The hymnal includes, besides the Lord's Prayer, some standard prayers, such as the Sursum Corda, from the *Book of Common Prayer* and the *Alternative Service Book.*

[58]von Allmen, *Worship,* p. 293.

[59]Catechism of the Catholic Church, no. 2770.

[60]Brunner, *Worship in the Name of Jesus,* p. 202.

[61]See the works of Anscar Chupungco, *Liturgies of the Future: The Process and Methods of In-*

*culturation* (New York: Paulist, 1989), and *Liturgical Inculturation,*

[62]The official, comprehensive Catechism of the Catholic Church on the one hand and a personal, perspectival one like Edward Norman's *An Anglican Catechism* (New York, London: Continuum, 2001) on the other illustrate the broad range of possibilities of catechetical training.

[63]Liturgical *inculturation* (nowadays the preferred term in addressing theological issues in crosscultural settings) covers not only theological content but also ritual actions, liturgical texts, rites and music. Calls have been made to find local "dynamic equivalents," for example, to bread and wine in the eucharistic celebration. See Anscar J. Chupungco, "Inculturation," in *The New SCM Dictionary of Liturgy and Worship,* ed. Paul F. Bradshaw (London: SCM Press, 2002), pp. 244-51. In the area of music, inculturation has become quite normal, as can be seen in the newer denominational hymnals. On this, see C. Michael Hawn, *Gather into One: Praying and Singing Globally* (Grand Rapids: Eerdmans, 2003). I have restricted myself to raising the contextual question with regard to the content of the catechism, as this seems to be an area that most concerns evangelicals.

[64]Cf. Catechism of the Catholic Church, nos. 2115-17.

[65]Bradshaw, *Search for the Origins,* pp. 161-84. See also Johnson's introductory essay in Whitaker, *Documents of the Baptismal Liturgy,* pp. xiii-xxi.

[66]Kavanagh, *Shape of Baptism,* p. 115.

[67]Cyril of Jerusalem *Catechetical Lectures* 20.4.

[68]For an account of early Christian practice see Herman Wegman, *Christian Worship in the East and West: A Study Guide to Liturgical History,* trans. Gordon W. Lathrop (New York: Pueblo, 1985).

[69]Turning east does not just occur in the baptismal ritual but is also the determinate direction of the liturgy of the sacrament. It underscores the eschatological direction of the church. See chapter six, below.

[70]Alexander Schmemann, *For the Life of the World: Sacrament and Orthodoxy* (Crestwood, N.Y.: St. Vladimir's Seminary Press, 2000), p. 70.

[71]In the *Rite of Christian Initiation of Adults,* this occurs when new believers are accepted into the catechumenate (no. 73).

[72]For a concise summary of the various meanings and practices associated with confirmation, see *On the Way,* pp. 64-69. For a discussion of the relation of water baptism with Spirit baptism, see Kavanagh, *Shape of Baptism,* pp. 25-26.

[73]The temporal separation between baptism and confirmation was a result of reforms under Charlemagne in the ninth century, which required confirmation by the laying on of episcopal hands. See Nathan D. Mitchell, "Dissolution of the Rite of Christian Initiation," in *Made, Not Born: New Perspectives on Christian Initiation and the Catechumenate* (Notre Dame, Ind.: University of Notre Dame Press, 1976), pp. 55-56.

[74]See, e.g., Max Turner, *The Holy Spirit and Spiritual Gifts in the New Testament Church and Today,* rev. ed. (Peabody, Mass.: Hendrickson, 1998), and James D. G. Dunn, *Baptism in the Holy Spirit* (London: SCM Press, 1984).

[75]The oneness of and distinction between baptism and confirmation provides a better explanation of the Pentecostal doctrine of subsequence than the one usually given by classical Pentecostals, that Spirit baptism is "distinct from and subsequent to" the new birth, which makes Spirit baptism separate from conversion. See Simon Chan, *Pentecostal Theology and the Christian Spiritual Tradition,* Journal of Pentecostal Theology Supplement Series (Sheffield, U.K.; Sheffield Academic Press, 2000), pp. 53-54, 87-93.

[76]Mitchell, "Dissolution of the Rite," p. 57, quoting A. P. Milner, *Theology of Confirmation* (Notre

Dame, Ind.: University of Notre Dame Press, 1971), pp. 19-22.

[77]Mitchell, "Dissolution of the Rite," p. 58.

[78]Enrico Mazza's study of Theodore of Mopsuestia's mystagogical sermons has noted that his sacramental realism is explained in terms of the action of the Spirit (*Mystagogy: A Theology of Liturgy in the Patristic Age,* trans. Matthew J. O'Connell [New York: Pueblo, 1989], pp. 85-93).

[79]Tertullian *On Baptism* 4.

[80]Ibid., 20.

[81]This point was noted by Louis Bouyer many years ago in *The Spirit and Forms of Protestantism* (London: Collins, 1956).

[82]Philip Seddon, *Gospel and Sacrament: Reclaiming a Holistic Evangelical Spirituality,* Grove Spirituality Series 89 (Bramcote, Nottingham, U.K.: Grove, 2004), p. 5.

[83]The loss of mystery and transcendence is replaced by a "contrived intimacy" (ibid., p. 6).

[84]Cyril *Catechetical Lectures* 19-23, in *Nicene and Post-Nicene Fathers,* second series, vol. 7, ed. Philip Schaff and Henry Wace (1894; reprint Peabody, Mass.: Hendrickson, 1995). The situation may be different in the modern church context, where the unbaptized are usually not physically excluded from the eucharistic event, although still excluded from partaking. In the Catechism of the Catholic Church, mystagogy seeks to deepen what has already been learned in prebaptismal catechism: "deepening [the neophystes'] grasp of the paschal mystery and . . . making it part of their lives through meditation on the Gospel, sharing in the eucharist, and doing the works of charity" (244).

[85]Cyril *Catechetical Lectures* 19.4-8.

[86]Ibid. 29.6, 8.

[87]Ibid. 20.5.

[88]Ibid. 21.1.

[89]Ibid. 22.6.

[90]Ibid. 23.20

[91]Ibid. 23.21, 22.

[92]Mazza, *Mystagogy,* pp. 1-8.

[93]Ibid., p. 25.

[94]Ibid., pp. 9-13. Egeria described the exposition of the Scripture and the creed as "first literally, then spiritually" (*Egeria's Travels,* p. 144).

[95]For examples, see William Harmless, *Augustine and the Catechumenate* (Collegeville, Minn.: Liturgical, 1995), chap. 8; See Jean-Marie Tillard, *Flesh of the Church, Flesh of Christ: At the Source of the Ecclesiology of Communion,* trans. Madeleine Beaumont (1992; reprint, Collegeville, Minn.: Liturgical, 2001), chap. 2.

[96]Mazza, *Mystagogy,* pp. 45-104. It is noteworthy that Theodore is usually thought of as belonging to the Antiochene school of literal interpretation as opposed to the Alexandrian school of allegorical interpretation. But Mazza has shown that the distinction is not so clear cut.

[97]Ibid., pp. 61-62.

[98]Ibid., p. 62, cf. pp. 165-74. Mazza shows that two theologies are at work to handle the issue of sacramental realism and efficacy. One is the theology of imitation or representation, cited above, and the other is the *epiclesis,* the work of the Holy Spirit effecting Christ's work of redemption (pp. 71-76). It is the latter rather than imitation that is the basis of sacramental realism.

[99]See, e.g., Susan K. Wood, *Spiritual Exegesis and the Church in the Theology of Henri de Lubac* (Grand Rapids: Eerdmans / Edinburgh: T & T Clark, 1998).

[100]I can speak only from my limited experience of churches in several parts of Asia.

[101]Aidan Kavanagh, "Christian Initiation of Adults: The Rites," in *Made, Not Born: New Perspectives on Christian Initiation and the Catechumenate* (Notre Dame, Ind.: University of Notre Dame Press, 1976), p. 122.

[102]Kavanagh, *Shape of Baptism,* p. 120.

[103]Paul Hiebert, "Conversion, Culture and Cognitive Categories," *Gospel in Context* 1, no. 4 (October 1978): 215-20.

[104]Ibid., p. 219.

[105]Besides Darrell L. Guder, *The Continuing Conversion of the Church* (Grand Rapids: Eerdmans, 2000), see Gordon T. Smith, *Beginning Well: Christian Conversion and Authentic Transformation* (Downers Grove, Ill.: InterVarsity Press, 2001); Robert E. Webber, *Journey to Jesus: The Worship, Evangelism and Nurture Mission of the Church* (Nashville: Abingdon, 2001), and *Ancient-Future Evangelism: Making Your Church a Faith-Forming Community* (Grand Rapids: Baker, 2003). Smith identifies seven components in "good conversion": intellectual (belief), penitential (repentance), affective (trust), volitional (commitment), sacramental (baptism), charismatic (Spirit baptism) and corporate (membership in a church; pp. 138-41). Webber seeks to apply the ancient catechumenate to the present-day church.

[106]Even today in primal religious contexts, a sacramental view of reality is still prevalent. See Harold Turner, "The Primal Religions of the World and Their Study," in *Australian Essays in World Religions* (Bedford Park, S.A.: Australian Association of World Religions, 1977), pp. 27-37.

[107]See chapter seven below, pp. 147-50.

### Chapter 6: The Sunday Liturgy

[1]For brief but helpful suggestions on integrating structure and spontaneity, see Jeremy Fletcher and Christopher Cocksworth, *The Spirit and Liturgy,* Grove Worship Series 146 (Cambridge, U.K.: Grove, 1998). See also Robert E. Webber, *Planning Blended Worship: The Creative Mixture of Old and New* (Nashville: Abingdon, 1998).

[2]Paul F. Bradshaw notes that eucharistic prayers have a characteristically twofold structure: *anamnēsis* (remembering the Christ event) and *epiclesis* (invocation of the Holy Spirit). *Early Christian Worship: A Basic Introduction to Ideas and Practices* (London: SPCK, 1996), pp. 45-50.

[3]E.g., see Daniel Albrecht, *Rites of the Spirit: A Ritual Approach to Pentecostal/Charismatic Spirituality,* JPT Supplement Series 17 (Sheffield, U.K.: Sheffield Academic, 1999).

[4]Fletcher and Cocksworth, *Spirit and Liturgy,* p. 21. The phrase is from John Leach, *Liturgy and Liberty* (Eastbourne, U.K.: MARC, 1989), p. 155.

[5]See Simon Chan, *Pentecostal Theology and the Christian Spiritual Tradition* (Sheffield, U.K.: Sheffield Academic Press, 2000), pp. 92-96. Many liturgical traditions have a liturgy of healing. E.g., the new Church of England *Common Worship* has a separate "A Celebration of Wholeness and Healing" liturgy and another order incorporated into the regular Sunday eucharistic celebration. See *Common Worship: Pastoral Services* (London: Church Publishing House, 2000), pp. 13-23, 27-39.

[6]Constitution on the Sacred Liturgy, in *Documents of Vatican II,* ed. Walter M. Abbot and Joseph Gallagher (New York: Guild Press, 1966), pp. 137-78.

[7]Richard Bauckham has argued that the only reference to the Lord's Day *(kuriakē hēmera)* in Revelation 1:10 is to Sunday rather than to the eschatological event for which the usual phrase is "the Day of the Lord" *(hēmera tou kuriou)*. See "The Lord's Day," in *From Sabbath to Lord's Day,* ed. D. A. Carson (Grand Rapids: Zondervan, 1982), pp. 225, 232-33.

[8]To say that Sunday is not the sabbath is not to deny the value of the rest principle; rather, it is to recognize that the primary thrust of Christian Sunday theology is not to be derived from

the Old Testament sabbath. The confusion of Sunday with sabbath may be due to the fact that Sunday did become a holiday, a day of rest, later in the post-Constantinian age.

[9]Bauckham, "Lord's Day," pp. 236-38.

[10]Gordon W. Lathrop, *Holy Things: A Liturgical Theology* (Minneapolis: Fortress, 1993), p. 40.

[11]Jean Lebon, *How to Understand the Liturgy,* trans. Margaret Lydamore and John Bowden (London: SCM Press, 1987), p. 103.

[12]Peter Brunner, *Worship in the Name of Jesus,* trans. M. H. Bertram (St. Louis: Concordia, 1968), p. 222.

[13]Most of the elements are taken from Faith and Order Commission, *Baptism, Eucharist and Ministry* (1982; reprint, Geneva: World Council of Churches, 2001), Eucharist no. 27. The structuring of the elements, however, is adapted from various sources.

[14]Lathrop, *Holy People,* p. 21.

[15]Alexander Schmemann, *For the Life of the World: Sacraments and Orthodoxy* (New York: St. Vladimir's Seminary Press, 2000), p. 27.

[16]See chapter one, above.

[17]Lathrop mentions many "juxtapositions" or "dualisms" within the *ordo* of the liturgy, all of which highlight and are based on the basic eschatological nature of the liturgy (*Holy Things,* pp. 54-83).

[18]Brunner, *Worship in the Name of Jesus,* p. 134.

[19]In an extensive critique of the songs from the Vineyard Christian Fellowship, Percy Martyn notes that unlike Charles Wesley's songs, which are essentially didactic, Wimber's songs are essentially existential (p. 64). The songs seem to be aimed at inducing an "unresisting and submissive character" toward a divine power conceived as "coercive and exclusive" (p. 77), a "brute force, rather than the ambiguous power of Calvary" (p. 79). *Words, Wonders and Power: Understanding Contemporary Christian Fundamentalism and Revivalism* (London: SPCK, 1996).

[20]Brunner, *Worship in the Name of Jesus,* p. 210.

[21]See below (p. 138) for a further explanation of performative acts.

[22]Jean-Jacques von Allmen, *Worship: Its Theology and Practice* (London: Lutterworth, 1966), p. 291.

[23]This is revived in the Roman missal. See n. 29 below.

[24]von Allmen, *Worship,* p. 292.

[25]E.g., Howard L. Rice and James C. Huffstutler, *Reformed Worship* (Louisville, Ky.: Geneva, 2001), pp. 79-80.

[26]Brunner, *Worship in the Name of Jesus,* pp. 207, 206.

[27]This is apparent when we compare the then Methodist Church's *Book of Worship for Church and Home* (Nashville: Methodist Publishing House, 1965) with the "Word and Table: Service 1" in the *United Methodist Hymnal* (Nashville: United Methodist Publishing House, 1989). The 1965 confession sees sin as primarily against God: "Almighty God, Father of our Lord Jesus Christ, maker of all things, judge of all men: We acknowledge and bewail our manifold sins and wickedness, which we from time to time most grievously have committed, by thought, word, and deed, against thy divine majesty. We do earnestly repent, and are heartily sorry for these our misdoings; the remembrance of them is grievous to us. Have mercy upon us . . ." (p. 17). The 1989 confession does not mention sin but refers to a failure to love: "Merciful God, we confess that we have not loved you with our whole heart. We have failed to be an obedient church. We have not done your will, we have broken your law, we have rebelled against your love, we have not loved our neighbors, and we have not heard the cry of the

needy" (p. 8). The sense of God's majesty and holiness is conspicuously missing from the newer prayer.

[28]The Orthodox liturgy, too, has a much stronger sense of the holiness of God compared with modern Protestant liturgies. Cf. the Divine Liturgy of St. John Chrysostom.

[29]*Daily Roman Missal* (Manila: Studium Theologiae Foundation, 1989), p. 563.

[30]Brunner, *Worship in the Name of Jesus,* p. 133.

[31]Richard C. Eyer, *They Will See His Face: Worship and Healing* (St. Louis: Concordia, 2002), p. 16. There is a lingering suspicion among evangelicals that the use of words of absolution might return the church to sacerdotalism. But to say "In the name of Jesus, you are forgiven" does not imply that the minister has the power to forgive sin, any more than "In the name of Jesus, you are healed" spoken by the charismatic preacher implies that the preacher has the power to heal. The minister is not speaking in his or her own capacity but as representative of Christ *(in persona Christi).*

[32]Brunner, *Worship in the Name of Jesus,* pp. 127-41.

[33]Ibid., p. 153.

[34]Second Helvetic Confession 1.4, in *Reformation Era,* vol. 2 of *Creeds and Confessions of Faith in the Christian Tradition,* ed. Jaroslav Pelikan and Valerie Hotchkiss (New Haven, Conn.: Yale University Press, 2003).

[35]For a recent argument on this, see I. Howard Marshall, *New Testament Theology: Many Witnesses, One Gospel* (Leicester, U.K.: Inter-Varsity Press, 2004).

[36]Von Allmen notes that the canonization of Scripture owed much to the reading of the Scripture in worship (*Worship,* p. 134). See Lathrop, *Holy People,* pp. 24-25.

[37]This concern for "objective truth" finds expression in the doctrine of inerrancy, which, ironically, was developed to combat the "destructive" critical study of the Bible.

[38]See Enrico Mazza, *Mystagogy: A Theology of Liturgy in the Patristic Age,* trans. Matthew J. O'Connell (New York: Pueblo, 1989). Mazza points to Theodore of Mopsuestia, "a principal representative" of the Antiochene school, as an example of extensive allegorical interpretation of liturgical rites (pp. 55-66).

[39]See David C. Steinmetz, "The Superiority of Pre-critical Exegesis," in *The Theological Interpretation of Scripture,* ed. Stephen E. Fowl (Oxford: Basil Blackwell, 1997), pp. 26-38.

[40]See Susan K. Wood, *Spiritual Exegesis and the Church in the Theology of Henri de Lubac* (Grand Rapids: Eerdmans, 1998).

[41]Ibid., p. 22.

[42]The work of Brevard S. Childs has been largely responsible for the modern return to the canonical interpretation of Scripture. See his *Biblical Theology of the Old and New Testaments* (Minneapolis: Fortress, 1993).

[43]See, e.g., Stephen E. Fowl, *Engaging Scripture: A Model for Theological Interpretation* (Oxford: Basil Blackwell, 1998).

[44]Brunner, *Worship in the Name of Jesus,* p. 128.

[45]Ibid., p. 129.

[46]von Allmen, *Worship,* p. 133.

[47]*General Instruction of the Roman Missal,* 3rd ed. (Washington, D.C.: U.S. Catholic Conference, 2003), no. 29.

[48]Lathrop, *Holy People,* p. 22.

[49]The word *lector* is used to avoid confusion with *reader,* who in some traditions is a lay minister.

[50]The Reformer Ulrich Zwingli retained the practice. See von Allmen, *Worship,* p. 135.

[51]*General Instruction of the Roman Missal,* no. 62.

[52]Brunner, *Worship in the Name of Jesus,* p. 130.

[53]*General Instruction of the Roman Missal,* no. 29.

[54]Jean Lebon, *How to Understand the Liturgy,* trans. Margaret Lydamore and John Bowden (London: SCM Press, 1987), pp. 9, 101.

[55]Brunner, *Worship in the Name of Jesus,* pp. 131-32.

[56]Jürgen Moltmann, *The Church in the Power of the Spirit,* trans. Margaret Kohl (London: Harper & Row, 1977), pp. 74-75, 82.

[57]Ibid., pp. 97-98.

[58]*General Instruction of the Roman Missal,* no. 70.

[59]Lebon, *How to Understand,* p. 115.

[60]The *Alternative Service Book* (1980) locates it before the eucharistic prayer, while the Roman Missal places it just before the breaking of bread.

[61]*Alternative Service Book,* p. 128.

[62]Ibid., p. 128.

[63]Brunner, *Worship in the Name of Jesus,* p. 162,

[64]Robert W. Jenson, *Visible Words* (Philadelphia: Fortress, 1978), p. 93.

[65]Irenaeus *Against Heresies* 4.18.5.

[66]Carlos Messerli and Philip H. Pfatteicher, *Manual on the Liturgy: Lutheran Book of Worship* (Minneapolis: Augsburg, 1979), p. 232.

[67]Brunner, *Worship in the Name of Jesus,* p. 202.

[68]Schmemann, *For the Life of the World,* pp. 37-38.

[69]Ibid., pp. 39, 37-38.

[70]*Common Worship* (London: Church Publishing House, 2000), Eucharistic Prayer F, p. 198.

[71]Brunner, *Worship in the Name of Jesus,* p. 168.

[72]*Common Worship,* Prayer G, p. 203.

[73]"A Service of Word and Table 1" of the United Methodist Church: *The United Methodist Church Hymnal* (Nashville: United Methodist Publishing House, 1989), p. 10.

[74]*Common Worship,* Prayer F, p. 200.

[75]*Alternative Service Book,* p. 142.

[76]Bradshaw, *Early Christian Worship,* p. 78.

[77]*Common Worship,* p. 181.

[78]*Daily Roman Missal,* p. 699.

[79]See chapter four, above.

[80]Lathrop, *Holy People,* pp. 16-18.

[81]Justin Martyr *First Apology* 66.1-2.

[82]Cf. Brunner, *Worship in the Name of Jesus,* pp. 172-73. Modern Lutherans, however, seem to take a more agnostic view of the "how" question while affirming the mystery of the real presence. See the Evangelical Lutheran Church in America's *The Use of the Means of Grace: A Statement on the Practice of Word and Sacrament* (Minneapolis: Augsburg, 1997), p. 37.

[83]Bradshaw notes that the use of "realistic" language is older than the "symbolic" and appears to have been motivated by the attempt to refute any form of docetism (*Early Christian Worship,* p. 60).

[84]Ibid., pp. 62-63.

[85]Cf. ELCA, *Use of the Means of Grace,* p. 47.

[86]Schmemann, *For the Life of the World,* p. 42, emphasis author's.

[87]Ibid., pp. 42-43, emphasis author's.

[88]Brunner, *Worship in the Name of Jesus,* p. 136.

[89]In recent years, the influence of the Third Wave has resulted in a revival of this magical attitude, especially among non-Western Christians who have only recently been converted from the world of animism. For a critique of the Third Wavers' animistic worldview, see Paul G. Hiebert, "Healing and the Kingdom," in *Wonders and the Word* (Winnipeg, Canada: Kindred, 1989), pp. 109-52.

[90]Moltmann, *Church in the Power of the Spirit,* p. 273.

[91]The eucharistic presence is both a real presence and a real absence because of the ascension. On the significance of the ascension for the Eucharist, see Douglas Farrow, *Ascension and Ecclesia* (Grand Rapids: Eerdmans, 1999), pp. 15-40.

### Chapter 7: Active Participation

[1]Constitution on the Sacred Liturgy, in *Documents of Vatican II,* ed. Walter M. Abbot and Joseph Gallagher (New York: Guild Press, 1966), no. 30.

[2]Susan J. White, *The Spirit of Worship: The Liturgical Tradition* (Maryknoll, N.Y.: Orbis, 1999), pp. 21-28. Cf. Philip H. Pfatteicher, *Liturgical Spirituality* (Valley Forge, Penn.: Trinity Press International, 1997).

[3]Richard C. Eyer, *They Will See His Face: Worship and Healing* (St. Louis: Concordia, 2002).

[4]E.g., Philip H. Pfatteicher, *The School of the Church: Worship and Christian Formation* (Valley Forge, Penn.: Trinity Press International, 1995).

[5]Ibid., pp. 104-5.

[6]Joyce Ann Zimmerman, *Liturgy as Living Faith: A Liturgical Spirituality* (Scranton, Penn.: University of Scranton Press, 1993), p. viii.

[7]Ibid., p. viii.

[8]Ibid., p. xii.

[9]Cf. ibid., pp. 127-28.

[10]Cf. the two ways of praying in chapter four, above.

[11]See Don E. Saliers, "Spirituality, Liturgical," in *The New SCM Dictionary of Liturgy and Worship,* ed. Paul F. Bradshaw (London: SCM Press, 2002), p. 448.

[12]Craig Douglas Erickson in *Participating in Worship: History, Theory and Practice* (Louisville, Ky.: Westminster John Knox, 1989) identifies six modes of engagement: spontaneous involvement, silent engagement, interiorized verbal participation, prophetic verbal participation, lay leadership, and multisensate participation through sights, sounds and gestures (p. 21).

[13]W. Jardine Grisbrooke, "Towards a Liturgical Spirituality," *Studia Liturgica* 17 (1987): 77-86.

[14]Ibid., pp. 84-85.

[15]See Patrick Keifert, *Welcoming the Stranger: A Public Theology of Worship and Evangelism* (Minneapolis: Ausburg, 1992).

[16]Whether this particular rubric is in fact universally Presbyterian or just a local idiosyncrasy is another question.

[17]Erickson suggests a scale of liturgical participation with "ritualism" at one end of the scale (zero participation) and "synergistic ritual" at the opposite end, where persons, church and liturgy are involved "in a cooperative relationship of mutual enrichment" (*Participating in Worship,* p. 15).

[18]*Redemptionis Sacramentum* 39 (April 23, 2004), available at http://www.vatican.va/roman _curia/congregations/ccdds/documents/rc_con_ccdds_doc_20040423_redemptionissacramentum _en.html>.

[19]Leaders are not only the clergy but include those who exercise a leadership role at any point in the liturgy, such as the lector, intercessor, cantor and choir.

[20]Putting it another way, the roles of church leaders must be defined in relation to their lot *(cleros)* within the liturgical assembly, and this role is distinguished from that of the people. See Gordon W. Lathrop, *Holy Things: A Liturgical Theology* (Minneapolis: Fortress, 1993), pp. 185-95.

[21]See the discussion of John D. Zizioulas on the nature of ministry in *Being as Communion* (Crestwood, N.Y.: St Vladimir's Seminary Press, 1985), pp. 214-24, where he argues that the liturgical "amen" of the congregation is indispensable to the orders of the ordained ministry (p. 218).

[22] Cited by Lathrop, *Holy Things*, p. 194.

[23]*General Instruction of the Roman Missal,* 3rd ed. (Washington, D.C.: U.S. Catholic Conference, 2003), no. 35.

[24]Bryan Spinks notes the high level of lay ministry that the *Alternative Service Book* allows. The same could be said of most modern liturgies. Bryan Spinks, "The Liturgical Ministry of the Laity," in *A Kingdom of Priests: Liturgical Formation of the People of God,* ed. Thomas J. Talley, Grove Liturgical Studies 5 (Bramcote, Nottingham, U.K.: Grove, 1988), pp. 24-25.

[25]See Percy Martyn, *Words, Wonders and Power: Understanding Contemporary Christian Fundamentalism and Revivalism* (London: SPCK, 1996), pp. 77-81.

[26]Alasdair MacIntyre defines practice as "any coherent and complex form of socially established cooperative human activity through which goods internal to that form of activity are realized in the course of trying to achieve those standards of excellence which are appropriate to, and partially definitive of, that form of activity, with the result that human powers to achieve excellence, and human conceptions of the ends and goods involved, are systematically extended." *After Virtue: A Study of Moral Theory* (Notre Dame, Ind.: University of Notre Dame Press, 1981), p. 175.

[27]Robert W. Jenson, *Visible Words* (Philadelphia: Fortress, 1978), p. 57.

[28]Pfatteicher, *School of the Church,* pp. 14-27.

[29]Jenson, *Visible Words,* pp. 57-58.

[30]Dietrich Bonhoeffer, *Life Together,* trans. John W. Doberstein (New York: Harper & Brothers, 1954), pp. 56-57.

[31]*General Instruction of the Roman Missal,* no. 38.

[32]Ibid., no. 32.

[33]*General Instruction of the Liturgy of the Hours,* no. 19, available at <http://www.ewtn.com/library/CURIA/CDWGILH.HTM>.

[34]Pfatteicher, *School of the Church,* p. 88.

[35]Quoted in ibid., pp. 101-2.

[36]Ibid., p. 30.

[37]See *General Instruction of the Roman Missal,* no. 45.

[38]Pfatteicher, *School of the Church,* pp. 66-72.

[39]Quoted by J. Gelineau, "Music and Singing in the Liturgy," in *The Study of Liturgy,* rev. ed., ed. Cheslyn Jones et al. (New York: Oxford University Press, 1997), p. 496.

[40]Ronald P. Byars has noted the shrinking of Word and sacrament in many Protestant churches in *The Future of Protestant Worship: Beyond the Worship Wars* (Louisville, Ky.: Westminster John Knox, 2002), pp. 68ff.

[41]Gelineau, "Music and Singing in the Liturgy," p. 496.

[42]*General Instruction of the Liturgy of the Hours,* no 109.

[43]Ibid., no. 103.

[44]Ibid., no. 107.

[45]Ibid., no. 108.

[46]Don E. Saliers, *Worship Come to Its Senses* (Nashville: Abingdon, 1996).

[47]See Jonathan Edwards, *A Treatise Concerning Religious Affections,* in *The Works of Jonathan Edwards,* vol. 2, ed. Perry Miller (New Haven, Conn.: Yale University Press, 1959).

[48]Saliers, *Worship Come to Its Senses,* pp. 23-28.

[49]Peter L. Berger, *A Rumor of Angels: Modern Society and the Rediscovery of the Supernatural* (Garden City, N.Y.: Doubleday, 1969).

[50]Ideally, the liturgy should overflow into daily living. It should be the place in which Christians experience awe and from which they encounter divine awe in creation. The fact that it does not happen in this way, that "signals of transcendence" (themselves signs of God's grace) are needed to lead people back to true worship, is an indication of the weakness of the modern church as a traditioning community. For many modern Christians, the church is only one of many communities they inhabit, and not even the most significant one.

[51]See Simon Chan, *Spiritual Theology* (Downers Grove, Ill.: InterVarsity Press, 1998), pp. 125-27.

[52]Pfatteicher, *School of the Church,* p. 75.

[53]*General Instruction of the Roman Missal,* no. 42.

[54]Pfatteicher, *Liturgical Spirituality,* pp. 110-14.

[55]For a summary discussion of the origins of daily prayer, see Paul F. Bradshaw, *The Search for the Origins of Christian Worship: Sources and Methods for the Study of Early Liturgy* (Oxford: Oxford University Press, 1992), pp. 185-92.

[56]*General Instruction of the Liturgy of the Hours,* no. 11.

[57]Bradshaw is of the view that the morning, noon and evening pattern was the more universal. Other communities adopted the divisions of the day in the Roman Empire—the third, sixth and ninth hours—and these two patterns were later brought together into the fivefold pattern in the third century (*Search for the Origins,* pp. 190-91).

[58]Constitution of the Sacred Liturgy, no. 89a.

[59]Perhaps one reason unemployment is so demeaning is that it breaks this deeply built-in rhythm.

[60]Christopher Cocksworth and Paul Roberts have noted that the sixteenth-century Reformers and seventeenth-century Puritans had a strong sense of the liturgical context of daily prayers. See *Renewing Daily Prayer: An Introduction to Celebrating Common Prayer,* Grove Worship Series 123 (Bramcote, Nottingham, U.K.: Grove, 1992), pp. 10-11.

[61]The Constitution of the Sacred Liturgy calls the daily office "the public prayer of the church" and "the voice of the church" (nos. 90, 99).

[62]This is what the new Anglican *Common Worship: Daily Prayer* (London: Church House Publishing, 2002) seeks to do. It includes a form of daily prayer ("Prayer Through the Day") that blends the traditional elements of the daily office and the "quiet time" that evangelicals are at home with. See Christopher Cocksworth and Jeremy Fletcher, *Common Worship Daily Prayer: An Introduction,* Grove Worship Series 166 (Cambridge, U.K.: Grove, 2001), pp. 11-12. Note: This study predated the publication of *Common Worship: Daily Prayer* itself.

[63]Constitution of the Sacred Liturgy, no. 83.

[64]Ibid., no. 84.

[65]*Redemptionis Sacramentum,* no. 41.

[66]*Common Worship: Daily Prayer,* p. 88.

[67]*Alternative Service Book,* p. 81.

[68]*Book of Common Prayer,* p. 117; *Common Worship: Daily Prayer,* p. 94.

[69]*Book of Common Prayer,* p. 112.

[70]For a brief explanation of occasional meditation, see Chan, *Spiritual Theology,* pp. 180-85.

[71]From the *Alternative Service Book.*

[72]Ibid., p. 70.

[73]Constitution of the Sacred Liturgy, no. 102.

[74]For a brief explanation of the Christian calendar and the meanings of the major and minor feasts, see James White, *Introduction to Christian Worship,* 3rd ed. (Nashville: Abingdon, 2000), pp. 47-80.

[75]The Roman calendar includes the period between Epiphany and Lent as "ordinary time."

[76]Pfatteicher, *Liturgical Spirituality,* pp. 135-36.

[77]See chapter one, above, "The Living Tradition" section.

[78]For examples of themes for Christian living corresponding to the church calendar, see Robert E. Webber, *The Worship Phenomenon* (Nashville: Star Song, 1994), p. 114; Zimmerman, *Liturgy as Living Faith,* pp. 117-22.

[79]Cf. *General Instruction of the Liturgy of the Hours,* no. 12.

[80]Zimmerman, *Liturgy as Living Faith,* pp. 124-26. See the section "The Eschatological Orientation of the Liturgy" in chapter three, above.

[81]Zimmerman, *Liturgy as Living Faith,* p. 114.

[82]Henry E. Horn, *Worship in Crisis* (Philadelphia: Fortress, 1972), pp. 34-39.

[83]See Pfatteicher, *School of the Church,* pp. 9-10; Horn, *Worship in Crisis,* p. 62.

# Name Index

# Subject Index

# Scripture Index